WHAT WENT WRONG

with

AMERICA...
AND HOW
TO FIX IT

WHAT WENT WRONG

with

AMERICA...
AND HOW
TO FIX IT

Reclaiming
the Power
That Rightfully
Belongs to You

Darrell Ankarlo

with a foreword by Glenn Beck

CUMBERLAND HOUSE
NASHVILLE, TENNESSEE

WHAT WENT WRONG WITH AMERICA...AND HOW TO FIX IT
PUBLISHED BY CUMBERLAND HOUSE PUBLISHING
431 Harding Industrial Drive
Nashville, Tennessee 37211

Library of Congress Cataloging-in-Publication Data

Ankarlo, Darrell, 1959–
    What went wrong with America—and how to fix it : reclaiming the power that rightfully belongs to you / Darrell Ankarlo ; with a foreword by Glenn Beck.
        p. cm.
    Includes bibliographical references.
    ISBN 1-58182-411-4 (hardcover : alk. paper)
    1. Political participation—United States. 2. Politics, Practical—United States. 3. United States—Politics and government—2001– I. Title.
JK1764.A525 2004
323'.042'0973—dc22

2004011114

Printed in the United States of America
1 2 3 4 5 6 7—09 08 07 06 05 04

To my wife, Laurie—my best friend and gift from God.
You have helped define me.

To my kids: Kris, Adam, Ben, and Katie.
No better children could a man have.
You have refined me.

CONTENTS

Foreword by Glenn Beck   *ix*

Acknowledgments   *xiii*

Introduction   *xv*

An Answer to the Question   *xix*

PART 1: LOST VISION—WHAT WENT WRONG

1. The Brewing Storm   *5*

2. They Lied to Us   *11*

3. A Clear and Present Danger   *27*

4. The Separation of Church and State Myth   *49*

5. No More Springfields!   *57*

PART 2: LOST DIRECTION—WHERE WE ARE NOW

6. The Absurdity of It All   *67*

7. Blame the Bogeyman!   *79*

8. The Slope to Destruction   *83*

9. All Fed Up! Red States–Blue States   *95*

10. Special Interests and America's Culture War   *103*

11. Oh, the Hypocrisy!   *109*

12. Does "The Star-Spangled Banner" Still Make You Cry?   *113*

13. What Could Happen If Conservatives Throw in the Towel   *119*

14. The Heartland Responds   *129*

15. You Work for Me!   *135*

16. Talk Radio Saved Democracy—Sort Of   *139*

PART 3: RECLAIM AMERICA—HOW TO FIX IT!

17. The Tennessee Governor's Gone Mad!
     The Beginning of the Tennessee Tax Revolt   *147*

18. Reclaiming the Power   *155*

19. The Politics of It All   *157*

20. A Citizen Politician   *166*

21. Madame Mayor—You Were Supposed to Lose!   *187*

22. Q&A with Political Pros   *197*

23. People Can Make a Difference, Even in America   *211*

24. Can I Get a Volunteer?   *229*

25. A Soccer Dad Comes Through   *234*

26. Texas United!   *240*

27. Winning Event Strategies from a Premier Promoter   *248*

28. Operation Enduring Support   *253*

29. Good PR Is Not Magic   *255*

30. The Rainbow That Is America   *273*

Conclusion   *277*

Notes   *279*

FOREWORD

MY SEVENTY-SIX-YEAR-OLD father and I had a conversation the other night. We talked about family, friends, politics, and global events. I was feeling pessimistic. "Dad," I said, "there are days that I wish the kids and I were your age." He laughed knowingly. But his response surprised me.

He told me that he had been driving earlier that day and listening to someone on the radio explain the day's events in the Middle East. (I was temporarily distracted by the terrifying thought that he was still a licensed driver.) His own thoughts turned to how glad he was to be at the end of his time here. The world seems so dangerous, with problems getting bigger and solutions proving elusive. There seem to be more days than ever when we lose that wonderfully American trait . . . optimism.

We fear, but not for ourselves. When this country was created, our Founding Fathers assembled a Constitution for "ourselves and our posterity." Since September 11, I think most of us have been focusing on the latter. What will life be like in the land created through Providence in fifty years? If we change as much from now through 2054 as we have since 1954, America will be almost unrecognizable. Are we leaving our children a secure nest egg of freedom, prosperity, and security? Or have we saddled them with the slavery of ignorance, debt, and terror? I don't know about you, but I feel as our Founding Fathers did: if there are to be hard times, strife and struggle, let's deal with it now and leave our children an easier and safer life.

However, there is a cacophony of voices vying for attention, creating a country of confusion. And the most important voice of all is the one we hardly pay attention to anymore—our own. A farmer friend was telling me about the "blessings" of mowing his lawn a few days back. He said, "There is nothing better than being atop my John Deere and mowing the lawn. No matter how loud the kids scream or how many times the phone rings, I can't hear any of it. For an hour a week, I am alone with my thoughts." I had never thought of it that way. It makes me want to buy a John Deere. Of course it still wouldn't make me want to mow my lawn, but I could just start it up and sit in the driveway.

How often do we turn off the TV, put down the magazine, and spend time thinking about our hopes and dreams? When was the last time you planted common decency, pure goodness, or hope in the life of a neighbor? I know it has been too long for me. Instead of doing good, we make ourselves feel good by getting the quick fix of shopping, going to a movie, or surfing the Internet. Our lives focus on entertainment and stuff instead of ideas and dreams. But we needn't forget that it wasn't "stuff" that built the America of fifty years ago. It was people. It was values. It was family.

Everything we surround ourselves with tells us we are incomplete unless we wear this shirt, drive this car, and live in this neighborhood. We have slowly lost touch with who we are. We have become a nation of image and sound bites. Nothing is as it seems, and we seem to prefer it that way.

I read a poll recently that stated that 60 percent of conservatives thought the economy was good and getting better, while only 35 percent of those on the Left reflected that hope. How is that possible? The facts are what they are; the economy is good and getting better. This type of pessimistic thinking is the Achilles' heel of the liberal Left. They believe themselves to be in the majority when in fact they are not.

When our Founding Fathers were drafting the Constitution, Ben Franklin sat at his desk in Independence Hall in Philadelphia. For months he stared at the chair occupied by George Washington. On it was the object of Franklin's obsession: a carved sun. Later Franklin shared that all through the proceedings he had wondered if that sun was setting or rising. After the Constitution was signed, he knew. He stood and stated that it was a rising sun. I believe it is still rising; it is still morning in America.

Hope, however, is a difficult elixir to find in today's "mainstream" America, or so you would think. While I was living in Tampa, Florida, I read about an elderly couple who went to Busch Gardens for a little R and R. Both were in their seventies and had just returned from a mission for their church. They decided to travel south to enjoy some sun. As they opened the door to their motel room, a man forced his way in and beat them both nearly to death. All for $117.

I remember reading this story and feeling as though I were surrounded by "bad guys." Could we really have lost the war of good versus evil without knowing it, or was I simply being pessimistic again? I wasn't sure. I wondered aloud on my radio program if others had noticed this trend. Are there a few good people surrounded by evil, or is it the other way around? In an effort to replace the stolen money, I asked listeners to bring one dollar down to the studio before I left the air. I wanted to see if I could find 117 good people. I didn't. Within two hours, more than six thousand good people found me.

I am reminded of a story a friend told at church about a lesson she learned from her husband. One Saturday afternoon their house was egged. They saw who did it and immediately recognized him as the son of a neighbor who lived two doors down. He had a tough family life and was regarded as the terror of the neighborhood. Upon hearing the eggs hit the house and seeing the boy scamper through the bushes, the woman immediately shouted to her husband to call the police. Instead, he suggested they follow the markings on their oldest child's arm bracelet that read WWJD. They sat down and discussed it. They decided they would bake a batch of cookies as a family and deliver them to the boy's house with a note that said: "Next time you want to use eggs, knock on the door, and we'll make cookies together."

This seems a pretty calm reaction to having your house egged. In fact, if you're anything like me, you'd have baked the cookies, ate them, and then choked the neighbor's kid to death in a sugar high. But they took the "Frank Capra Movie People" option and it worked. They can't claim that it changed the kid's life, but it did change his behavior. Wouldn't you love to be the type of person whose first instinct is to respond to rudeness with kindness?

To quote Ralph Waldo Emerson: "Who you are speaks so loudly, I can't hear what you're saying." Shouldn't this be the goal of us all? To be so true to our core values that we would never have to tell people "who" we are; they would know just by our actions.

Last spring John Kerry tried over and over to separate himself from his faith. He repeatedly made the statement that his religious beliefs were "his personal life" and separate from "his public life." What? Are your core beliefs a jacket that you can put on and take off? Consider that what Emerson said applies to both the good and the bad. We can talk all we want about the "real America," but until we live it ourselves, no one will be able to hear our words over the drumbeats of who we are.

Darrell Ankarlo demonstrated this principle to me the spring before the war in Iraq began. He was tired of screaming at the protesters on TV but not doing anything about it. He wanted to be the person who bakes the cookies and gives them away, not the person who eats them. He decided to stop talking to the TV and take action.

The result was Texas United, a calling together of like-minded Americans who wanted to stand up to support the troops and our president. By standing up for what he believed in, thirty-five hundred people were empowered to do the same thing on a rainy Tuesday afternoon just outside Dallas. His success gave me the idea to try this nationally. When all was said and done, more than three hundred thousand people stood in their public squares from coast to coast to support the troops and rally for America. All it took was one voice and the courage to be real to get that ball rolling in Dallas.

Now it's your turn. Who are you? What do you believe in? What do you hope America looks like when our children are our age?

Glenn Beck

ACKNOWLEDGMENTS

Personally, I am who I am because of the strength of my family. Dad and Mom were always there for me and taught me the value of love. They are waiting for me.

I couldn't have asked for better brothers and a sister than George, Orville, Loren, Steve, and Star. If you add my name as the fourth child and put the first initials of our names together it spells out the phrase GOLD STARS. Yep, my parents planned it that way, and oh, by the way, did I mention they were a little crazy? A person will never laugh harder than when spending time with those people.

Jeanne, Robbie, and Shane are the epitome of the kind of in-laws a family hopes for, and Lona was a godsend.

Professionally, a man doesn't work in the radio and television business, write books and columns, have terrific website exposure, and do the amount of public speaking I do without a lot of help from a lot of people. Obviously, I can't list everyone who has touched my life during a twenty-six-year career, but there are a few folks who deserve to be acknowledged with regard to this publication.

I've had a lot of producers in a number of cities, but the top three, in no particular order, have helped to clarify my radio show and to make *Ankarlo Mornings* the force that it is. AnnMarie Petitto is my "go to" person in Dallas. I can't think of anything or anybody she doesn't have in her handy Rolodex. She knows how to keep me "up" during the show (which is a necessity for morning radio), and she makes me laugh. Boy, does she make me laugh. Cory Berry served the show in three markets and has been through all the ups and downs with me and defines loyalty. Lisa Ferrari broke into New York City media as my producer when I worked with Sony and has gone on to become an entrepreneurial goddess. She is a cherished friend.

The best program directors I've had the pleasure to count as friends and great bosses are David Rimmer and Jeff Hillery. In particular, David headhunted me from Philadelphia to New York City in a move that profoundly changed my life. Under Jeff's direction I have evolved to a whole new level. He has made me a better broadcaster.

Thanks to Chris, Ron, and Ed at Cumberland House. Chris kept suggesting that I write a book, Ron said, "Do it," and Ed made me look good.

Dick Whitworth was the first program director who saw something in me and gave me a chance—a long time ago. He has consistently lived a life of integrity to which I daily aspire.

To Nolan—an Internet genius. Just believe. To Keith—the best graphics guy in the business. To the many "A Team" members who have worked on *Ankarlo Mornings* over the years. You're the best.

Thanks for the legwork, Tamara.

Let me also acknowledge the Savior, as politically incorrect as that may be. You heard my prayers and answered them, but before I could even whisper a word, you gave me the gift of America!

INTRODUCTION

I CAME TO LOVE America as the middle child of a small-town preacher in the country's heartland. My father never made a lot of money, but the church where he pastored gave him a month of vacation. With few exceptions, every summer of my youth found Dad and Mom loading up the station wagon with us six kids, filling the trailer, and heading to new places to discover and explore the world around us. Each of my brothers and my sister will recount at least one time when my parents had no idea where we were going, even as we made our way from the house and onto the town's main drag—Highway 159. There Dad would park the car by the side of the road, and he and Mom would debate our direction. If they remained at an impasse for more than a few minutes, Dad would get back on the road and start driving, leaving us all to guess our final destination.

With uncertainty as our backdrop, we were fortunate enough to visit every state in the Union with the exception of Alaska and Hawaii. When the money was running short, which it always was, my parents would pull into a gas station, a public park, or a stranger's yard, and after getting permission to stay, my mom would cook the evening meal before getting us ready for bed. Strangers who became friends stretched from coast to coast. My parents believed in hospitality and commonality. In other words, since we all belonged to the same country, we should all go out of our way to help one another.

In our hometown it was not uncommon for someone who was passing through and down on their luck to happen upon Reverend Ankarlo's house. Of course, my first awareness of our new houseguest would be when I was awakened by sounds of snoring from the bunk below. It was well known that George and Isabelle never turned anyone away.

This is how I learned about America. I experienced its towns, its landmarks, and its people. Later, as an adult, I chose the broadcast field and for more than twenty-five years lived in a variety of places, from Chicago to Nashville and from New York City to Philadelphia, before landing in Dallas/Fort Worth. I've had the distinct opportunity to experience our country as a guest in some of its towns and as a deep-rooted citizen in others.

In life, we model what we know. I was privileged to have parents and a support system that exemplified respect, honor, and personal responsibility. Those last two words are almost curse words in today's society. My hometown—Maryville, Illinois—was less than a dot on the map; in fact, when I lived there, we weren't even on the map. With a population of about seven hundred people, it was typical small-town America. I remember how easy it was for a kid to find himself in trouble because everyone knew everyone, along with their children and virtually every detail of their lives. I could not begin to count the number of times I heard a neighbor lady from blocks away shout, "Hey Ankarlo boy! I am calling your father on you, so you better get home and tell him what you've been doing." My trouble was usually innocuous, but it was trouble nonetheless.

Those innocent mischievous romps and, more specifically, getting caught at them taught me this valuable key to life: a single person can truly be responsible for only himself. However, it does not stop there. As a part of the corporate body known as America, I must be willing to look out for the other guy, too. Don't get me wrong. I don't believe I should take on the complete burden of responsibility for others, but I should be willing to help when needed. I have had many disagreements with liberals who feel it is society's chore to prop up people. They just don't understand that our system wasn't built that way and cannot flourish with such a mindset.

Our country continues to dominate the world because we are a proud people who have been willing to work hard in order to indulge in success. If I am rewarded for refusing to look for employment, having children out of wedlock, sneaking over the border, or crying about the color of my skin, then any motivation to excel has been diminished.

As a father I remember vividly what it was like to look into a cupboard that had only enough rice to feed four members of my family of six. On those occasions, my wife and I went without. I have felt the pain of unemployment along with the fear of uncertainty that is married to it. But I also knew that work would not come looking for me. I

had to hunt it down. So I fought hard for the next paycheck by applying myself ten to fifteen hours a day, six days a week, until work was
mine. Yes, family and friends were there to help, and for that I am
blessed. But had I taken their benevolence to extremes and moved into
their homes and demanded daily sustenance along with a healthy al-
lowance of spending money, there is no doubt I would have been
shown the door and felt a boot in the process.

Personal responsibility. Hard work. Determination. Looking out
for the other guy. America came into prominence on the backs of such
powerful thoughts. America's position in the world relies on regular
citizens embracing these common, everyday values.

Though I've had my share of celebrity and success, I believe it is my
average existence as an American citizen that empowers me to write this
book because we can still make a
difference even if we are only
"average." Not only is it within
the ability of each of us to do so,
it is our mandate as citizens of
the greatest free nation in the
world to do so.

Over the years I have been
told that I have been used to
change the minds of politicians,

> ### WHAT WENT WRONG WITH AMERICA
>
> While writing this book I polled my listeners both in
> terms of "what went wrong with America" and "how
> to fix it." Interspersed throughout the first two parts of
> this volume are their comments in sidebars such as this
> with either a "what went wrong" or a "how to fix it"
> heading. (D.A.)

the plans of a reckless governor, and the perception of a nation. I have
helped to cause entire cites to stop dead in their tracks when a wrong
went unchecked, and I have stood firm when it wasn't the popular
thing to do. Each of us has the same ability. We alone choose whether
or not to use our powers to create positive change and to impact our
communities for the better. This is my story, but this is not a book
about me.

What follows is a story about you and your neighbor and the folks
on the next block—about each of us finding our place of significance.
It is a tome about regular folks who made this land great and how that
same spirit will keep us moving forward.

When you have finished reading this book, I am sure you will feel
the same sense of pride I felt after seeing the stories of how typical citizens chose to remain silent no longer. But it doesn't stop there. I have included some specific suggestions for you to help return America to its

God-inspired roots. Since I am a longtime member of our nation's much maligned media, I have outlined ways for you to get grass-roots support by including others in your causes. There is no doubt that when "We The People" hear the truth and know that others feel the same way, we are more than willing to join the fight. This book is about the fight and how you can help win it. This book is about becoming significant.

The strength of many raised this country to its position as a world power, and though forces are out there trying to stamp out the fire that is America, we are still here and we are still faithful enough to keep up the fight.

We are just average Americans who still believe.

AN ANSWER TO THE QUESTION

I AM THE MORNING-DRIVE personality at Talk Radio 570 KLIF in Dallas/Fort Worth. Sure, I do other things—like write books, run businesses, and watch my kids grow up—but for more than twenty-five years I have been a radio and TV guy. I think I've had my share of success because early on I learned to listen to the voice of the people. You—more than all the leaders, statesmen, and politicians—know the real score. Oh, you sometimes play coy, but in the end, you know exactly what's going on.

As an important element to this book, I decided to hear how average Americans responded to its title. So I posed two questions to my vast audience in Texas and throughout the world via my newsletter and streaming website: What went wrong with America? How would you fix it? I then encouraged listeners and readers to submit their solutions in one paragraph. And the letters poured in. It took me three days to read them all, but I did get through every one. And just as I suspected, folks had a solid handle on the situation.

But there was a line from one lady that summed it up brilliantly. It's going to hurt a little, and some probably won't like what she said. In fact, many probably won't believe it—not at first anyway. Soon they will. And then we might just be able to get onto the path to reclamation.

When I asked the question: "What went wrong with America?" it was Brenda G's five-word answer that hit with the force of a crashing ship: "I say we gave up."

Open the book. Take a look. See if she's right. Read what some of the others said, because I have included a few of them as well. What do you have to lose—except the rest of your freedoms?

WHAT WENT WRONG

with

AMERICA...
AND HOW
TO FIX IT

PART ONE

• •

LOST VISION

What Went Wrong?

Foolish is the man who gains knowledge but chooses to lock it away
instead of setting it free to impact others.
—*DARRELL ANKARLO*

I

· ·

THE BREWING STORM

AMERICA IS AT WAR today. And though it is a war for our survival, many refuse to recognize the enemy because they have been lulled to sleep by the very freedoms that we promised to protect at all costs.

We are a lost people. A clueless people. A people without an identity.

Think about it: What is an American? Who are we? What are we? The truth is, we don't know. The tragic and unadulterated truth is, we don't even know that we don't know. The enemy has us in a stranglehold and has no plans to let go until we are six feet under.

But there is some good news. Some of us still have life in our bones and a flicker of hope in our hearts. We are not just Americans; we are angry Americans, and we have decided that it is time for a change—while there still is time.

This country is in the throes of a culture war like never before. Morality has become something that is scoffed at, not embraced and cherished as a most prized possession. The more outrageous and debased a person is, the more books he will sell and the greater his influence will be. What a sad commentary on a nation that once served as a moral beacon on which the world could rely.

The election of 2000 will be reviewed by historians not as one of the biggest squeakers ever but as a warning that this nation is ripping apart at the seams. Many will say a few hanging chads in Florida put one man in the White House and dangled the carrot of "not this time" in front of the other. It wasn't about that at all; the personalities were the byproducts, the sideshow, nothing more. It only seemed that things centered on them.

The hostility that clouded the aftermath of the election was about a divided country. Some call it the phenomenon of the red states versus the blue states, big cities versus little towns, Democrats versus Republicans. Though all of those divisions certainly played a part, the resentment ran deeper. The election was just the boiling point for feelings buried too deep and too long.

Regular Joes can smell the winds of change in the air; there is a storm brewing. Conservative Americans are livid every time we conjure a mental image of a president having illicit sex in the Oval Office and then lying about it afterward. We are equally angry at liberals who argued that such conduct was "normal," "blown out of proportion," and "not that bad." Conservative Americans are tired of consigning all our income for the first half of a year to the government coffers so yet another social program will be funded.

On the other hand, liberals don't just "not care" about conservatives; they loathe us. They hate us. Big government enthusiasts cannot tolerate anyone who suggests scaling back redundant social programs; they won't be happy until every American is hooked on the cocaine that is government dependence. Elements of the Left despise the Right because we have something they don't, because we question their need to legitimize something that isn't legitimate. In this same society, Christians have become lepers. A hardworking, taxpaying, patriotic family with a few kids and a dog and a yard was once the goal for many. But today that family portrait is a laughingstock.

WHAT WENT WRONG WITH AMERICA

We told God we didn't want him here anymore! We told him that he no longer had a place in our government, in our schools, in our states, in our cities, or in our lives. We took him completely out of the equation. When you tell God you don't want him there, I guarantee he won't be there. Then we have something like 9/11 happen, and then we have the audacity to question God and ask him why HE let that happen? Come on! This is exactly what is wrong with America! It's like draining all the oil out of your car and wondering why it doesn't run anymore. (Cheryl J.)

America is at a cultural crossroads. Can two ideologies that have drifted so far apart ever work hand in hand again? Granted, we have always had differences, and just as iron sharpens iron, those distinctions have only helped to keep us strong. But now, I fear, the two sides are so polarized that we are on the verge of something terrible.

Federal judges have become activists, stealing states' rights issues away from their rightful jurisdictions. Look at the Ten Commandments battle that took place in Alabama in 2003. Since when does a federal court unilaterally decide a state issue? Liberals applauded. Conservative Americans scowled.

In 2004 gay activists turned the marriage bed into a battleground as cities and states broke laws and tradition to reach out to their downtrodden "domestic partners" by offering marriage licenses. In most cases it was against the law; in all cases it was against the will of the people. But somehow it became an equal rights issue, and the war escalated another notch. Liberals pranced in the streets with overflowing joy. And Conservatives scratched their heads in disbelief.

After the September 11 attacks, the president (that would be George W. Bush, though liberals still discount him) declared a war on terrorism. During his 2002 State of the Union address, he vowed to fight terrorism on all fronts while naming three nations

> ## HOW TO FIX IT
>
> Begin teaching true history. When people read the Mayflower Compact, the story behind the famous painting of George Washington kneeling in a forest, the three-hour prayer session that opened the first Continental Congress, or the diaries of the Founding Fathers, they will know that we are truly a nation founded on Christian principles. One of our Founding Fathers said that this government is for a "moral and religious people." It won't work for people who are not moral and religious. So the farther we move from our religious heritage, the more we will fall apart. (Jackelyn S.M.)

as an "axis of evil." Then he was forced to defend his use of the phrase for months, though all three nations have been genuine threats to world peace for years. In February 2003, as President Bush made his case for Iraq to comply fully with several longtime UN resolutions, he used sixteen words: "The British government has learned that Saddam Hussein recently sought significant quantities of uranium from Africa."

Immediately, Left-leaning news organizations and liberal celebrities tried to assassinate the character of the commander in chief, calling him a liar, a manipulator, and a man set on war at any cost so he could vindicate his father and former president. When conservative Americans spoke out on the president's behalf, they were ridiculed widely as kooks, wackos, and extremists.

What went wrong with America? How did we get so far out of balance? Is there still time to put the pieces back together? The questions are many, but the answers are few. Still, we have to search, we have to struggle for the solution. That is the spirit of America, and it is our drop of sunshine in the deep, dark hole that has slowly enveloped us.

We are well past finger-pointing. I can only imagine that during the Civil War, as a Union soldier held up his Springfield rifle to kill his Confederate enemy, he must have routinely questioned the wisdom in shooting a onetime friend and neighbor. As he took aim to fire, he had to think to himself, *He's an American, too.* With that fleeting thought, he squeezed the trigger, and red became the color of the grass and flowers.

Is this where the United States of America is heading? Does our anger consume us so much that what naturally follows is the escalation of our philosophical and political differences to the point of physical conflict? We would like to think we have become sufficiently sophisticated to not repeat such a sad saga in American history, but I'm not so sure we have evolved that much. The rage within Americans toward other Americans is palpable.

I see myself as an average American. I'm certainly not a spokesman for anyone other than myself, but I am fully aware that my feelings are shared by millions. We're just regular people—dads, moms, sons, and daughters—who want to lift the sense of despair from our great land. I won't suggest that I don't despise the actions of the loudmouths who articulate the liberal agenda—because I do. I abhor their actions, run from their ideologies, and cringe at the thought that they are fast-tracking a slavelike future for my children. I also admit that I look at my Left-leaning liberal neighbors and ask how they can be so foolish to believe as they do. But I also know that they look at me with the same question.

I am equally disgusted at so-called conservatives who rush to the center on issues that are deciding the fate of the country. Find your place and stick with it. It has been said that a double-minded man is unstable in all he does. This doesn't mean we should not seek to understand people with different agendas and beliefs, but when we seek to placate or join them, we lose our heading.

I'm not soft on liberalism. I believe it has sucked us into the pits of hell through extreme permissiveness. But even though the death rattle clatters in our deepest souls, I still believe. I believe in the human spirit. I believe in America. I believe in the people who are America.

Most Americans, be they liberals or conservatives, want happy families, good jobs, and a hope for a better tomorrow. The problem lies in the fact that most Americans relinquished their involvement in the process a long time ago. We are the body, but the mouths who represent the extreme Left and the extreme Right are the ones causing the greatest disturbance. Most of these spokespeople are on someone's payroll and recognize that their stake in the game rises every time they increase the noise and conflict levels. While we need leadership and cheerleaders, we also need something greater than all of that. We need to get involved.

When I talk to someone whose principles are opposite from mine, my first thought isn't to attack their positions. I want to understand how they arrived at their conclusions and how they built a philosophy around such tenets. It is only after I have this key knowledge that I can develop dialogues and debates with them to effect change, or at the very least, have them understand my positions, too. You are me. You feel the same way.

> ## WHAT WENT WRONG WITH AMERICA
>
> We Americans allowed ourselves to be taken down the wrong path when we gave our permission to have prayer removed from our lives! This country was founded on principles that our founders believed were extremely important. Our belief in God as the Creator and example for us was important enough to those Founding Fathers that they passed this belief system along to us in both the Bill of Rights and our Constitution. When we allowed the courts to disrupt our belief system and take prayer and religion into the "realm of separation," we then started the long road down the never-ending track to denial of God and the loss of our core beliefs. We are becoming a Godless society with no moral foundation. (Gene A.)

I have a battle to fight, a war to win. Right now it looks like it's going to be a bloody conflagration, but what if many of us, millions of us, jumped into the combat? What would happen to the temperament of the country if we could open dialogues across our many chasms of disagreement? Our leaders may be angry, but isn't there a chance this could offer the greatest possibility to save our nation? I don't know about you, but I am willing to try this route, because what we've been doing up to now isn't working.

To best understand what went wrong with America, we'll start with a trip back in time. For many, your eyes will be opened to this country's beginnings in ways that have mysteriously been lacking from our textbooks for decades. It doesn't matter that you do or don't agree with what you find; all that matters is truth. On the pages that follow you will read the truth that has been stolen from us. What you do with it is up to you.

At the beginning, be prepared for words you don't see that often. Words like: *church*, *Christian*, *Bible*, and *Jesus Christ*. Fair warning: As much as it is not my desire to offend you, it may just happen, especially if you've bought into the mumbo jumbo of those who have twisted the details of our early days.

> ## HOW TO FIX IT
>
> Someone once said that it is impossible to take an oath if you don't believe in something greater than yourself. Who will you swear by if you are an atheist? Who do you have to fear if you don't believe in God?...Who can you respect if you can't respect God? What would I do about our loss? I'd try to help people see that if we are to survive as a society, we must raise our children up in the admonition of the Lord God, and we ourselves must be an example for them to follow. I'd plaster the Ten Commandments everywhere and remind people that they are commandments, not suggestions. Once enough of us get it right, then those that refuse to follow will become outcasts. (Tom J.)

This book is divided into three parts: (1) an exploration of our history, (2) a look at the country through the lens of today's issues, and (3) some ideas for changing things for the better. To me the third section is the key to everything you are about to read because it highlights real people (just like you) who chose to make a difference in their community. This third section is rife with ideas, suggestions, and solutions—which is the major purpose for this book to begin with.

Read. Learn. Save our country. Change the world.

2

· ·

THEY LIED TO US!

In the name of our Lord Jesus Christ . . .
—CHRISTOPHER COLUMBUS

A̲MERICA WAS NOT FOUNDED on Christian principles!" I had just finished giving a speech about patriotism and politics, and the charging
man, who looked like he would have been willing to don a cape and fly if
that would let him confront me any sooner, was ready to pounce. Startled by his abruptness, I couldn't help but engage him in conversation.
Of course he was ready to provide quotes from Thomas Jefferson and
Benjamin Franklin to prove they weren't Christians, and if you assumed
he was about to pull out the typical and all-too-worn cliché "Most were
deists, and God isn't mentioned in the Constitution," you would have
been right. I think one day I will market a T-shirt that reads, "Blah, blah,
blah . . ." because that's all I heard as he attacked my character and IQ,
right-wing "dumb asses," and the sad condition of the country. Blah,
blah, blah. The problem with his "this country has always been secular"
argument is that it is flat wrong. As you will soon see, the freedom of religion concept isn't exactly right either.

America was founded not on religious liberty alone but specifically to
serve as a colony of Christianity. It is vitally important that we understand
this point because every part of our identity is mapped to it. This chapter
will go a long way in proving that, because of our Christian heritage, we

fought and won the Revolutionary War, developed laws that are still on the books, and created a Constitution that is known as one of the greatest founding documents in the history of the world. Detractors will say that it is a wholly secular constitution. I submit that it can't be, based on the events leading up to its creation as well as the men who did the work of bringing it into existence. You were most likely never taught what I'm about to tell you, which sadly is too real a barometer of how far our nation has veered from its original course.

> **WHAT WENT WRONG WITH AMERICA**
>
> What went wrong in America? We got away from what our forefathers said and believed. (Paula W.)

Even as I write this book I am mindful of the diversity of hands that will turn its pages. But diversity wasn't always the case in our history. From the days of the Pilgrims and up to the ratification of the Constitution, approximately 80 to 85 percent of all citizens attended regular weekly church services—Christian church services.

MOVE OR DIE!

THE ORIGINAL passengers who boarded the *Mayflower* from England and the *Speedwell* from Holland knew what they were risking but agreed even death would be better than living under the thumb of a church and government that tortured its people. Of the 102 people aboard the *Mayflower*, three-quarters of the women, half the men, a third of the boys, and a few of the girls died within their first year in the New World. Imagine the fear and anxiety they shared as they boarded the ships. They had sold their businesses, homes, and possessions and were leaving their friends, families, and churches behind. What a scary thought—on one hand, abandon everything and search for a new home; on the other, stay where you are and face an uncertain future.

The Church of England was the dominant force throughout Britain, and though the government tolerated the Puritans with their strict interpretation of the Bible and separate church services, there was only so much the leaders would tolerate. These Christians fought openly about specific doctrines and traditions like sacraments, marriage, baptism, holy days, and church organization, but they were also forced to flee to the shadows for fear they would be identified and imprisoned. For years families would sneak from one home to the next, using codes and passwords to avoid the eye of the government. They wanted to practice Christianity in its purest form; the government liked it the way it was. Finally, when James I came into power in 1604 he went to work to stop what he thought was madness. Those who did not worship and think as the Church of England dictated were arrested, persecuted, jailed, and even executed.

Not that long before the Puritans, Martin Luther used the term "horribly corrupt" to describe the affairs of a national church. Routinely, death came by hanging, drowning, or burning. Under Protestant British monarchs, Jesuits like John Ogilvie[1] (1580–1615) were under constant watch, because Catholicism was deemed "unpatriotic." When the leaders had had enough, they hanged Ogilvie and disemboweled him as an example to those who dared follow in his path.

In 1630 a Puritan was arrested and sentenced to life imprisonment, but not before his property was confiscated, his nose slit, an ear cut off, and his forehead branded "S.S." (sower of sedition). His crime? He and his fellow believers wanted to be sure the full truth of the Bible was taught.

One of the world's greatest Bibles, the Tyndale Bible, was translated by John Rogers,[2] a Catholic priest who converted to Protestantism. Shortly after Queen Mary took the throne, she heard John Rogers preach the gospel. Mary was so outraged that she had him arrested on a charge of heresy and demanded that he be burned alive, making Rogers the first Protestant martyr in Britain.

Europe was definitely not the place to be if one wanted to worship freely. So on pure faith and a hope for a better life, immigrants headed to America.

MORE THAN FREEDOM OF RELIGION

OBVIOUSLY, NOT everyone boarding vessels for the New World did so for reasons of religious freedom. Political rebels, indentured men, and "maidens pressed" also set sail. Yet history shows that most who made the trip did so because of their deeply religious faith—a Christian faith. The original agreement between the early settlers of Massachusetts, also known as the Mayflower Compact[3] (1620), clearly demonstrates which God they served. Read carefully its first paragraph:

> IN THE NAME OF GOD, AMEN. We, whose names are underwritten, the Loyal Subjects of our dread Sovereign Lord King James, by the Grace of

God, of Great Britain, France, and Ireland, King, Defender of the Faith, &c. Having undertaken for the Glory of God, and Advancement of the Christian Faith, and the Honour of our King and Country, a Voyage to plant the first Colony in the northern Parts of Virginia; Do by these Presents, solemnly and mutually, in the Presence of God and one another, covenant and combine ourselves together into a civil Body Politick, for our better Ordering and Preservation, and Furtherance of the Ends aforesaid: And by Virtue hereof do enact, constitute, and frame, such just and equal Laws, Ordinances, Acts, Constitutions, and Officers, from time to time, as shall be thought most meet and convenient for the general Good of the Colony; unto which we promise all due Submission and Obedience. IN WITNESS whereof we have hereunto subscribed our names at Cape-Cod the eleventh of November, in the Reign of our Sovereign Lord King James, of England, France, and Ireland, the eighteenth, and of Scotland the fifty-fourth, Anno Domini; 1620.

The early settlers were unashamed to proclaim their Christian principles even in matters of government and community. Historical documents refer to the New England colonies as "Bible Commonwealths."[4] Here is how one presentation from the Library of Congress describes their motivation:

> They enthusiastically supported the efforts of their leaders to create "a city on a hill" or a "holy experiment" whose success would prove that God's plan for his churches could be successfully realized in the American wilderness. Even colonies like Virginia, which were planned as commercial ventures, were led by entrepreneurs who considered themselves "militant Protestants" and who worked diligently to promote the prosperity of the church.[5]

Other American documents point to the Bible as the settlers' source for law and order. The primary document used was called *The Body of Liberties*,[6] which was compiled and drafted by Nathaniel Ward, a lawyer turned minister who was the son of a Puritan preacher. Of special interest is that much of the content came from the Old Testament and church teachings. Among these can be found several of the rights that surfaced later in the Bill of Rights. This is a critical link between the Bible and the Constitution. The document was also the foundation for the laws and Constitution of Massachusetts[7]; the same state that has been in the heat of battle over the legalization of gay marriage in 2004.

Lately we have been bombarded by the notion of political correctness. Many of those who are devoted to this concept are among the first to preach that this country was founded on secular or "freedom of religion" principles. But they are mistaken. We evolved into secular thought and slowly opened the doors to religious choice. Those decisions have slowly degraded the foundation that tied us together. Newspaper headlines frequently scream about the efforts to keep "under God" out of the schools, the Ten Commandments away from public buildings, and the holy Scriptures from the history we learn. Two hundred years ago such thoughts would have been construed as diabolic.

If the red-faced man who confronted me at the beginning of this chapter were standing here now, I am sure he would be jabbing his finger at my chest and proclaiming that America has worked all these years because we adhere to the rule of law. "Look at the Magna Carta!" he'd assert. So I'll indulge him.

The Magna Carta (1215) is the documentary basis for order in England, and it was a resource our constitutional framers. It is also the document that William Penn relied on during the founding of Pennsylvania. But liberals fail to mention a couple of key points when they trumpet the Magna Carta over Christian principles. Penn was an outspoken Quaker who called the the city of Philadelphia a "Holy Experiment," and the Magna Carta has God stamped all over it.

HOW MUCH MORE CHRISTIAN CAN A NATION BE?

THE MAGNA CARTA was a reactionary document created when England emerged from the Middle Ages and the country gravitated toward a representative form of government instead of the typical king-rules-all system. The document provided a framework for the British constitution and would later aid in the development of American law. As you will note, God and church are front and center in the language:

KNOW THAT BEFORE GOD, for the health of our soul and those of our ancestors and heirs, to the honour of God, the exaltation of the holy Church, and the better ordering of our kingdom, at the advice of our reverend fathers . . . and other loyal subjects:

FIRST, THAT WE HAVE GRANTED TO GOD, and by this present charter have confirmed for us and our heirs in perpetuity, that the

English Church shall be free, and shall have its rights undiminished, and its liberties unimpaired. That we wish this so to be observed, appears from the fact that of our own free will, before the outbreak of the present dispute between us and our barons, we granted and confirmed by charter the freedom of the Church's elections—a right reckoned to be of the greatest necessity and importance to it—and caused this to be confirmed by Pope Innocent III.

The evidence proving this country's Christian disposition is indisputable. In 1776 eleven of the thirteen colonies required that a person be a Christian to run for political office. In 1777 the war with Britain cut off the flow of Bibles, so the Continental Congress voted to spend $300,000 to purchase Bibles. The charters of Virginia, Massachusetts, Connecticut, Pennsylvania, and others referenced Christianity or Christ in their language. The constitutions of Pennsylvania, Mississippi, Maryland, Massachusetts, New Hampshire, North Carolina, Connecticut, South Carolina, and Georgia also place God as their central focus.

To see just how up front the framers of the state constitutions were about their Christian faith, look at this oath required of all officeholders in Delaware (1776): "I, ____, do profess faith in God the Father in Jesus Christ His only Son, and in the Holy Ghost, one God blessed for evermore; and I do acknowledge the Holy Scriptures of the Old and New Testaments to be given by divine inspiration." All charters and constitutions had similar language, and most required an oath or statement of faith. New Jersey's charter is another prime example. It required that all members of the legislature have "a belief in the faith of any Protestant sect."

In addition to the documents, state constitutions, and various charters, the words that flow directly from our country's historical leaders leave no room for doubt. Christopher Columbus, in a letter to the Spanish monarchs, is unambiguous about his Christian faith: "That there shall be a church, and parish priests or friars to administer the sacraments, to perform divine worship, and for the conversion of the Indians."[8] In his journal, Columbus further stated that his reasons for exploring "undiscovered worlds" was to "bring the Gospel of Jesus Christ to the heathens [and] . . . bring the Word of God to unknown coastlands."[9]

Supreme Court Justice John Jay, one of the architects of the U.S. Constitution, noted: "Providence has given to our people the choice of their rulers, and it is the duty, as well as the privilege and interest of our Christian nation, to select and prefer Christians for their rulers."[10]

"It cannot be emphasized too strongly or too often that this great nation was founded, not by religionists but by Christians, not on religions, but on the gospel of Jesus Christ," stated Patrick Henry.[11]

Noah Webster said, "Almost all the civil liberty now enjoyed in the world owes its origin to the principles of the Christian religion."[12]

In May 1776 Congress proclaimed a "day of Humiliation, Fasting and Prayer," which was to be observed annually throughout the Revolutionary War. In the proclamation Congress urged the citizens to "confess and bewail our manifold sins and transgressions, and by a sincere repentance and amendment of life, appease [God's] righteous displeasure, and through the merits and mediation of Jesus Christ, obtain his pardon and forgiveness." Massachusetts furnished churches throughout the colony with ample supplies so all could join the effort.

> **HOW TO FIX IT**
>
> I personally would fight to reestablish the fact that our nation was founded on a belief in God and reinstitute God into our schools, communal gatherings, and most of all, into the lives of all Americans. The separation of church and state does not exist. Our Judeo-Christian belief system is an integral part of our heritage and our future. Anyone who doesn't like prayer, belief in God, and allowing the Ten Commandments to be displayed and used for the purpose of directing our lives should get a grip on themselves and thank God for all they have and for the freedom we enjoy each day. When God is back in this nation, we will once again have the direction and ability to live our lives and become who we are destined to be: the greatest nation on earth, allowing everyone to become and live free. (Gene A.)

The following year, Congress set December 18, 1777, as a Day of Thanksgiving[13] so the American people "may express the grateful feelings of their hearts and consecrate themselves to the service of their divine benefactor" and on which they might "join the penitent confession of their manifold sins . . . that it may please God, through the merits of Jesus Christ, mercifully to forgive and blot them out of remembrance." Congress also suggested that Americans petition God "to prosper the means of religion for the promotion and enlargement of that kingdom which consisteth in righteousness, peace and joy in the Holy Ghost."

History shows that all roads heading to America had the church, Christ, or God leading the flow of traffic. Keep in mind that my goal is to show you how our past has been covered up and remodeled. This information will have a significant bearing on your decision to involve yourself in helping to direct America's future.

Those who argue that America was and is secular in nature usually point to Thomas Jefferson, Ben Franklin, and a few others as deists. A deist is one who believes God placed the universe in motion and then abandoned it, leaving us to handle things ourselves. Jefferson believed God was evident through reason and nature. He was no doubt a deist in the defined sense of the word, but Franklin's life is open to much greater interpretation. What is interesting, though, assuming that each man was a deist, is how they routinely looked to the Bible for counsel.

> ## HOW TO FIX IT
>
> Remove the Ten "Suggestions" from our homes, schools, churches and businesses, and society's representatives. Bring forth the Ten Commandments or call them the Ten Aspirations. Simple to read and comprehend, maybe difficult to adhere to and follow, but most rewarding for all. (Michael)

One of the best examples has to do with the Seal of the United States.[14] Congress appointed Franklin, Jefferson, and John Adams "to bring in a device for a Seal for the United States of America." Franklin's proposal modified the biblical story of the Israelites and their wilderness experience, while Jefferson went to the same story but included the cloud by day and a pillar of fire by night. Jefferson liked Franklin's idea better and endorsed it to Congress. A different seal was adopted eventually, but the example serves to point out the important role Christianity played, even in the decision-making process of religious liberals, leaving no doubt Christianity was the major influence of the day.

AMERICA'S LAWS SET US APART—BUT WHERE DID WE GET THE LAWS?

AT SOME point we have all read or at least skimmed one of this country's greatest treasures, the Declaration of Independence. It was penned in large part by Thomas Jefferson, though four others also comprised what was later called the Committee of Five, the group designated to draft the document. Each man had long ago lent his pen to many letters and documents espousing the teachings of Christ and the importance of the Bible in the lives of citizens. One of the five, Roger Sherman, wrote, "I believe that there is only one living and true God. . . . That the scriptures of the old and new testaments are a revelation from God and a complete rule to direct us how we may glorify and enjoy Him."[15] Each man understood the importance of the task as well as society's deep love for God, and therefore, I believe, could not operate without faith entering the equation.

Review the opening lines of the Declaration, and already God is evident. Why would secular writers working on a secular, godless document dare to mention the Creator—unless they were devoted to a higher calling?

> When, in the course of human events, it becomes necessary for one people to dissolve the Political Bands which have connected them with another, and to assume among the Powers of the Earth, the separate and equal Station to which the Laws of Nature and of Nature's God entitle them, a decent Respect to the Opinions of Mankind requires that they should declare the causes which impel them to the Separation.
>
> We hold these Truths to be self-evident, that all Men are created equal, that they are endowed by their Creator with certain unalienable Rights, that among these are Life, Liberty and the Pursuit of Happiness.[16]

What our schoolbooks have omitted for many years is that Jefferson's inspiration for his outline of the Declaration of Independence came from another Virginian. Plantation owner and patriot George Mason drafted a list of rights for Virginia, later known as the Virginia Declaration of Rights. Copies were distributed to the other colonies, and the ideas caught on in the streets as citizens convened meetings just to read what was about to come to their region. The Declaration of Rights contained sixteen sections that gave citizens control over their lives. The sixteenth, in yet another "secular" document, says that "religion, or the duty which we owe to our Creator, and the manner of discharging it, can be directed only by reason and conviction, not by force or violence. Therefore all men are equally entitled to the free exercise of religion, according to the dictates of conscience; and that it is the mutual duty of all to practise Christian forbearance, love, and charity toward each other."[17] Mason was a devout Christian who helped raise funds to build his church. In many historical circles he is listed as the "Father of the Bill of Rights."

Now we have two sources, including the *Body of Liberties*, which lead from Scripture to our most central founding documents. But we're never told this. God, religion, the Bible, Christ, and heaven have been systematically deleted by liberal leaders for far too many years. Too bad someone forgot to tell George Mason that his country was devoid of God; he may have reconsidered the words of his last will and testament: "My soul, I resign into the hands of my Almighty Creator, whose tender mercies are overall His works, who hateth nothing that He hath made and to the Justice and Wisdom of whose dispensation I willingly and cheerfully submit, humbly hoping from His unbounded mercy and benevolence, through the merits of my blessed Savior, a remission of my sins."

AMERICA ADVANCES BECAUSE OF ITS FAITH

AMERICA AS we know it would not have been born without God-fearing men and women who came to this continent on faith alone. But without widespread Christian influence, America would have been wiped out by the British during the Revolutionary War. Let me explain.

In the 1730s and 1740s a religious fervor spread throughout England and Scotland and eventually made its way to America where the people were prepped for "an outpouring from God." This movement has been studied by theologians and historians for more than two hundred years because of the unbelievable impact it had on the colonies. The Great Awakening, as it is known, created an almost frenzied atmosphere where colonists openly encouraged one another in their faith and evangelized others to join them. As a result, churches were built at a record pace, and more Christians and ministers joined themselves to civil and cultural affairs than at anytime up to that point. Their creed was simple: "Go ye into all the world, and preach the gospel to every creature" (Mark 16:15).

A new breed of church grew from the awakening with denominations like the Baptists, Presbyterians, and Methodists, all very evangelical in nature, flourishing while Anglicans, Congregationalists, and Quakers diminished because of their inability to catch the vision of the newfound passion.

GOD WON THE REVOLUTIONARY WAR!

BY THE time the American Revolution was in full war mode, Americans had been basking in the glory of their faith for more than two decades, and this may have turned the tide in favor of the rebels. Ministers routinely preached not just a message of salvation from their pulpits but also sermons that directed citizens to believe in their country and get involved in the fight for freedom. One scholar noted, "By turning colonial resistance into a righteous cause, and by carrying the message to all ranks in all parts of the colonies, ministers did the work of secular radicalism and did it better."

The war for freedom from the tyranny of the king and the dictates of English law was fought by most as a righteous cause. Men and women wanted to be free, but their new and improved sense of God's provision gave them the courage to believe that he would deliver them just as he had the children of Israel in the Bible stories they had read. In a certain sense, the Revolutionary War took on almost a holy war sense of urgency, with families leaving and selling property to join the fight while right alongside them in many instances were their pastors and elders, encouraging them in the call to battle.

The Continental Confederation Congress, a legislative body that governed the United States from 1774 to 1789, was composed almost exclusively of deeply religious men. And the work they did for the country almost always included a way to impact the world with the gospel. During this time Congress sponsored Bible publication and distribution (which later led to the creation of the American Bible Society),[18] appointed chaplains for the armed forces while imposing Christian morality on all soldiers,[19] established national days of prayer, and worked on a principle that the stronger the faith of the people, the stronger the resolve to succeed would be. This "secular" institution, as today's textbooks label it, actually followed an extremely religious edict known as the "Covenant Theology," which was a Reformation doctrine that claimed God himself had entered into an agreement for victory if his people would humbly seek his face. This was a much beloved doctrine of the New England Puritans.

In the end, these bands of American patriots, most of whom had little or no military training, fought one of the mightiest and most revered armies in the world and won. America was now its own entity because the Christian faith of the citizens compelled them to believe that God would help them triumph!

DISMISSING GOD WHEN WE NEEDED HIM MOST

HOW DID this New World—discovered, settled, and governed by Christians (not including Columbus)—turn away from its roots and toward secularism overnight? How did its Christian leaders decide—during wartime, mind you—that religion should no longer play a role in society, although all original colonial charters show a direct link? What happened that caused 80 percent of churchgoing Americans to chuck it all for some system devoid of God? Those questions are continually fed to us as fact, and most Americans have no clue how to answer. Let me point out that these questions represent things that never happened. None of it happened. Nothing changed. But for some reason liberals have thoroughly indoctrinated us to believe our founders somehow turned away from God—or never knew him in the first place.

We know that our leaders were God-fearing, Bible-believing people from the founding of the colonies up to and during the ratification of the Declaration of Independence. That was 1776. The Constitution was written less than ten years later, with nine of the original thirteen colonies ratifying it in 1789. Every state demanded the Bill of Rights be attached for full acceptance, because they wanted several personal rights issues to be resolved, and they did not want the government to keep them from their faith. Isn't it odd that we have been led to believe that a majority of the early Americans as well as their political leaders wanted an amendment (the First Amendment) to keep God, the Bible, and the church out of the affairs of the state and federal governments? This is one of the biggest lies ever perpetrated, and to this day it is treated as fact. It just doesn't make sense.

Remember the guy at the beginning of the chapter? He hung around a while longer, claiming that our highly intelligent and most influential deist leaders shifted the language to keep the church from getting involved in the affairs of government. Let me debunk this thought process once and for all. As I briefly mentioned, Thomas Jefferson was most likely a deist. So what? He was just one man. Just one guy who did a great service to America, but he did not act alone. He never acted alone. There were more than two hundred founders. Check the numbers: Fifty-five were at the Constitutional Convention, ninety helped to frame the First Amendment and the Bill of Rights, and fifty-six signed the Declaration. The mathematical odds that all, or even a majority, switched from their godly lives to ardent secularists are almost incalculable. Somehow we are supposed to believe that they distributed Bibles, held national days of prayer, helped out at their churches, volunteered to fight in a war, while also deciding that God meant nothing to the nation they were involved in founding. Such contentions are complete fabrications, but that's what our schools and news media have been preaching to us for decades. And many of us believe them.

Here are a few more examples of our nation's Christian heritage. In the spring of 1785 Congress proposed that each town's central section be used for education and that "the Section immediately adjoining the same to the northward, for the support of religion. The profits arising therefrom in both instances, to be applied for ever according to the will of the majority."[20] It's hardly likely that nonbelievers who allegedly wanted nothing to do with God made provisions for churches to be situated in the center of town—right next to schools. Go figure.

Then there was the Northwest Ordinance from the summer of 1787. Article 3 says: "Religion, Morality and knowledge being necessary to good government and the happiness of mankind, Schools and the means of education shall be forever encouraged."[21] Those founders whom liberals believe wanted religion out of society just kept tossing it right back into the mix. Their answer was clear: Christianity developed America.

> ## WHAT WENT WRONG WITH AMERICA
>
> Our problem? The whole anti-religion movement and the total lack of personal morals, convictions, and personal responsibility. Compare where we were fifteen to twenty years ago to where we are today, and you'll see a drastic difference. And it's not a good difference either. We are slowly turning into one of the Godless societies we fought against back in the 1950s. If we don't change and take back this once proud country, we will end up like Communist China or the old Russia, where nearly everyone, with the exception of a few, lives in poverty and no one believes in a higher being. Our country was built on principles of a higher power, like it or not. (Monte R.)

THE SUPREME COURT'S INCONSISTENCIES

WE HAVE seen citizens and politicians embrace the religion of the land in the fabric of the founding of the nation. Finally, let's look at the courts before they sold out to liberalism.

In *Runkel v. Winemiller* the Supreme Court stated: "By our form of Government, the Christian religion is the established religion; and all sects and denominations of Christians are placed on the same equal footing, and are equally entitled to protection in their religious liberty."[22]

In another Supreme Court decision, the *Church of the Holy Trinity v. U.S.*, the justices quoted eighty-seven precedents in a sixteen-page document in making their case that Christianity was the religion of the country. These are just a few:

> Our laws and our institutions must necessarily be based upon and embody the teachings of the Redeemer of mankind. It is impossible that it should be otherwise, and in this sense and to this extent our civilization and our institutions are emphatically Christian. These and many other matters which might be noticed, add a volume of unofficial declarations to the mass of organic utterances that *this is a Christian nation*. . . .
>
> No purpose of action against religion can be imputed to any legislation, state or national, because this is a religious people. This is historically true. From the discovery of this continent to the present hour, there is a single voice making this affirmation. . . . The commission to Christopher Columbus . . . that it is hoped that by God's assistance some of the continents and islands in the ocean will be discovered. . . . The first colonial grant made to Sir Walter Raleigh in 1584 . . . and the grant authorizing him to enact statutes for the government of the proposed colony provided that they "be not against the true Christian faith." . . .
>
> We find everywhere a clear recognition of the same truth . . . because of a general recognition of this truth [that we are a Christian nation], the question has seldom been presented to the courts. . . . There is no dissonance in these declarations. There is a universal language pervading them all, having one meaning; they affirm and reaffirm that this is a religious nation.
>
> Those are not individual sayings, declarations of private persons; they are organic utterances; they speak the voice of the entire people. . . . While because of a general recognition of this truth the question has seldom been presented to the courts, yet we find that in *Updegraph v. The Commonwealth*, it was decided that, Christianity, general Christianity, is, and always has been, a part of the common law . . . not Christianity with an established church . . . but Christianity with liberty of conscience to all men. . . .
>
> And in *The People v. Ruggles*, Chancellor Kent, the great commentator on American law, speaking as Chief Justice of the Supreme Court of New York, said: The people of this State, in common with the people of this country, profess the general doctrines of Christianity, as the rule of their faith and practice. . . .

We are a Christian people, and the morality of the country is deeply engrafted upon Christianity, and not upon the doctrines or worship of those impostors [other religions]. . . . And in the famous Case of *Vidal v. Girard's Executors*, this Court . . . observed: It is also said, and truly, that the Christian religion is a part of the common law. . . .

These, and many other matters which might be noticed, add a volume of unofficial declarations to the mass of organic utterances that this is a Christian nation.[23]

In *U.S. v. Macintosh*, the Court said, "We are a Christian people . . . according to one another the equal right of religious freedom, and acknowledge with reverence the duty of obedience to the will of God."[24]

In *Zorach v. Clauson* (1952), the Supreme Court noted: "We are a religious people and our institutions presuppose a Supreme Being. . . . When the state encourages religious instruction or cooperates with religious authorities by adjusting the schedule of public events to sectarian needs, it follows the best of our traditions. We cannot read into the Bill of Rights a philosophy of hostility to religion."[25]

In *Abington School District v. Schempp* (1963) the Supreme Court stated: "The State may not establish a 'religion of secularism' in the sense of affirmatively opposing or showing hostility to religion, thus preferring those who believe in no religion over those who do believe."[26]

What other evidence is required? When every major facet of society points to the same source, the same religion, and when thousands of stories and lives bear witness too, then truth has been found.

> ## WHAT WENT WRONG WITH AMERICA
>
> In 1962 the Supreme Court, without precedent, ruled that children should no longer say a simple prayer in school. The prayer asked for God's hand in our schools, family, government, and country. If you look at the data from 1963, you will see that SAT scores plummeted, divorce became commonplace, STDs and drug use increased, and the country started a downward spiral. Parents were told to not discipline their children. We got involved in an unwinnable war. Leaders were assassinated. And people stopped going to church. (Trent B.)

America's population is pushing the three hundred million mark, and since we are greatly diversified by way of culture, race, and religion, it is a given that there is no way to return to an earlier, more simpler time. But that is not the point.

This chapter has been about debunking the liberal thought police, who have commandeered a religion and country right under our noses. Let this serve as a very specific warning: Incrementalism (that is, if you want to eat the whole cow, you must do it one bite at a time) is alive and well and is working to rid our culture of its Christian past. As soon as this goal is satisfied, then the move to take our freedoms and conservative philosophies will be easy pickings, since both are tied to our religious roots. Once the firsthand evidence has been destroyed, any story can be concocted, and we can't do anything other than accept it. Think about it. If such a monumental piece of history can be eradicated, then anything is fair game.

Since this has been a story of religion in America, let me close with a biblical example from the New Testament commonly called the Parable of the Ten Virgins:

> At that time the kingdom of heaven will be like ten virgins who took their lamps and went out to meet the bridegroom. Five of them were foolish and five were wise. The foolish ones took their lamps but did not take any oil with them. The wise, however, took oil in jars along with their lamps. The bridegroom was a long time in coming, and they all became drowsy and fell asleep. At midnight the cry rang out: "Here's the bridegroom! Come out to meet him!" Then all the virgins woke up and trimmed their lamps. The foolish ones said to the wise, "Give us some of your oil; our lamps are going out." "No," they replied, "there may not be enough for both us and you. Instead, go to those who sell oil and buy some for yourselves." But while they were on their way to buy the oil, the bridegroom arrived. The virgins who were ready went in with him to the wedding banquet. And the door was shut.
>
> Later the others also came. "Sir! Sir!" they said. "Open the door for us!" But he replied, "I tell you the truth, I don't know you."
>
> Therefore keep watch, because you do not know the day or the hour. (Matthew 25:1–13, NIV)

The moral? As America continues its slow slide toward a liberal "choice is everything as long as I feel good about myself" way of living, are you paying attention to the signs and tirelessly fighting for the future of your way of life, family, and country? Or do you sleep?

3

•••••••••••••••••••••••••••••••••••

A CLEAR AND
PRESENT DANGER

*Any twenty-year-old who isn't a liberal doesn't have a heart,
and any forty-year-old who isn't a conservative doesn't have
a brain.*

—WINSTON CHURCHILL

IN 1963 WE WERE at the height of the cold war. Spies gathered intelligence, Russia wanted to rule the world, and schoolchildren routinely practiced civil defense by crawling under their desks or hunkering down in school hallways. Looking back, I suppose the drills gave us at least some degree of security, albeit unrealistic. Even with all the anxiety over nuclear confrontation, there were some Americans who said, "It's all much ado about nothing" while those who despised America put their long-term plans into effect.

Fast-forward at least two generations, and the trouble that faced our representative democracy has only grown in size and complexity. Cavalier attitudes prevail now and threaten our future more than ever before. I'm not sure why, but too many Americans are intimidated by the bullies and thugs in society who consider conservatives to be second-class citizens because we value faith, family, and country. And the moment we express our opinions, those on the other side make sure we feel like idiots or, at the very least, uninformed.

Do not buy their rhetoric, not even for a moment, because your freedoms hang in the balance. I know I sound like an alarmist, but after you research the anti-family, anti-God, and anti-America groups, you will understand that the only way to keep the dream of this great nation alive is to fight both as individuals and dedicated teams.

It was a Thursday, January, 10, 1963, and a Florida Democrat had had enough. His country was careening out of control, and he wanted to make sure the thoughts he was about to share would not only be heard but would endure for generations to come. Albert. S. Herlong Jr., a twenty-year veteran of the U.S. Congress, asked his colleagues to accept into the Congressional Record a disturbing list that still makes this average citizen shudder with fear. His request won unanimous approval. "The Current Communist Goals," as the list would later be known, included forty-five ways to infiltrate the American system and ways to ultimately destroy it. The list was compiled from a book entitled *The Naked Communist*, which was published in 1958 by W. Cleon Skousen, a sixteen-year veteran of the FBI and a former university professor.[1] Skousen was one of the foremost experts on communism and went to great lengths to research his material, combining thoughts, goals, and lessons from more than one hundred leaders in the communist community.

I recently read the communist goals to my radio audience, and the response was overwhelming. Most people had never heard of Skousen or the list, even though his book sold more than one thousand copies a day and was reprinted more than nine times. There were also many who believed the list was contrived and irrelevant.

I am always dumbfounded by the reaction from our country's skeptics. What will it take to wake the foolish? The details in the document were sourced directly to the Soviet Union, a country dead set on wiping us out. The document was written almost a half century before I read a single word of it to my audience, and still some people thought it was immaterial or part of a right-wing conspiracy.

As you read through the list of communist goals, ask yourself if it reflects the changes made in America's direction over the last half century. Remember, the items on this list are from 1958 and include a communist thought process that reaches back to the 1940s:[2]

1. U.S. acceptance of coexistence as the only alternative to atomic war.
2. U.S. willingness to capitulate in preference to engaging in atomic war.

3. Develop the illusion that total disarmament by the U.S. would be a demonstration of "moral strength."
4. Permit free trade between all nations regardless of communist affiliation and regardless of whether or not items could be used for war.
5. Extension of long-term loans to the Soviet Union and Soviet satellites.
6. Provide American aid to all nations regardless of communist domination.
7. Grant recognition of Red China and admission of Red China to the UN.
8. Set up East and West Germany as separate states in spite of Nikita Khrushchev's promise in 1955 to settle the Germany question by free elections under supervision of the UN.
9. Prolong the conferences to ban atomic tests because the U.S. has agreed to suspend tests as long as negotiations are in progress.
10. Allow all Soviet satellites individual representation in the UN.
11. Promote the UN as the only hope for mankind. If its charter is rewritten, demand that it be set up as a one-world government with its own independent armed forces. (Some communist leaders believe the world can be taken over as easily by the UN as by Moscow. Sometimes these two centers compete with each other as they are now doing in the Congo.)
12. Resist any attempt to outlaw the Communist Party.
13. Do away with loyalty oaths.
14. Continue giving the Soviet Union access to the U.S. Patent Office.
15. Capture one or both of the political parties in the U.S.
16. Use technical decisions of the courts to weaken basic American institutions by claiming their activities violate civil rights.
17. Get control of the schools. Use them as transmission belts for socialism, and current communist propaganda. Soften the curriculum. Get control of teachers associations. Put the party line in textbooks.
18. Gain control of all student newspapers.
19. Use student riots to foment public protests against programs or organizations that are under communist attack.
20. Infiltrate the press. Get control of book review assignments, editorial writing, policy-making positions.
21. Gain control of key positions in radio, TV, and motion pictures.

22. Continue discrediting American culture by degrading all form of artistic expression. An American communist cell was told to "eliminate all good sculpture from parks and buildings," substitute shapeless, awkward, and meaningless forms.

23. Control art critics and directors of art museums. "Our plan is to promote ugliness, repulsive, meaningless art."

24. Eliminate all laws governing obscenity by calling them censorship and a violation of free speech and free press.

25. Break down cultural standards of morality by promoting pornography and obscenity in books, magazines, motion pictures, radio, and TV.

26. Present homosexuality, degeneracy, and promiscuity as "normal, natural, and healthy."

27. Infiltrate the churches and replace revealed religion with social religion. Discredit the Bible and emphasize the need for intellectual maturity, which does not need a "religious crutch."

28. Eliminate prayer or any phase of religious expression in the schools on the grounds that it violates the principle of separation of church and state.

29. Discredit the American Constitution by calling it inadequate, old-fashioned, out of step with modern needs, a hindrance to cooperation between nations on a worldwide basis.

30. Discredit the American Founding Fathers. Present them as selfish aristocrats who had no concern for the common man.

31. Belittle all forms of American culture and discourage the teaching of American history on the ground that it was only a minor part of the big picture. Give more emphasis to Russian history since the communists took over.

32. Support any socialist movement to give centralized control over any part of the culture—education, social agencies, welfare programs, mental health clinics, etc.

33. Eliminate all laws or procedures that interfere with the operation of the communist apparatus.

34. Eliminate the House Committee on Un-American Activities.

35. Discredit and eventually dismantle the FBI.

36. Infiltrate and gain control of more unions.

37. Infiltrate and gain control of big business.

38. Transfer some of the arrest powers from the police to social agencies. Treat all behavioral problems as psychiatric disorders that no one but psychiatrists can understand or treat.
39. Dominate the psychiatric profession and use mental health laws as a means of gaining coercive control over those who oppose communist goals.
40. Discredit the family as an institution. Encourage promiscuity and easy divorce.
41. Emphasize the need to raise children away from the negative influence of parents. Attribute prejudices, mental blocks, and retarding of children to the suppressive influence of parents.
42. Create the impression that violence and insurrection are legitimate aspects of the American tradition; that students and special-interest groups should rise up and make a united force to solve economic, political, or social problems.
43. Overthrow all colonial governments before native populations are ready for self-government.
44. Internationalize the Panama Canal.
45. Repeal the Connally Reservation so the U.S. cannot prevent the World Court from seizing jurisdiction over domestic problems. Give the World Court jurisdiction over domestic problems. Give the World Court jurisdiction over nations and individuals alike.

After reviewing this list, I am convinced each one has already been accomplished in this country, some to more extent than others. The proof is everywhere. Just look at the evening news. A group of California judges ruled that we can't mention God in the Pledge of Allegiance (though they were overruled by the Supreme Court), a Florida husband won a court's approval to murder his wife by removing her feeding tubes, Christ can't be mentioned at Christmastime but Muhammad can, special teachers are hired to teach parts of classes in Spanish because illegal immigrants deserve an education at taxpayer expense. Every day this list gets longer. Clearly, a shift has taken place in the United States. And the campaign put into effect more than four decades ago is now strangling us with its weeds of degradation.

Communism collapsed when President Ronald Reagan pierced the air with these words: "Mr. Gorbachev, tear down these walls." For the most part, communism is no longer embraced by Russia, a country that now has McDonald's, Starbucks, and popular music in cities everywhere. So why discuss a fallen system and a book written almost fifty years ago? I contend that the threat embodied in this list is as great today as it was then. Not because the plot itself continues, but because the byproducts of that plot persist. I believe these plans may have started with the Communists in Russia, but they took on a life of their own and have been perpetuated by a left-leaning liberal crowd that has pushed us to the edge of annihilation.

Take a look at another list. Had I proposed these goals in 1958, I would have been locked away in a padded cell. If anyone back then had believed the country would abandon its Christian principles, that wholesome groups like the Boy Scouts would become a target for the courts, or that the rights of citizens would take a back seat to the will of foreign powers, he would have been regarded as a kook.

PACIFIC JUSTICE INSTITUTE'S LEFT COAST HALL OF SHAME—2003[3]

1. Ninth Circuit reaffirms its earlier ruling that the Pledge of Allegiance is unconstitutional for public schools.
2. New law allows illegal aliens to acquire driver's licenses.
3. All foster-care parents in California must undergo homosexual sensitivity training in order to continue caring for children.
4. Ninth Circuit financially punishes Washington student because of his decision to major in theology.
5. California law no longer protects students from being interrogated about sex, family life, or religion without parental consent.
6. Ventura County United Way eliminates the Boy Scouts from their funding campaign.
7. Federal statute protecting churches ruled unconstitutional by California judge.
8. To show their support for homosexuality, school districts recognize a day of silence for gay students.
9. Anti-recall [the recall election of Gray Davis] union members beat women and threaten a nine-year-old boy while his dad is beaten up.
10. Christian students' club singled out and censored to prevent any religious quotes on posters or flyers.

At what point did the collective voice of the heart and soul of this country fall silent? A few protest signs or derogatory remarks about our conservative values, and we fold like a pup tent in a Texas windstorm. What is wrong with us? The next time the loudmouths caught up in everything that is destroying this country tries to stop you from sharing your opinion, do not just let it pass—debate them, chastise them, and debunk them. Do not quietly sit by hoping someone else will fight the fight for you; those people are too few.

Now take a closer look at the communist goals and realize that what you read in today's headlines was already in print in the 1950s. The radical changes that have come to our land have happened slowly and stealthily so as not to draw attention to the plan. Looking back at just a few of the individual goals is enough to make us wonder how our sentries left their posts:

11. PROMOTE THE UN AS THE ONLY HOPE FOR MANKIND. IF ITS CHARTER IS REWRITTEN, DEMAND THAT IT BE SET UP AS A ONE-WORLD GOVERNMENT WITH ITS OWN INDEPENDENT ARMED FORCES.

IN LATE 2003 there was little doubt that America was strategizing an invasion of Iraq to remove Saddam Hussein, the country's murderous dictator. Hussein was known to have systematically killed his own people by the tens of thousands while thumbing his nose at the world. After his 1991 defeat in Operation Desert Storm, Hussein was ordered to allow UN inspectors to search for new weapons development, which if found would be a violation of the conditions forced on him at the end of the war.

During the following decade he systematically broke the rules imposed on him in defeat, finally making it so difficult to prove any compliance that inspectors pulled out. The UN hit Iraq with at least seventeen resolutions demanding his cooperation, and seventeen times Saddam disregarded their edicts. When President George W. Bush decided it was time to act, many member nations in the UN rebuffed him, stating that another resolution should go forward first. The real truth behind the rejection was that those member countries were owed billions of dollars by Iraq, and an invasion could prevent them from collecting their debt. So this thing called the UN, which was supposedly established to promote peace and cooperation, was willing to turn a blind eye to mass rape, murder, and torture because of money.

Imagine if the dollars were high enough and multiple countries were affected. Could they not agree to stage a war for such a purpose? They have military machines set up both internally and in cooperation with the member countries. Articles 41 and 42 of the UN Charter contain interesting enforcement powers:

> Article 41: The Security Council may decide what measures not involving the use of armed force are to be employed to give effect to its decisions, and it may call upon the Members of the United Nations to apply such measures. These may include complete or partial interruption of economic relations and of rail, sea, air, postal, telegraphic, radio, and other means of communication, and the severance of diplomatic relations.
>
> Article 42: Should the Security Council consider that measures provided for in Article 41 would be inadequate or have proved to be inadequate, it may take such action by air, sea, or land forces as may be necessary to maintain or restore international peace and security. Such action may include demonstrations, blockade, and other operations by air, sea, or land forces of Members of the United Nations.[4]

The United States has a permanent seat on the Security Council with unilateral veto power, but what happens if our country continues its slide—would we not be in position to follow the plan? Or even if the United States were to veto such a move, the remaining member states can simply choose to make their move without the United States, which could lead to a world war between America and the UN.

17. GET CONTROL OF THE SCHOOLS. USE THEM AS TRANSMISSION BELTS FOR SOCIALISM, AND CURRENT COMMUNIST PROPAGANDA. SOFTEN THE CURRICULUM. GET CONTROL OF TEACHERS ASSOCIATIONS. PUT THE PARTY LINE IN TEXTBOOKS.

WHEN MY four children were in elementary and junior high school, I made it a practice to drop by a couple times a year to take them out for lunch. I went through the proper procedures with the school by sending a note stating my intentions and signing them in and out on the day of my visit.

One year my visibly upset son came to me the day before my visit to explain that his principal didn't want me to come by. When I asked why, all he knew was that the new policy didn't allow it. I was on the phone to that principal in about twelve seconds; ten of those were spent waiting for my touchtone to catch up with my blazing fingers. When I made contact, I was told, "It's a policy decision. Sorry." I told the principal to have the police ready to stop me, because I would be at the building the next day to take my son to lunch, and if it was a war he wanted, I would gladly provide it.

The next day, at the appointed hour, I went to the school office and asked that my son be called down. The shaky receptionist knew I was coming. "The principal said you would be coming—" I stopped her in midsentence. "Great. Call him down. I'll wait." She quickly moved to a back room where fast-paced whispering echoed under the door.

"He will be down shortly, but you must have him back by the end of his lunch period," she said when she returned, trying to suggest she was in charge. I thanked her for her cooperation and explained that, as his father, I would keep him as long as necessary. We had a fine lunch that day.

Can you imagine how many times a day that nonsense plays out in our schools—administrators and principals usurping the power of parents under the direction of high-powered liberal teachers' unions? It happens because we allow it. Don't get me wrong, there are many fine educators and rules that make sense. But too often those rules try to exclude parents.

The remainder of Goal 17 has also been fulfilled. We live in an age when everyone has to be included, regardless of their abilities. So when students can't handle the class, assignment, or quiz, we dumb down the process so they don't feel bad. In Nashville, Tennessee, a decision was made to do away with honor rolls because they cause students who don't make the list to feel inadequate.[5] "The rationale was, if there are some children that always make it and others that always don't make it, there is a very subtle message that was sent," Principal Steven Baum at Julia Green Elementary in Nashville explained. "I also understand right to privacy is the legal issue for the new century." Baum believes spelling bees and other publicly graded events are leftovers from the days of ranking and sorting students. "I discourage competitive games at school," he said. "They just don't fit my worldview of what a school should be."[6]

Give me a break! When I tried out for the tennis and track teams in high school, there were always faster and better players. If I wanted a spot, I had to excel. Period. I am shocked that most basketball or baseball teams don't have five hundred or six hundred members each so every member of the student body can boast on their résumés that they made the team.

Let's just dumb down everything since there will always be screwups and underachievers in every part of life and society. Pretty soon, we will be a land ripe for the picking.

As for the move to gain control of teachers' unions—it is already done. That was accomplished long ago, and anyone who knows anything about the National Education Association (NEA) is aware that it is one of the most left-leaning liberal organizations in America. And we let them have our kids' minds for six to eight hours a day.

20. INFILTRATE THE PRESS. GET CONTROL OF BOOK REVIEW ASSIGNMENTS, EDITORIAL WRITING, POLICY-MAKING POSITIONS.
21. GAIN CONTROL OF KEY POSITIONS IN RADIO, TV & MOTION PICTURES.

MOST PEOPLE still believe what they read and accept it as truth, though we complain about the "liberal press." It should go without saying that the easiest way to control the direction of a nation is to have countless members of the Left indoctrinating others with their worldview and perspectives. To counter this, we need quality reporters and editors to find jobs with the press so that, at the very least, the other side is represented when stories are selected and crafted.

22. CONTINUE DISCREDITING AMERICAN CULTURE BY DEGRADING ALL FORM OF ARTISTIC EXPRESSION. AN AMERICAN COMMUNIST CELL WAS TOLD TO "ELIMINATE ALL GOOD SCULPTURE FROM PARKS AND BUILDINGS" AND SUBSTITUTE SHAPELESS, AWKWARD, AND MEANINGLESS FORMS.

THIS ONE seems innocuous. Bad art, what's the big deal? Think about it for a minute. Removing or replacing treasures with meaningless forms dumbs down our expectations. When the government subsidizes artists to urinate in a cup, or fill a coffee can with feces, and displays their work as culturally significant, the state has become involved in sanctioning the mundane. When the public ponders the byproduct and thinks such things could be "art," then the door is opening for the argument that everything should be accepted or tolerated.

Is this a big jump? Consider a picture of a religious symbol buried in a pile of human waste, now open your mind to the belief that such is art. If this is art, then what other mental leaps are possible in the mind of the beholder? What's wrong with man-boy love, incest, or polygamy? Gone is any concept of an absolute, a standard. These are replaced with what-ifs, maybes, and why nots.

24. ELIMINATE ALL LAWS GOVERNING OBSCENITY BY CALLING THEM CENSORSHIP AND A VIOLATION OF FREE SPEECH AND FREE PRESS.

HOW IS it possible that displays of sexual intercourse, foreplay, mastur-bation, and triple-X-rated layouts were deemed inappropriate and ob-scene thirty or forty years ago, but now we can view these taboos as part of a prime-time lineup every night? If it was not acceptable then, what happened to our culture that suggests it should be acceptable now? Are we evolving toward enlightenment or devolving into degeneracy?

25. BREAK DOWN CULTURAL STANDARDS OF MORALITY BY PROMOTING PORNOGRAPHY, AND OBSCENITY IN BOOKS, MAGAZINES, MOTION PICTURES, RADIO, AND TV.

WHILE ACCEPTING a Golden Globe award in 2003, Bono, from the super group U2, thanked the foreign press by saying, "This is f—ing brilliant." NBC chose to not delete or bleep the word, and the Federal Communications Commission decided not to fine the network. Instead the FCC determined that the word *f—*, which had heretofore been one of the seven banned words in broadcasting, could be broadcast if it was used as an adjective. The commissioners argued that Bono certainly had not used the word to describe a sex act. They allowed it instead as an ex-pression of exuberance. Once again the government bureaucracy sanc-tioned the dumbing down of our culture. Only after conservatives petitioned the FCC by the tens of thousands did the agency make an abrupt about-face. (But more on that later.)

26. PRESENT HOMOSEXUALITY, DEGENERACY, AND PROMISCUITY AS NORMAL, NATURAL, AND HEALTHY.

IN 2003 the Massachusetts Supreme Court cleared the way for gay mar-riage, the first state in America to do so. The *New York Times* reported it this way: "The highest court in Massachusetts declared in an opinion is-sued today that only full marriage rights for gay couples—not just civil unions—would comply with the state's constitution."[7] Activists selected Massachusetts because they were aware that the law there did not use

"man and woman" language in defining marriage. When John Adams
helped to draft his state's constitution more than two hundred years ago,
he and his contemporaries understood that marriage involved a man and
a woman. Without the descriptive language, any couple in the state
could demand that Massachusetts sanction their marriage. Unless the
ruling is overturned in the Bay State, it and other states that follow suit
will be obliged to allow any couples to marry. It is reasonable to assume
that a father could marry his daughter, a brother could marry his sister,
and so on. This ruling opens the floodgates for further depravity in a nation that is increasingly ruled by it. Again, as conservatives joined forces
to speak with one voice, the Massachusetts legislature agreed to an
amendment to the state constitution defining marriage as a sacred union
between a man and woman.

Some of the most popular television shows in 2003 and 2004 are
Will and Grace, Queer Eye for the Straight Guy, and *Boy Meets Boy.* All
don't merely have gay characters, but the characters are written to sell
the viewing audience on how perfectly natural it is for such relationships
in the first place. I wonder if Skousen or Herlong envisioned just how
much pressure liberals would exert to make this practice acceptable.

27. INFILTRATE THE CHURCHES AND REPLACE REVEALED RELIGION WITH SOCIAL RELIGION. DISCREDIT THE BIBLE AND EMPHASIZE THE NEED FOR INTELLECTUAL MATURITY, WHICH DOES NOT NEED A "RELIGIOUS CRUTCH."

THIS COUNTRY used to rely on churches as a stopgap on moral slippage.
If a person's soul was hanging in the balance, the church supplied the answer. If a mother needed help to feed her children, it was the church that
stepped in. Families knew that when they graced the doors of their
house of worship, they would hear of the spiritual ills plaguing the community and how to turn from them.

Now we have megachurches and seeker-sensitive services. *Seeker-
sensitive* is a euphemism for dumbing down the message from God's
Word. Pastors say they have to do it because today's culture doesn't want
to attend a church that preaches too deeply. We have generations demanding quick messages, skits, snacks, and prayers in sixty minutes or
less. Pastor John MacArthur observed:

When churches sacrifice substance for style—when even well-meaning
pastors soft-pedal the gospel to keep people in the pews—churches stag-

nate and eventually die. Instead of being a place where men and women grow spiritually by coming under the influence of God's Word, seeker-sensitive churches become mere shells filled with false converts and malnourished Christians. Once a church exchanges its God-ordained mission to preach the Word, which is the only source of spiritual life, for a marketing manifesto to fill pews, it surrenders its claim to divine power along with its effectiveness in the world.[8]

There is a place for the tools used to bring seekers into the church. But when they become the rule instead of the exception, the church has transformed itself into a social gathering place and has sacrificed much of its spiritual center. Take away the church's power as a force against sin, and society has lost its greatest defense against obliteration.

Is this a communist plot? No. It is the church transforming itself to keep pews filled during a time when our culture is in flux. Civilizations will always have flux periods. But if churches change too much during these times, then the teachings of absolute truth will be lost. If churches ever needed to be relevant, it is now.

Instead, a nonbeliever may attend a Sunday morning pep rally, hear a nice motivational message, hit on a couple of cute babes in the back, then head to the shuttle that will drop him off at his car. The next day he'll join the throng laughing at pedophile priests, preachers having sex with secretaries, and televangelists who head to jail. When churches die, can the same thing not be far behind for the culture itself?

28. ELIMINATE PRAYER OR ANY PHASE OF RELIGIOUS EXPRESSION IN THE SCHOOLS ON THE GROUNDS THAT IT VIOLATES THE PRINCIPLE OF SEPARATION OF CHURCH AND STATE.

NOWHERE IN the U.S. Constitution is there a reference to the separation of church and state defined as the prohibition of a person's having or sharing his religious views. In fact, the First Amendment says the exact opposite: the government can't demand that we worship, pray, or experience God in a certain manner. This is most commonly called the establishment clause. I wish more Americans would grasp this truth, because many are flung around like sheets on a clothesline in a tornado. The government can't establish religion, but we can and should.

When my children were younger, their public school sent us a note that Christmas was going to be turned into a winter celebration so no one would be offended. Am I supposed to believe that elementary school kids are going to be forever damaged because someone mentions the word *Christmas*? The kids could sing "Winter Wonderland" and "Frosty the Snowman" but not "Joy to the World," "O Come All Ye Faithful," or other religious-oriented songs. Nor would students be allowed to wear Christmas-themed attire. I asked my kids how they felt about that, and they said they felt robbed. We told them if they wanted to wear their with "Jesus Is the Reason for the Season" sweatshirts, we would allow it. My wife, Laurie, looked at our small boys and told them to have the teacher call her if there was a problem. The issue went nowhere because the school knew there was no basis for this anti-Christmas policy.

> **HOW TO FIX IT**
>
> There is no constitutional right to not be offended. I would disbar any lawyer who files a frivolous lawsuit. If my kid drives his car into a tree in your yard, it's my kid's fault for driving crazy, not your fault for planting a tree in your yard. Yet nowadays the first thing that happens when an accident occurs is that some lawyers swarm to see who they can sue. Everyone knows hot coffee spilled on your lap will probably burn, but to blame the makers of the coffee? Give me a break. (Randal S.)

Since when did we begin to believe that separation of church and state meant that we couldn't demonstrate our faith publicly? Review the First Amendment carefully. Read each word out loud: "Congress shall make no law respecting an establishment of religion, or prohibiting the free exercise thereof." It does not say that I can't enjoy my faith, celebrate my faith, or demonstrate my faith. (More on this a little later.)

There is no doubt that our public schools are government controlled and influenced, and as such they work very hard to control what was once the religion of the people of America. During the very season when my kids couldn't sing about Christmas, they were encouraged to sing the dreidel song because students were learning about the Jewish culture, and we didn't want to offend them or their heritage.

The U.S. Supreme Court outlawed school-instituted prayers, and in 2000 the Court took it to the next level by asserting that young people who wished to lead fellow students in prayer at sports activities and school events were equally prohibited. Liberal Justice John Paul Stevens wrote the majority opinion: "The delivery of such a message—over the school's public address system, by a speaker representing the student body, under the supervision of school faculty, and pursuant to a school policy that explicitly and implicitly encourages public prayer—is not properly characterized as 'private' speech."[9]

Chief Justice William Rehnquist dissented, joined by Justices Antonin Scalia and Clarence Thomas. Rehnquist pointed out that not all student speech should be "content-neutral." He added, "The court [majority] distorts existing precedent to conclude that the school district's student-message program is invalid on its face under the 'establishment clause' of the First Amendment . . . but even more disturbing than its holding is the tone of the court's opinion; it bristles with hostility to all things religious in public life."

Chief Justice Rehnquist put the issue center stage when he said the Court's opinion bristles with hostility to all things religious. I realize the line included "in public life," but it's becoming very evident that to be outwardly religious in America is becoming a liability.

I don't want my kids to be led in a prayer to a god they do not know or serve, but I also do not want my kids to be intimidated or disciplined for taking time to thank God for his help and mercy.

As I write this, the most popular search engine on the Internet is called Google. For kicks I typed in the phrase "school prayer." Google found almost three million webpages dedicated to this topic, including stories about teachers disciplined for praying after September 11 and students expelled for praying over a meal in the cafeteria.

The communist plan has succeeded.

31. BELITTLE ALL FORMS OF AMERICAN CULTURE AND DISCOURAGE THE TEACHING OF AMERICAN HISTORY ON THE GROUND THAT IT WAS ONLY A MINOR PART OF THE BIG PICTURE: GIVE MORE EMPHASIS TO RUSSIAN HISTORY SINCE THE COMMUNISTS TOOK OVER.

THE VEIL known as communism was ripped asunder several years ago, but this plan is still being implemented. Its seeds have turned into full-sized plants. Instead of emphasizing Russia, these days we are engaged in daily indoctrination from Mexico and the Middle East. Because there are so many Muslims in America, we are constantly reminded to embrace them and the culture. The push is on to incorporate their ideals and beliefs into our system, and with time the process will be complete. Lobbyists went to work weeks after the September 11 tragedy to ensure that Arabs, Muslims, and other Middle Easterners were not viewed harshly. I may be politically incorrect, however, in reminding us that the deaths of three thousand people can be directly attributed to all three groups.

Meanwhile, Mexico has been chipping away at U.S. history from a different angle. Latinos do not like the way they were depicted in U.S. textbooks, so they have worked to change the language. Fox News reported it this way:

> "Remember the Alamo is a battle cry that Texans learn early in their formative years. But the call to remember the Texas revolution of 168 years ago has a new place in Texas history, somewhere in the back of the textbooks. That may now be changing, in part because some fear rampant pride will alienate the growing Mexican student population in their midst. We don't want our Hispanic kids, or any kids, to feel like we're teaching a bias approach," said Angela Miller, social studies curriculum manager for the Houston Independent School District.[10]

Dan Stein is the executive director of the Federation for American Immigration Reform, and he was outraged when news of the planned changes was announced. "There is only one way to teach Texas history and that's Texas history. Now, if you're going to teach Mex history or you're going to teach some other country's history, that's fine. But Texas history is Texas history." Many agree with Stein, certain that such a move sows seeds of doubt about Texas's past. "If you teach young people, who have allegiances not only to the United States but to Mexico, that Texas is stolen [property], you could be planting the seeds of a separatist movement thirty years from now or sooner," Stein added.

> ## WHAT WENT WRONG WITH AMERICA
>
> Trust went away when moral decay took over. The times when a handshake was as good as a contract are gone. With trust went our ability to function without worrying whether people in control were really acting in our best interest. Our mistrust hampers our leaders in their ability to do a good job even if that was their original intention. (Polly P.)

When Mexican president Vicente Fox campaigned for office in 2000, one of his stated missions was to create a single North American bloc. If Fox had his way, there would be no borders between Mexico and the U.S. or Canada. *Fox News Sunday* host Chris Wallace interviewed President Fox on January 11, 2004, and he continued to paint the picture: "Well, on the long, long term, yes, I think that would be the best for our two nations, or our three nations, including Canada. On the long term, this North American bloc can be the leading bloc on the world and be the most competitive bloc on the world by working together and, through that, be able to keep increasing the quality and the level of life of our citizens."[11]

How would Fox gain American cooperation on one of the most controversial ideas hatched on the continent? His answer is simple: "We must think long-term and change their culture."[12] Fox hopes to see a unified bloc by 2030, and he knows the only way to see his dream realized is through the continue influx of legal and illegal immigrants into the United States in an attempt to change public opinion. When groups sympathetic to the cause demand that textbooks be rewritten so as not to offend Hispanics, what these citizens are really saying is they are not opposed to plans that will ultimately lead to the loss of our national identity and our nation's sovereignty.

> ## WHAT WENT WRONG WITH AMERICA
>
> The failure to educate our children in the home (parents' failure to teach morals, honor, integrity, and personal responsibility). The education of our children in school. For three generations children have been taught a negative or a diluted version of our nation's history and culture. Parents and public education have failed to teach our children that success requires commitment, integrity, and personal responsibility. Few children know or understand the honor and high privilege they have as citizens to dedicate themselves to a mission higher than themselves. Our children do not understand that liberty, freedom, and the American way of life come at a price. These are not free or cheap, and they will fail as will our American culture if they do not step up and take responsibility for protecting it. (Mary-S G.)

Clear-thinking Americans understand this plan could easily be implemented over three decades if the battle is waged from the inside. If you don't believe that's possible, then reread some of the communist goals outlined above. Did anyone four decades ago believe this country could possibly change as much as it has?

40. DISCREDIT THE FAMILY AS AN INSTITUTION. ENCOURAGE PROMISCUITY AND EASY DIVORCE.

THE FAMILY has always been a bedrock institution capable of enduring the vilest of offenses and personal tragedies but, at the same time, fragile enough that it crumbles with a lustful look or a full-blown lie. Yet this institution is under attack as never before, with every conceivable pressure weighing it down.

Look at where we are forty years after the communist goals were entered into the record. Almost one of every two marriages end in divorce, with no-fault divorce a key option in a number of states, making it a simple and repeatable procedure. Obviously, if the fundamental foundation of a family is unstable, then the institution itself becomes shaky and open to question.

WHAT WENT WRONG WITH AMERICA

America has moved away from faith, family, and personal accountability. (1) Without a faith-based belief system you lose morality. Faith drives our moral compass. That's why we have more perversions, less willingness to be compassionate to our fellow man.
(2) The family unit provided the environment for nurturing and accountability. Without it, Americans "do what feels good" regardless of how it may affect others.
(3) People are no longer held accountable for their actions or lack of actions. It's always someone else's fault, which feeds the engine of our litigious society. Because there is no personal accountability, Americans believe "I am entitled to...," which throws us into a vicious circle that has caused the country to spiral out of control. (J.F.A.)

On too many occasions in the last few years, schoolchildren have walked into their classrooms with weapons blazing, declaring that they feel purposeless and that no one cares. In several instances the killer kids blame bullies who pushed them over the edge. Think about it. Those bullies come from somewhere, don't they—like a broken or bruised home.

On Sunday, February 1, 2004, pop music dominated the halftime show of one of the most watched sporting events in the world, the Super Bowl. With more than 150 million viewers in the United States alone, rappers and singers performed pseudo sex acts and pseudo masturbation scenes while writhing to the beat of pornographic songs. The act culminated with heartthrob Justin Timberlake ripping away a piece of fabric from superstar Janet Jackson's top to fully expose her breast, complete with pierced nipple. More than 200,000 people complained to the Federal Communications Commission, forcing congressional hearings on decency standards.

It seems the message of the day is evoke radical change by pushing the limits of decency bit by bit by bit. For example, for sheer publicity, singer Madonna kissed two female performers young enough to be her daughters during a national awards show. Publicity in its crassest form is all about creating a buzz, and apparently the raunchier and less family friendly the better.

More than 93 percent of all public high schools currently offer courses on sexuality or HIV.[13] I'm in favor of educating our kids about sex and disease, but I want parents to have that conversation with their children. Since when did government agencies become surrogate parents? The answer is academic: when parents gave up because the public schools made them feel inadequate. After people are repeatedly told how bad and unnecessary they are, they will eventually give in and let others take control. This is an epidemic that has controlled the families in this nation for too long.

The teen pregnancy rate in America is more than double the rate of any other Western industrialized country. More than a million teens become pregnant each year.[14]

One in four of America's youth contract a sexually transmitted disease by the age of twenty-one—the highest rate of STDs in any age group.[15]

HIV infection is increasing most rapidly among young people. In the United States 25 percent of all new infections occur in people younger than twenty-two.[16]

The number of people who contracted AIDS from 1981 to 2002: 886,575.[17]

The number of AIDS cases in America in 1963: 0.

A war wages for the heart of America's families. Adult videos bring in $500 million to $1.8 billion in annual sales, and the Internet chalks up another $1 billion in business. Meanwhile, pay-per-view pornography accounts for $128 million, and smut magazines have sales estimated at $1 billion. With all categories combined, we consume almost $4 billion worth of pornography each year,[18] though *Forbes* magazine quoted numbers as high as $10 billion per year in a 2003 article. Putting it in perspective,

WHAT WENT WRONG WITH AMERICA

Everything wrong with America goes back to the perversion of our legal system. America has come to value the law over morality. This has resulted in the sense that if the legal system says you are not guilty (even if you are indeed guilty of the crime), you are thus absolved of your sin and can actually make yourself believe you are innocent. This has led to the erosion of personal responsibility. It has also has led to the moral relativism that values personal rights over the greater good, and thus the deterioration of patriotism (i.e., I value mine over yours or ours). The sad thing is that these "terrorists" use our own tool (the Constitution) against us. (Luis S.)

in the 1990s there were more than five hundred porn magazines and tens of millions of porn pages on the Internet. In 1963 approximately thirty soft-core porn magazines, most hidden from public view, were available, and the Internet had not yet arrived.[19] In the 1960s only a handful of porn movies were released; most of them as underground stag films or in seedy adult theaters. In the 1990s approximately fifteen hundred sex films were produced a year. In 2004 the number of porn films jumped to fifteen thousand per year.

HOW TO FIX IT

Take the blame and make a stand. Accountability is the key. I accept that I've failed my country, but I vow to do what's right. I will become anti-complacency. I will make my voice heard and encourage others to do the same. (Jerry W.)

Very few doubt that communism is defunct, and I don't believe this fifty-year-old list of goals represents a stealth attempt by some rogue nation to take over America in the twenty-first century. What I do believe is that this blueprint has been adopted as the agenda of the Left in this country, though most liberals aren't aware that their platform and beliefs stem from plans originally designed to destroy America. As I have demonstrated with expositions on only a few of the forty-five listed items, today's headlines scream at us to sit up and take notice. Over time, when we hear something repeatedly, we will come to accept it as truth. The truth is, most of the points outlined in this chapter will ultimately destroy the greatest country ever to dot a map.

Those citizens who fight to remove parental authority, scrap the Constitution, legalize gay marriages, and institute the many other goals on the list of communist goals do so without respect for history. If they would review what happened to communism, they would see a wall that was shattered in Berlin, a Soviet Empire that is no more, and a China that is begging to host the Olympics so they can join the rest of the world. Those citizens would notice that their acceptance of a forty-year-old agenda is a recipe for the downfall of our civilization.

We may not be able to stop the Left. We may not be able to kill each issue outlined here, but if we take on one or two issues, learn all there is to know about those issues, and become vocal about them, and if others do the same, we may still have a fighting chance. Read the list again and then ask yourself what you have done to stop the movement to destroy America. If not you, then who?

RANT—SOMEONE TELL SUSAN SHE'S NUTS!

There was no doubt in my mind that what I was watching would be a significantly polarizing event as America positioned itself for war in Iraq. It was early February 2003 when on my TV screen popped a major star from Hollywood, Susan Sarandon. And within the first ten seconds of hearing her liberal-laced foolishness, I was fuming with anger. In fact, very few things have made me as angry as when she advocated a series of moves meant to derail President George Bush as our troops massed for the beginning of Operation Iraqi Freedom.

Sarandon's presentation was sponsored by the Win Without War[20] coalition, which is just another mouthpiece for the Left-leaning establishment. Take a look at a few of its supporters, and the picture gets very clear: Feminist Majority, Greenpeace, MoveOn, National Gay and Lesbian Task Force, National Organization for Women (NOW), Rainbow/Push Coalition, Sierra Club, and more than thirty others. Celebrities like Sarandon did not speak as private citizens, but on cue they delivered the lines required by their agenda-centered organizations.

She looked so serious while acting out her lines while I, with my TiVo in instant-replay mode, sat on my couch replaying her pitch time and again. Each time I replayed the piece, my blood pressure inched up another point or twenty. Finally, after about the tenth time or so of hearing her nonsense, I flung my remote across the room and screamed at the television: "Go ahead, say it again with all the heart and soul your drama instructors taught you to emote, 'What did Iraq do to us?'"

How dense could she be? We're on the brink of war, and she's asking why we wanted to kill the people of Iraq. Our troops were poised to *liberate* the Iraqis. We wanted to set them free from firing squads, mass graves, rape rooms, and torture chambers. "What did Iraq do to us?" she asked. It was never America's ambition to wipe out the people of Iraq, and we proved it time and again in the early days of war when we used precise surgical strikes in Baghdad so as to not knock out power grids, water supplies, or annihilate entire neighborhoods.

We can say what we want in America; that's one of the great benefits of living in a free society. But timing is everything. When it is done in a place, time, and fashion that will cost lives, then this greatest of freedoms must be used with discipline, wisdom, and forethought. Sarandon's timing was terrible. Her words and those of other liberals and Hollywood elitists helped to stir anti-war and anti-American sentiment worldwide, with hundreds of thousands protesting in the streets.

I have publicly stated numerous times that I believe America and Saddam Hussein changed strategies because of the large protests. First, we declared we would use a strategy dubbed "Shock and Awe" in the opening stages of the war.

The chairman of the Joint Chiefs of Staff, Gen. Richard Myers, said, "If asked to go into conflict in Iraq, what you'd like to do is have it be a short, short conflict. The best way to do that is have such a shock on the system, the Iraqi regime would have to assume early on the end is inevitable."[21] But the initial strikes were answered by Tariq Aziz, the deputy prime minister of Iraq, who declared that Iraq would "fight to the last bullet; and to the last breath."[22]

I believe the Bush administration played it safe because of the intense pressure from the Left, but the bad boys in Iraq amped things through the roof to show their defiant spirit, aided in part by France, Germany, Russia, and celebrities like Susan Sarandon. If I were Saddam Hussein, I would have been on my knees several times a day in thanksgiving to my new support team. America searched for allies before going into Iraq; Saddam's gang had new enlistees daily, with "stars" like Sarandon, the Dixie Chicks in Britain, Michael Moore, and former President Bill Clinton's remarks in France. All during wartime.

Sarandon told an interviewer, "I lost a very dear friend in the Twin Towers on 11 September and thought the shock was so huge that American arrogance would be diminished."[23] Wait a minute. Let me get this right: America is arrogant for trying to free the oppressed? I wonder how World War II would have turned out if Sarandon would have been leading the charge. It probably would have sounded something like this: "America's arrogant for declaring war on the Japanese after Pearl Harbor, and anyway, why are we exploiting this misunderstanding to pick on the Germans? What did the Germans ever do to us?" Meanwhile the corpses of millions of Jews were dumped into open pits. "American arrogance would be diminished"?

Sarandon can run around like a lunatic as she did in *The Rocky Horror Picture Show* or drive her car off a cliff like she did in *Thelma and Louise.* She can do whatever her heart tells her. All I ask is that she and her Hollywood elitist friends save their acting for the movies and television shows, because in the real world, people die. And many more die when naive people tell responsible people to do nothing.

Sarandon's nonsense had a greater and quite different impact than she expected. But more on that later.

4

· ·

THE SEPARATION OF CHURCH AND STATE MYTH

The Christian religion, in its purity, is the basis and the source of all genuine freedom in government. . . . I am persuaded that no civil government of a republican form can exist and be durable, in which the principles of Christianity have not a controlling influence.

—JAMES MADISON

ONCE THE SLOW DEGRADATION of the American Dream began, things deteriorated rapidly. The process is similar to a master thief trying to crack a safe: give him enough time and he will succeed. Such is the case when one group uses the Constitution and the accrued body of laws to search out loopholes that give undue aid to the few. One lawsuit sets precedent for the next and the next and the next.

How many passengers aboard the *Mayflower* could have imagined that their descendants a few generations later would be fighting to keep God far away from the public square? Here's a case in point.

Frequently when I'm asked to speak to a group or convention, my host will ask if it is okay to allot time for a question-and-answer period at the conclusion, especially if my material is current-event laden. It is not often that I know the makeup of my audience beforehand, but on this rainy Texas night I did, because many had already introduced themselves to me. To say that I was a little intimidated would be an understatement, for before me were some of the area's finest judges, lawyers, and politicians. I almost always include legal and Founding Fathers stories in my repertoire, so the reaction this night would be very interesting.

My presentation went well, and the audience responded to all my hand movements and facial expressions. Laughter happened in the right places as well as quizzical looks. It was when the blonde at one of the front tables hit me with her question that I felt the room shrink and knew that my words were being parsed by great legal minds. For a moment I was a college student again, and I had just been transported to the dean's office. The woman softly whispered, as though she knew her question would be analyzed by the rest of the listeners. "Could you explain what *separation of church and state* means?" she quizzed me.

> **WHAT WENT WRONG WITH AMERICA**
>
> We ask God for help in our times of need, and then we kicked him out of our lives, our schools, our governments, and our public facilities. We no longer remember the Ten Commandments. We've turned from God to worship the idols of public opinion. We're throwing away the republic for which we stand. (Arlan D.)

I have answered this question a thousand times, but not before this kind of company. Beads of sweat appeared from nowhere. I took a breath, composed myself, and launched into the only answer I have—the right answer.

The First Amendment, which was actually the third because the first two were never ratified, says: "Congress shall make no law respecting an establishment of religion, or prohibiting the free exercise thereof; or abridging the freedom of speech, or of the press; or the right of the people peaceably to assemble, and to petition the Government for a redress of grievances." Though this sentence is packed with a series of rights, the religion clauses continue to be used to stifle faith-based laws and church involvement in almost anything public—especially if there is a government building within a hundred miles.

We have worked overtime to make these clauses the most difficult to understand: "Congress shall make no law respecting an establishment of religion, or prohibiting the free exercise thereof." These were placed in the Constitution because the last thing our leaders ever wanted was to return to the days of disemboweling and public burnings that so-called heretics suffered at the hands of state-sponsored churches. The settlers of America escaped that kind of tyranny. Though all colonies reflected a love of Christ, over time and while weighing the significance of the founding document, the authors of the Constitution agreed to use somewhat ambiguous language. There is no question that ambiguity exists, because debates have swirled around these sixteen words for more than two hundred years.

The original language as adjusted by the House of Representatives read: "Congress shall make no law establishing religion, or to prevent the free exercise thereof, or to infringe the rights of conscience."[1] In the Senate the adopted section read: "Congress shall make no law establishing articles of faith, or a mode of worship, or prohibiting the free exercise of religion."[2] The hope was to stay true to the deeply religious (and very Christian) roots of those who signed the Mayflower Compact and penned the colonial charters and constitutions while ensuring that no government or secular interference would be tolerated.

The first clause of the First Amendment became known as the establishment clause; that is, the government shall not establish a state religion. History shows that Christianity was the religion of the people, so there really wasn't a way for the newly formed government to create something already created. It was a safeguard for the people, a way to celebrate one's faith without fear of reprisal. A main desire of James Madison, one of the original authors of this amendment, was to let states continue to deal with religious issues as they always had. Up to and past that point, states routinely funded church-based efforts and provided property for religious activities.

A discussion about the First Amendment and its meaning can never take place without someone raising Thomas Jefferson's wall-of-separation letter. Remember, there is no mention of the separation of church and state in the First Amendment. Those debating this issue with you (and they will argue with you until you pass out from fatigue) point to Jefferson's 1802 letter to the Danbury (Conn.) Baptist Association as proof that it was implied. First, it was a private letter, and second, it was written in response to a letter the association addressed to Jefferson in 1801. In part, this is what the Danbury Baptists stated:

> Our Sentiments are uniformly on the side of Religious Liberty—That Religion is at all times and places a matter between God and individuals— That no man ought to suffer in name, person, or effects on account of his religious Opinions. . . . But Sir our constitution of government is not specific. Our ancient charter together with the Laws made coincident therewith, were adopted on the Basis of our government, at the time of our revolution; and such had been our Laws & usages, and such still are; that

Religion is considered as the first object of Legislation . . . If those, who seek after power & gain under the pretense of government & Religion should reproach their fellow men—should reproach their chief Magistrate, as an enemy of religion Law & good order because he will not, dare not assume the prerogatives of Jehovah and make Laws to govern the Kingdom of Christ.[3]

It was in response to that loaded and very specific letter that Jefferson penned the words that have caused many to argue on behalf of a wall of separation between church and state. This is the meat of Jefferson's reply, minus all the pleasantries both sides indulged in:

Believing with you that religion is a matter which lies solely between Man & his God, that he owes account to none other for his faith or his worship, that the legislative powers of the government reach actions only, & not opinions, I contemplate with sovereign reverence that act of the whole American people which declared that *their* legislature should "make no law respecting an establishment of religion, or prohibiting the free exercise thereof," thus building a wall of separation between Church & State. Adhering to this expression of the supreme will of the nation in behalf of the rights of conscience, I shall see with sincere satisfaction the progress of those sentiments which tend to restore to man all of his natural rights, convinced he has no natural right in opposition to his social duties.[4]

Somehow these few words, coupled with the First Amendment, have given the liberals in America a license to persecute anything Christian. And in some cases they prosecute anything merely religious. How many times have we heard the rallying cry of "separation of church and state" when a display of the Ten Commandments needs to be removed, an invocation is requested at a school event, or a child is prohibited from using "under God" in the recitation of the Pledge of Allegiance? The answer: every single time!

With the passage of time, secular and liberal warriors have effectively argued and created precedents that continue to take this amendment into areas never anticipated. I believe our Founding Fathers would stand at the microphone at high-school graduations to lead a prayer or read a Bible passage and never think ill of any request to do so. They did not have the thousands of make-believe religions we have today, so a decision to incorporate faith was not uncomfortable for anyone. They didn't have to hear the nonsensical utterings of the ACLU, the American Atheist movement, or any of the thousands of other groups who seem to want to live by codes created out of exceptions to the rule instead of the rule itself.

I have four children. Any parent knows how they can play games to get their way. "Why can't I go over to John's house?" questions one while another chimes in from the other room, "Ah, let him go. You let me." "Wait a minute, you let Charlie go?! Well then I should get to go." The argument continues for minutes, hours, days, depending on the game plan. You already have one instance when you made an exception with one child, so you give in. Bad move. Now you have a firmly planted precedent, and every time a similar request comes up, you are reminded that you have already made an exception to the rules. We all wish we could make certain decisions again, because as soon as we relented, we were on the path to defeat in a variety of areas—especially if we dare suggest that we are fair parents.

WHAT WENT WRONG WITH AMERICA

Gradually "unalienable rights endowed by our Creator" have been stolen from us. God has been and is being cut out from the fabric that is America. As God is removed from the equation, it is logical to conclude that the rights "endowed" by him will be that much easier to be eradicated. This is precisely what the Founding Fathers were trying to evade. Activist judges imposing their liberal agendas and legislating from the bench have cut away at the Constitution, rewriting it through precedent, to remove God and instill communist goals in an effort to turn this into a socialist nation. (Jonathan T.)

Take that same argument to government and its citizens. With hundreds of millions of people, millions of lawyers (and paralegals and judges), and tens of millions of requests, it can only be assumed that a judge or jury somewhere will make a wrong decision and *boom*—the groundwork has been laid for a variety of other bad decisions until the spirit of the law is not even a memory.

We have abandoned our faith-based roots, and as a result, the religion clauses of the First Amendment have been diverted from their original course. In their purest sense, they were meant to keep the government out of the life of its people—*not* the other way around.

I remember attending a Christmas, er, I mean "seasonal" musical at my son's high school in a Philadelphia suburb. Kris came home very disturbed. He and the other performers were warned that no Christmas carols could be performed because it would be offensive to families who didn't share "that" religion. Inserted were a few snow, reindeer, and crackling fire songs. Parents were outraged. We petitioned the school, but our protests were summarily dismissed. On the two songs that once had "Christ" or "Savior" in the lyrics, the music was to play and the kids were to hum instead of sing. How moronic is that! We protested all the way up the ladder and were turned down each time. It was a chilly Sunday afternoon as families crowded into the cramped hall. The kids had been warned that they would flunk the choral chorus if they dared to sing the banned words. None wanted to fail, so they planned to submit to the pressure put in place years prior by some uninformed person who argued against Christmas celebrations as a First Amendment issue.

When the musical began, the kids complied. Then during the outlawed use of the Messiah's name, a lone parent stood up. She was petite and trembling, but she began to sing the words. And she sang them loudly! Up popped another parent and another. Within moments we were all on our feet and singing at the top of our lungs. Our kids joined us as tears and smiles owned the room. The band leader threw his baton down, turned, and led us all in the songs.

No one complained. Not the Jewish families. Not the Muslim families. Not the families whose kids never attended church. Everyone understood what the "seasonal" event was about, and those who did not share the faith were able to join in a community atmosphere and create a teaching environment. Imagine that—parents were teaching their kids about something they had all experienced. What a concept.

That afternoon we all learned a lesson. The school was trying to abide by a mandate to separate church from state because someone foolishly suggested that a Christmas carol blurred the line. But the citizens refused to be trod upon. The citizens stood up for their rights and better understood and articulated a long-argued sixteen words in the founding document of their nation.

Now back to my speech to the judges and lawyers—after I explained my position on the separation of church and state to my questioner, two judges and a lawyer sought me out afterward to say they wished all of America could hear this truth, "because people blindly follow a definition that can't be found." Be informed. Get involved. Leave your mark.

RANT—EVEN OUR KIDS KNOW SOMETHING IS WRONG!

One of my most vivid memories of comfort from when I was a small child came from a small framed prayer that my grandmother and mother had on their walls. It was a simple poem, but for some reason it always made me feel like I wasn't alone. Later, my wife proudly mounted a similar plaque for our kids. It is credited as an eighteenth-century bedtime prayer and is familiar to most of us:

> Now I lay me down to sleep,
> I pray the Lord my soul to keep;
> If I should die before I wake,
> I pray the Lord my soul to take.
> Keep me safely through the night
> And wake me with morning light.

In 1992 another prayer made the rounds after it appeared in the *Washington Times*. In 1993 the *Detroit News* ran a similar version, and for more than a decade the poem spread across the country via the Internet. Each time some of the phrases were updated to keep current with the latest tragedy in our youth culture, but with little exception, it has always been credited to "an anonymous student." Whether or not it is from the pen of a student is something we may never know, but this doesn't take away from the stark reality that things have changed for the worse in our once innocent and God-fearing country.

The New School Prayer

> Now I sit me down in school
> Where praying is against the rule
> For this great nation under God
> Finds mention of him very odd.
> If Scripture now the class recites,
> It violates the Bill of Rights.
> And anytime my head I bow
> Becomes a federal matter now.
> Our hair can be purple, orange, or green,
> That's no offense; it's a freedom scene.
> The law is specific, the law is precise.

Prayers spoken aloud are a serious vice.
For praying in a public hall
Might offend someone with no faith at all.
In silence alone we must meditate,
God's name is prohibited by the state.
We're allowed to cuss and dress like freaks,
And pierce our noses, tongues, and cheeks.
They've outlawed guns, but FIRST the Bible.
To quote the Good Book makes me liable.
We can elect a pregnant Senior Queen,
And the "unwed daddy," our Senior King.
It's "inappropriate" to teach right from wrong,
We're taught that such "judgments" do not belong.
We can get our condoms and birth controls,
Study witchcraft, vampires, and totem poles.
But the Ten Commandments are not allowed,
No word of God must reach this crowd.
It's scary here I must confess,
When chaos reigns the school's a mess.
So, Lord, this silent plea I make:
Should I be shot, my soul please take!

Even our kids know something is wrong . . .

5

• •

NO MORE SPRINGFIELDS!

A piece of spaghetti or a military unit can only be led from the front end.

—GEN. GEORGE S. PATTON

FOR EACH OF US there's a time when we realize we have to join the fight for what is right—no matter what others say or think about us. The first time we do it, there is a major learning curve because, for most of us, we are out of our comfort zone. However, this one single experience can empower us in such a dramatic way that we continue to develop our skills for citizen action for the rest of our lives. My realization came in a little town in Missouri, and the lessons I learned were some of the most valuable I have ever learned, opening the door for many a future battle.

Long before rapper Fifty Cent was bragging about his nine bullet holes from the guns of neighborhood thugs and fellow dope dealers, and years before hothead rap star Eminem would be out of high school, there was 2 Live Crew. Gangsta rap was still underground, and hip-hop was a decade away from hitting the big time, but Miami was offering this nasty little rhyme team, and they had their sights set on forging new standards in the music world and in society.

It was the fall of 1990 and 2 Live Crew was set to play a little club near downtown Springfield, Missouri. I was the manager and morning personality of a radio station I founded there and was aware of the group but hadn't heard any of their songs. Their reputation, however, was known throughout the music industry. This was a group that believed filth would be their claim to fame. For 2 Live Crew, the nastier the better.

In the late 1980s and early 1990s Springfield was a quiet town with Sunday blue laws and churches everywhere. The Queen City of the Ozarks, as it is still called, is home to major religious denominations, Christian schools, and international ministry headquarters. But it is also the temporary stopping point for more than twenty thousand students who attend Southwest Missouri State University (SMS) as well as another fifteen thousand who attend other colleges and universities in the area, and when the weekend comes they are the first in line looking for a party. The city has always been able to snag popular performers without too much difficulty because they can be assured of at least a reasonable turnout. But this notch in the Bible Belt had never seen anything like the band heading through Joplin and about to get off at the Glenstone Avenue exit.

We have freedom of speech in this country, and though I didn't care for 2 Live Crew's porn-laced junk, I wasn't sure it was my place to tell an adult-oriented band they could not play a set or two for an adult audience. So I read the papers with interest and heard the scoop on the street, but that was about it. I certainly had no desire to jump into the middle of a fight. But that was about to change.

Word came to me that 2 Live Crew would perform two shows, the latter featuring their infamous pelvic thrusts, pseudo sex acts, and filthy lyrics. An earlier show would offer a good sampling of the same, but for the teenage crowd. Now they had my attention.

When I do battle, I want to be assured that mine is a strong position. I am not the kind of guy who jumps into a fight without knowing who's on the other side and without gathering the facts. The Internet was still in DOS mode, and upstart America Online took no less than five minutes for a full news report to load at 14K speed, so finding out about the rap group required more than a mouse click or two. Instead, I went to the SMS library and read a few articles by and about the band and its crude leader, Luther Campbell. My curiosity was piqued. I needed to hear the lyrics. Big mistake. Suffice it to say that I have found more worthwhile projects at the bottom of my cat's litter box. These guys were pigs, and they were set to play a concert to the young people in my community.

The next day I went on the air with my information and read from a lyric sheet that required heavy redacting. The segment went something like this: "As I told you yesterday, a rap group is coming to town in a couple of weeks, and you need to know what they have to offer to your kids. I would like to read the words to one of the raunchy songs they perform—if you can call it a 'song'—and I am aware that some of you may need to turn your radios off." I proceeded to play a few seconds of the hook, minus the vulgarities, and then read from the lyric sheet.

The first line is "Sittin' at home with my d— on hard,"[1] and the rap goes downhill from there, describing a guy studying his little black book while he goes on the prowl for sex. As the tune progresses, the "horny" subject of the song explains to his girlfriend that he plans to leave her "f—ed and deserted," but only after persuading her to lie to her parents about where they are going and what they plan to do. Nothing is left to the imagination as the rap works overtime to sell the bankrupt concept that lies, immoral sexual relations, objectifying women, and unsafe sex are A-Okay. The rapper concludes by telling his girlfriend that he wants her to suck his "d— and my a—hole too."

> **WHAT WENT WRONG WITH AMERICA**
>
> As Americans we have lost respect for ourselves and the notion of what is right and wrong. By not respecting ourselves, we have lost any sense of right and wrong, which has led to a selfish, "anything goes" society. (Arthur R.)

How I chose to respond to the group, its filth, and the anger from the community may be the turning point in my life. It happens to most of us—eventually. It's the moment you recognize that you have no choice but to roll up your sleeves and jump into the fray.

I had always followed news and events but had never immersed myself to the point of doing something to change what I perceived to be absolutely unacceptable. The further into the song I went, the angrier I became, and by the time I finished, I was seething with indignation. My white-bread all-American Christian town followed suit. Every phone line at the station flashed red and demanded immediate attention as if to say, "Answer me now because the guy holding the receiver is going to explode." After several minutes a caller challenged me with the implication that I had chosen a single song to make the group look like pimps— the pimps I would prove they were. "You think I rigged it? Good enough. You get to tell me when to stop." My voice rang with fervent sincerity as I pulled out the CD cover and started reading the titles: "Me So Horny," "Put Her in the Buck," "D— Almighty," "Dirty Nursery Rhymes," "I Ain't Bullsh—in'," "Get Loose Now," "The F— Shop," "If You Believe in Having Sex," "Get the F— Out of My House," and "Bad A— B—" were just a few. I had to bleep out the offensive words so the band's stench didn't rub off on me. The caller hung up.

As each caller made it onto the show, I knew there were thousands who were working themselves into a frenzy but couldn't dial in. Eventually it would not be enough to just call a radio station; the public would demand action. Suddenly, in the midst of the uproar, it seemed everyone's attention turned to me. The cry went out: "Ankarlo, what are YOU going to do about this?!" What was I going to do? Me? I'm just a radio personality; it's not my job to play Moses to these people—or so I thought. But the calls kept coming; first by the tens and then by the hundreds. I finally relented. "Let me think about this overnight, and tomorrow I'll have an answer for you," I told all who listened. I flipped off my microphone at the end of the show and thought, *What have I gotten myself into?*

> **WHAT WENT WRONG WITH AMERICA**
>
> There are many factors, but one stands out in my mind: We forgot how to be ashamed. We began to accept and adopt unacceptable behavior because "everyone does it." We learned to lie, to make excuses, to just plain not care. We forgot that "the fault lies not in our stars, but in ourselves." (Fred S.)

In times of trouble and confusion people will always look for a leader, and if they can't find one who is grounded and wise, they will appoint almost anyone. Most folks are quite happy to be followers; just be sure to show them the back of the line. The cry goes out for the fight to begin, but make sure someone else leads the charge. I know this sounds rough, but it's accurate. As you read this book make a promise to yourself to accept the challenge, find the beginning of the line, and be that great leader if the opportunity arises. If you can't lead the attack, at least look long and hard for a strong candidate who will.

For the next twenty-four hours I called trusted friends and community leaders, seeking their counsel. By the end of the day I knew what needed to be done. There was something bubbling up inside that didn't want to wait until the next morning to tell the already inflamed audience; an audience that was looking for protests, street marches, and full censorship of the Crew's event.

Calls stacked up as I started my shift. "Well, Ankarlo, what are WE going to do?!" Before answering their pleas I decided to read the lyrics to one of the group's brand-new pieces called "Face Down. A— Up."[2] The second verse began with more of the same perverted slime: "Face down, a— up, that's the way I like to f—."

Where is this song headed? It's all about men using women to get their sexual kicks through oral and anal sex. How could clear-thinking adults tolerate such an assault on the children in their community? To suggest that this song was acceptable—when aimed at kids—was beyond my comprehension.

All over town people started flipping over to my show, and I wasn't even to the third verse. I am convinced the boys in the band would have been running for the border to avoid a lynching had they been in the city that day. I read each word for emphasis, substituting letters for rank words where needed. I wanted the full impact of the sleaze to drip from radios citywide before describing our plan of action.

As the last foul line hung in the air I lowered my voice to an emphatic whisper: "We are not going to do anything. I am not going to orchestrate any large-scale protests or efforts to shut down the concert. This group was around before Springfield, and they will be around afterward. It is OUR job to know what our kids are facing. It is OUR job to educate and lead them. It is OUR job to stand in the gap for them. Go home and love your kids and talk to them and ask to listen to their music with them. When you have finished, if you still have an interest, you are welcome to join me on the night of the concert. I will be standing on a street corner about five miles from the concert site. My wife and four children will be there too. If no one comes, that's okay. If everyone comes, that's okay too. It's about time someone stands up for the standards of this community."

Before my radio show had ended, reporters were on the lines, television crews were putting us on their assignment boards, and people were talking. Boy were they talking.

What were we thinking? Mine was a new station that had been on the air for a matter of months, yet it was taking on a national band with a strong following.

I used the phrase "stand up for standards" intentionally. I knew it was both a strong phrase that described the event perfectly as well as one that would solicit immediate involvement. Asking parents to talk to their kids was a risky move because most are afraid to venture there, but I believed by inviting them to join my family and me on a dark street corner on a brisk October night, I was letting them see how they could be a part of something bigger than any of us could be as individuals. The only thing I asked was that each person bring a candle or a flashlight as an emphasis of our need to be lights in a dark world.

Next, I made certain that all the media outlets were aware of the radio segments along with factual information and quotes for their stories, as well as an insight into the degree of disgust the adults were expressing. Each day I gave a few more details about the event while stressing the strong desire to keep it apolitical and nonviolent in structure. I rejected all suggestions to start a march at the rappers' concert hall. If we were to get our point across, it had to be systematic and it had to be done on my terms. I was the leader in this fight.

During the next several days I was interviewed by various news channels and radio stations and became the fodder for newspaper articles and opinions. I didn't care; this had become a mission. *USA Today* called. ABC News flew in. AP, the *Kansas City Star*, and the *St. Louis Post Dispatch* all wanted a piece of the story.

Finally, the night arrived. The event was set for 7:00 p.m. with no certainty of what would happen. The time was chosen so it was early enough for families with children but late enough for parents to get home from work, eat, and load up the car. At 5:30 p.m. I decided to head over to the selected site, candles in hand. As I turned the corner of Sunshine and Kansas Expressway, a surge of electricity shot through me like never before. There, standing in perfect formation and not uttering a word, were fifteen hundred moms, dads, sons, and daughters. Stand Up for Standards was already a success, and the official starting time was still ninety minutes away. To say that I freaked out is an understatement.

These people knew this was their chance to make a difference; it was their time. I'm sure the desire had always been there, they just didn't know how to get moving. Now they were empowered to do battle. As complete darkness fell, a sea of people filled every available spot, and cars stretched for miles. From every direction hundreds of individuals orderly assembled. Before the evening turned to night, more than eight thousand people stood side by side for an event that featured no scheduled singing, talking, chanting, or posters; only silence. Authorities said the line stretched for almost three miles.

That night, as eight thousand of us stood quietly, reverently, for a full hour, a lone demonstrator with a bullhorn and placards made his way to the opposite side of the road. He thought we all were a bunch of censorship zealots. A few wanted to shout him down, but before the situation escalated I walked over to the man and acknowledged his right to present his side. "You are on the wrong side of this issue, sir," I reasoned, "but go ahead and preach your beliefs." After several minutes of baiting the crowd, he disappeared.

A minivan came by, and the driver invited me to jump in so I could get a glimpse of all who came. As I passed the crowd, a lump formed in my throat and tears welled in my eyes. This was unbelievable. The public had caught the vision and had taken ownership. This was monumental. Huge. Spectacular. Just then I heard a lone mother softly singing lines from a familiar chorus as she huddled with her two small children, and the event became intimate and personal: "O beautiful for spacious skies. For amber waves of grain, for purple mountain majesties above the fruited plain." Others in the formation joined in as the song echoed into the horizon: "America! America! God shed his grace on thee, and crown thy good with brotherhood from sea to shining sea . . ." As the song wafted through the air I wept for my country. *This is the power of being an American*, I thought. *This is why we are the greatest nation in the world.*

The next day, the *Kansas City Star*'s reporter wrote a piece stating that 2 Live Crew performed a couple of shows and had as many as eight hundred in attendance while about sixty-five protesters demonstrated across town. The local paper said we had only fifteen hundred, which is a lot better than sixty-five, but obviously still wrong. I called both reporters and their editors. The first call went out to the Springfield paper. When the reporter answered, I laughed at him. "You interviewed me three times last night. You saw the crowd grow. Where did you get the

> **WHAT WENT WRONG WITH AMERICA**
>
> The rights of the individual have become more important than what is best for America as a society. This has led to the decline of parental authority over children. There's an overemphasis on free-speech rights, which now includes vulgarity and pornography. We've become a society of individuals who set their own standards—which means there are no standards. Tolerance has been overemphasized, making people afraid to disagree on politically correct issues for fear of being labeled a bigot. One who tolerates everything believes in nothing. Truth is intolerant. (Valerie A.)

number you printed?" I asked. "Darrell, that's how many you said were there. Don't you remember?" he answered. "Oh, I remember. But it was fifteen hundred strong almost two hours before the event started. Clearly, you left early or can't count, and I'm not sure which is worse," I chided as I hung up the phone.

Next, it was time to speak to the writer at the *Kansas City Star*—a paper that once had a little of my respect. The reporter answered the phone in the typical harried and somewhat intimidating manner that most do. I explained who I was and could hear his disdain for me and my cause with only a few intonations.

I lit into him. "Explain your numbers and think before you speak because I am taking notes and the next call is to your paper's editor." I was now in charge of the intimidation game. "You stated that this nasty rap group sold out their shows while sixty-five of us protested?!" I snapped. "What is your agenda, sir? You no doubt have one." He cleared his throat as if to interrupt, but I wasn't going to have any of that. "Admit to me right now that you went to their show and never came down to our end of town. Admit it!" I demanded.

At first he tried to make excuses. "You are burying yourself, pal," I scolded. "Be a man and admit it. You didn't even come down to our side. You made it all up." As he feigned anger that I would be so tough on him, I launched into him again: "You are why these porn peddlers get away with their stuff. Don't worry though, one day you will be a father, and you will wish to have last night back." I hung up and called his editor in an attempt to set the record straight. The perception that our event was orchestrated by a right-wing group led the editor to tell me he would investigate, but I knew it would go nowhere. It didn't matter. I knew the truth, and so did the reporter and his editor, and perhaps they would think twice before telling partial stories next time.

Though the press had the story wrong, those who stood for the cause knew we had made a difference. All ages, sexes, races, and religious affiliations were represented. Our candles lit the corridor, and that night, as far as the eye could see, were thousands of lights blending into one.

Two days later the bold-type headline from the front page of local paper read: "2 Live: No More Springfields!" Because of the huge outpouring of support, the foulmouthed prostitutes of music vowed to never return again. The people chose to Stand Up for Standards, and this time they had won.

PART 2

· ·

LOST DIRECTION

Where We Are Now

6

· ·

THE ABSURDITY
OF IT ALL

I have become comfortably numb.

—PINK FLOYD

WHEN A SAILBOAT LOSES its rudder, the crew has to radically join together to steer the vessel to safety. Everyone works harder, the sails have to be aligned in a specific order, and as weather conditions change, things can get tense. Home port is possible but not guaranteed since the rudder provides the steering or the direction capabilities, good weather or bad.

Imagine a country without a rudder. Just for kicks, let's give the country a name. Let's call it America. In the beginning it had everything going for it: faith, unity, a strong work ethic, and a determination to succeed. As the little country developed, there were growing pains and questions about routines. Not a problem; that's to be expected. But over time, as problems surfaced, key people in the wrong places made bad or unsophisticated choices, and the whole steering mechanism started to fall apart. Judges. Courts. Citizens. Politicians. All were to blame. As the winds of change started to blow, the rudder snapped, and the upstart country was left to flounder. Clueless. Directionless.

When we lost our vision, the next thing to follow was our sense of purpose—our direction. Remember playing Pin the Tail on the Donkey when you were a kid? You were blindfolded, spun around several times, and then told to pin a tail on a paper donkey. Remember how lost you felt? This is what happened to America.

Instead of going back through two hundred years of history for examples of a country losing its direction, let's look at a few recent stories. Tell me these don't represent a problem with our national rudder.

OPERA "PRO-LIFE," NOT "ANTI-ABORTION"
(ORIGINAL HEADLINE SOURCE: REUTERS)

LOS ANGELES TIMES music critic Mark Swed sent his latest piece to his copyeditor, clicked off his computer, and called it a night. He had just seen a Richard Strauss opera and opted to use the term "pro-life" to describe its theme. In this case, pro-life was supposed to mean the opera celebrated life. Swed was more than a little angry when, as he opened the next day's paper, his two words had been changed to "anti-abortion."

"It's about children who aren't born yet screaming to be born—not abortion," Swed responded. "Somebody who didn't quite get it got a little bit too politically correct . . . and we had a little breakdown in communications."

A "little breakdown in communications"? Can you spell *understatement*? What happened here was a perfect example of the liberal media working overtime to mollify their base and change the way we think in the process. The "error" happened because the *LA Times* had recently implemented a new policy that disposed of the phrase "pro-life" because it offended those who believe in abortion. Yes, you read that correctly. The two-syllable word offends people who aren't offended by the actual killing of babies. No, I don't get it either. Anyway, the copyeditor looked at his list of acceptable phrases for the newly illegal line and came up with "anti-abortion," which of course changes the meaning of the whole piece Swed wrote about an opera.

> ## WHAT WENT WRONG WITH AMERICA
>
> When this country began to focus on being politically correct, as to not hurt anyone's feelings or pride, we created a monster. Good feelings and pride can only come from achievement. But instead of keeping our standards high, we lowered them to accommodate the few so they would feel good. We did not raise the bar for them to become proud of being in America, the greatest nation on earth, but lowered the bar to the point that they feel they can condemn this country but continue to reap all of the benefits. (Isabelle T.)

The *Times* ran a correction the next day that led people to believe the mistake was Swed's. He threw another fit, so the paper issued another correction to clear up the situation. The second note, however, violated another policy at the *Times*. It seems the paper has a rule against identifying the person at fault, which forced a memo to remind employees that corrections will not assign blame.

I'm glad they cleared up both issues. Lord knows, we don't want anyone to be offended.

PARENT SIDELINES LITTLE LEAGUE PLAYER OVER REFERENCE TO GOD[1]
(ORIGINAL HEADLINE SOURCE: *SEATTLE TIMES*)

THIS *SEATTLE TIMES* headline says it all. Josh Benaloh decided he didn't like the fact that his son, Steven, was being asked to recite the Little League Pledge, so he benched him. You see, Dad is an agnostic, and his feelings get hurt when he hears of such religious discrimination.

"We don't feel comfortable and welcome in the organization," Benaloh said. "I'd like to think that a baseball organization would be inclusive of the people wanting to play." Someone apparently needs to tell the families of the 2.6 million U.S. children who play Little League every year, because they all are perfectly fine with the pledge. Sure, two or three parents question the "appropriateness" of the pledge every year, but none have gone as far as Steven's dad. Poor kid can't play baseball because his pop's not happy having his son read a couple of lines that do nothing more than instill great American values. What a fine example of a broken rudder.

> **WHAT WENT WRONG WITH AMERICA**
>
> The people in authority have completely allowed too many unmerited lawsuits and agendas to be priorities. There are some things that should never be tampered with, and the people in power need to use some common sense when dealing with unscrupulous claims and/or lawsuits. (Cathy A. B.)

LITTLE LEAGUE PLEDGE

I trust in God.
I love my country and will respect its laws.
I will play fair and strive to win.
But win or lose I will always do my best.

"GODLESS AMERICANS" LAUNCH POLITICAL GROUP
(ORIGINAL SOURCE: WORLDNETDAILY NEWS)

ELLEN JOHNSON, president of the American Atheists, a group formed in 1963 by Madalyn Murray O'Hair, has taken over as executive director of a newly formed political action committee known as GAMPAC, which is short for the Godless Americans Political Action Committee. She asserted that the time is right for "nonbelievers to assert themselves in the nation's capital."

Johnson's plan is straightforward: "Now, atheists, freethinkers, secular humanists, and other nonbelievers have another alternative in giving voice to our concerns and letting candidates for public office know that they must now start recognizing *us* as a potential force in American politics." She continued, "Everyone else has a 'place at the table' in the democratic process. It's now our turn."

As we read her last line, the odds are that most of us nod in agreement with her position. We don't like what she stands for, but we think she has every right to believe it. So the question follows: Is this an example of a country slowly learning to "tolerate" everyone or a snapshot of a nation that continues to be brainwashed? If GAMPAC had popped up fifty, one hundred, or two hundred years ago, would we have embraced it or shown its members a ship to sail on?

> ## WHAT WENT WRONG WITH AMERICA
>
> Recently a co-worker who describes himself as an atheist-libertarian said, "You Bushies are just warmongers. There was no need to use force to remove Saddam; the UN just needed more time." I asked, "Do you believe that diplomacy will always work?" "Yes," he replied. "If you enter negotiations with sincerity, you can negotiate with anyone." "So," I asked, "suppose Randall Terry of Operation Rescue was in the next room. Could you negotiate a settlement concerning abortion with him?" "Are you crazy? You can't reason with those radical Christians." He then departed. So it seems you can reason with the likes of Saddam, Hitler, Mao, Stalin, Pol Pot, and Osama bin Laden, but not a Christian. (Kenneth A.S.)

SHARON OSBOURNE: I WISH I HAD A "GAY" CHILD
(ORIGINAL HEADLINE SOURCE: WORLDNETDAILY NEWS)

THE FIFTEENTH annual Gay and Lesbian Alliance Against Discrimination (GLAAD) Awards were held on March 27, 2004, as some of Hollywood's stars took a moment to speak out about gay marriage laws in the United States.

Christina Ricci told *USA Today* she finds it "offensive and disgusting" that people have politicized gays' desire to marry and said she and her boyfriend, Adam Goldberg, will "vote even more Democratic than we usually vote" this year. Ricci's latest role was that of a lesbian lover.

Garry Marshall took a shot at conservatives with this line: "California is open to every lifestyle—except Republicans"; and Sharon Osbourne, wife of heavy-metal rocker Ozzy, drew raves when she said, "My only regret in life is that none of my children are gay."

That's terrific stuff, Sharon, you know, wishing your kids were gay and all, but isn't that a slap in the face to the people in the audience laughing and joking with you? Aren't they the ones who hated being gay kids?

Performer Alanis Morissette told the paper she went online to get her ordination papers because "My fantasy would now be to marry some of my gay couple friends."

Actor Antonio Banderas picked up the Vanguard Award for "promoting equal rights for lesbian, gay, bisexual, and transgender people." In his acceptance speech he enthusiastically declared, "I am going to be tonight very strongly on the side of those who are fighting for a legal frame in which they can develop their relationship normally in their lives." Before leaving the stage he shouted the words all participants wanted to hear: "In other words, gay marriage—yes, please! Absolutely yes!"

GLAAD used the awards show as the opportunity to roll out its new pro-same-sex marriage campaign called I Do, which includes a national competition to create a thirty-second television spot to push for the legalization of homosexual marriage.

> ## WHAT WENT WRONG WITH AMERICA
>
> Hollywood is at the center of what went wrong with America. Immoral values were touted and made to look like the norm: adultery, homosexuality, murder, rape, etc. Men were made to look weak and foolish, and women were encouraged to be immodest, aggressive, and to sell themselves. Family-centered living was not promoted as being the normal, unifying process in life, and stay-at-home mothers were criticized and child-care centers were praised. Marriage was a convenience instead of a commitment. (Karen K.)

"In a year where the enemies of equality want to define the American family by how many people they can exclude from it, the stakes are high for all of us," said GLAAD executive director Joan M. Garry.

"But each of you has the power and the opportunity to make a difference—by using the power of your stories to build a vision of America where equality, fairness, and love are values that all Americans share."

Remember—Hollywood does *not* have an agenda . . .

COURT WEIGHS EFFECT OF "CUTDOWN" ON PROCEDURE FOR LETHAL INJECTION
(ORIGINAL HEADLINE SOURCE: ASSOCIATED PRESS)

THE U.S. Supreme Court heard arguments in early 2004 that executions by lethal injection may be cruel and unusual punishment.

The case centers on Alabama death-row inmate David Larry Nelson, who claims that his veins—damaged by drug use—cannot handle the insertion of the needle used in the execution process and would need a "cutdown" procedure to carry out the execution. A cutdown occurs when a medical practitioner makes an incision into the arm to expose veins for insertion and, according to doctors, can be done under general anesthesia. Nelson's attorneys argued such a move is cruel and unusual because the state isn't set up to handle it.

> **HOW TO FIX IT**
>
> People must be more educated, more involved, and more willing to act to ensure that the liberal minority does not assume control of our country. It's not enough to just vote for a presidential candidate—the real work takes place at the local level. By retaking control of our local governments, we'll create the foundation needed to restore sensibility at the state and national levels. (Clayton J.)

Lethal injection is available to inmates in thirty-seven states and viewed as more humane than hanging, electrocution, and the gas chamber. Fourteen states use the cutdown procedure.

Cruel and unusual is the argument. Someone should have mentioned that to Nelson when he killed a cabdriver and then shot and killed another man while the man was having sex with Nelson's girlfriend. The girlfriend, who was also shot, testified that Nelson had set up the sex scene so he could rob the murdered man.

Nelson has been on death row for more than twenty years—that's about two decades more than his victims.

In a rare unanimous decision, the Supreme Court on May 24, 2004, ruled that Nelson could challenge the constitutionality of lethal injection—yet again placing his execution on hold.

SUPER BOWL STREAKER ARGUING NO ONE SAID NOT TO

(ORIGINAL HEADLINE SOURCE: ASSOCIATED PRESS)

THERE WAS another "flesh" incident that occurred at the same Super Bowl where Janet Jackson exposed her breast to the world. Thirty-nine-year-old Mark Francis Roberts dashed onto the field in a tear-away referee's uniform, ripped off his clothes near the kicking tee, and started dancing and displaying an online casino advertisement just as the second half was gearing up. Roberts was leveled by a New England Patriots linebacker and arrested by police.

> ### HOW TO FIX IT
>
> Individuals must be accountable for their actions and accept responsibility. If this can't be done on an individual basis, there's no way to expect the country to address it as a whole. We cannot roll back the clock to a simpler time, nor can we force people to care about anything in particular. But how we act and what we say can remind folks that the freedoms we enjoy allow us make these personal decisions responsibly. (TJN)

At a brief court hearing where he was charged with criminal trespass and public intoxication, Roberts's defense was that no one told him he was not allowed on the field. "It's on video, so there's no question as to what happened," attorney Sharon Levine said. "Under trespass you're entitled to a warning that entrance is forbidden." And Roberts said he saw no such warnings, "Nothing at all."

Some are calling it the "No one told me not to" defense. Sounds like something a six-year-old would say. But then I suppose our laws have boiled down to that.

On June 26, 2004, Roberts was found guilty and fined one thousand dollars. Janet Jackson's defense was very similar to Roberts's, but she was able to sell a few extra CDs because of her brush with nakedness.

COURT: EVIDENCE OK IN SOME NO-WARRANT SEARCHES

(ORIGINAL HEADLINE SOURCE: *HOUSTON CHRONICLE*)

THE FIFTH U.S. Circuit Court of Appeals ruled that police do not need an arrest or search warrant to search homes and buildings for evidence—a ruling that two dissenting judges called "the road to hell."

The ruling stems from a Louisiana case, where a Denham Springs man was arrested in October 2000 on federal gun charges after allegedly threatening to kill unidentified judges and police officers. Officers went to the man's trailer without a search or arrest warrant but were allowed in the door by another resident. Once in, the deputies conducted a sweep of the property to ensure their safety and subsequently found a weapons cache.

According to the court, any evidence discovered during that search is now admissible in court as long as the search was a "cursory inspection." They also stipulated that law enforcement would need an acceptable purpose to enter a home.

Someone must have forgotten that we have something called the Constitution, which includes a little thing called the Fourth Amendment. It says, "The right of the people to be secure in their persons, houses, papers, and effects, against unreasonable searches and seizures, shall not be violated, and no Warrants shall issue, but upon probable cause, supported by Oath or affirmation, and particularly describing the place to be searched, and the persons or things to be seized." It's sad when even a conservative court like the Fifth U.S. Circuit is making such horrific decisions.

HOW TO FIX IT

In the Internet, we have a weapon that can drag these nameless, faceless judges into the light of public scrutiny. We need a website that within moments of a ridiculous ruling will have the judges' images, bios, work and cell phone numbers, fax numbers, and e-mail addresses available for the world to see. Ronald Reagan said it best: "They may not see the light, but they can surely feel the heat." (Lee)

"I have no doubt that the deputy sheriffs believed they were acting reasonably and with good intentions," Judges Harold DeMoss Jr. and Carl E. Stewart wrote. "But the old adage warns us that 'the road to hell is paved with good intentions.'"

AT TRIALS ACROSS THE NATION, DOCTORS ATTACK LAW AS BANNING MOST SECOND-TERM ABORTIONS
(ORIGINAL HEADLINE SOURCE: MLIVE.COM)

THREE SIMULTANEOUS trials were under way in April and May 2004 in New York, Nebraska, and California as lawyers fought the Partial-birth Abortion Ban Act by putting doctors on the stand to make their cases.

In Lincoln, Nebraska, Dr. William Fitzhugh testified that he would "probably continue" performing abortions even if the law is upheld. "I'd have to take my chances."

In New York, Dr. Amos Grunebaum testified, "I would go to prison for doing a procedure I consider safer." Grunebaum, a specialist in maternal fetal medicine who has practiced medicine for thirty years and performed at least one thousand second-trimester abortions, admitted that the fetus is sometimes still alive as it is brought outside the body.

The Associated Press reported, "He said the process of pulling the fetus partially out of the woman's body and then puncturing the skull to collapse the soft tissue and squeeze the head out is often the safest method available."

Grunebaum went on to explain that in the early days of abortion, doctors would hide the dead fetus, but in the late 1970s and early 1980s studies showed that women grieved less if they could see the fetus after a failed pregnancy. "It is the same as any baby dying. People want to hold the fetus," he said. As another act of "compassion," Grunebaum said he goes so far as to put a cap on the head of the fetus just as he would a newborn.

It all sounds oddly similar to a scene in one of those R-rated slasher movies, doesn't it? You know the ones. The masked lunatic runs through a room, chopping off body parts and then "poses" his victims in a specific manner to prove he's the wild killer. I guess our guy likes baby caps as a trademark.

On June 1, 2004, U.S. District Judge Phyllis Hamilton declared the Partial-birth Abortion Ban Act was unconstitutional. The judge said the argument over pain suffered by a fetus was "irrelevant," adding, "The

> ### WHAT WENT WRONG WITH AMERICA
>
> The so-called Greatest Generation just assumed their kids would pick up their values. They had seen how precious life is and didn't want their kids to have to do what they did. So they spoiled their children, and those children spoiled my generation. Those children grew up to be spoiled adolescents who didn't believe in right and wrong and brought us free love, drugs, and war protests. They continue to be a bunch of spoiled brats. They gave us abortion, the liberal media, took prayer and discipline out of school, took God out of the public arena, and you name it. The baby boomers either hate America and what she stands for or they sit and do nothing while the rest of their generation moves us toward socialism. I know so many of them that care more about sports and how much stuff they have than informing themselves and voting. This is propagated by the liberal media and our fast-food mentality. I also know too many people who get their information from news blurbs or from the mainstream liberal media. They just take it in and go on about their day without stopping to think about whether it is true or whether they are getting the full story. (Jimmy W.)

act poses an undue burden on a woman's right to choose an abortion." By the way, this is the same federal judge who ruled in December 2003 that it was permissible for a California middle-school teacher to "require" her students to recite a Muslim prayer. Court records also show that the teacher read the Koran to the pupils in addition to the Muslim prayers. Yes, this happened in the same country where the Ten Commandments were outlawed.

The more I think about it, the more I'm convinced these are not just recent news stories. These are the signal flares sent up from an incapacitated sailing vessel. The waves are pounding, our sails are ripping, and our rudder has sunk to the ocean floor. We are in desperate waters and peril surrounds us.

The absurdity of it all is that we know we need a new rudder, but everyone is afraid to connect it back to the ship.

Mayday! Mayday! Mayday!

RANT—"OSAMA! OSAMA!"

*In times of prosperity friends will be plenty; in time of adversity
not one in twenty.*—ENGLISH PROVERB

The crowds screeched, jeered, and blew whistles, and then up from its bowels came the whisper—very soft at first: "Osama." A few more in the group joined in, and a few more, and within seconds the chant had grown into a roar: "Osama! Osama!" They waved their banners and flags and flipped off the Americans as though they were the bitterest of enemies. What Arab nation had my attention this time? Iraq? Sudan? Saudi Arabia? No. Try a "friend" closer to home.

The scene was straight from the Olympic men's soccer qualifying tournament in Guadalajara in February 2004, and the taunting, hate-filled fans were mostly from Mexico. "Osama! Osama!" They screamed the name meant to cause the most grief, not because they thought it would give their team the edge, they didn't need such help this day; they were already thrashing the U.S. soccer hopefuls terribly. No, our neighbors to the south were enjoying the new global sport called anti-Americanism. The rules are easy: act like you're our friends when you are in dire straits, but let your true colors show when you feel that the coast is clear.

Ah, Mexico! Viva la Mexico! Our pals to the south struggle economically because they have raped themselves with corrupt government after government for at least a century, and when things really get tough Uncle Sam rides to the rescue. That third-world nation suffers from earthquakes; America sends relief. That country can't compete globally, so America embraces NAFTA. That land of great opportunity, which continues to squander its existence when it should be the crown jewel of Latin America, gives up on its own people by sending more than a million illegals across the border into America every year. In return, we give them health care, food, and possibilities. Ah, *that* country!

It takes quite a lot for me to turn my back on someone, but after I do, it takes much longer for me to turn around again. I wonder if it is time for America to finally arrive at the conclusion that Mexico is abusing our friendship, to signal that we're dangerously close to turning our backs on them for a while.

When the United States needed support in our efforts to stop Saddam Hussein, we went to our Spanish-speaking cousin, which flatly rejected our request, even though, according to our intelligence community, terrorist organizations still operate from that nation. Illicit drugs still flow freely from the land of tequila. When our border patrol picks up their lawbreaking immigrants and ships them back home, they are detained for mere moments, if that long, and then released. I spoke to a seasoned border patrol officer, and he told me it is not unusual to detain and send back a Mexican illegal only to re-arrest that same person another time or two on the very same night.

While I enjoy the people and culture of Mexico and enjoy visiting that country, I don't demand that Mexicans speak English, change their laws, and adjust their culture to fit my needs. I am a visitor and know my place. If I were ever to move there, I would learn the laws and the language of the land. America has a multitude of prominent citizens with roots to Mexico, and most who are U.S. citizens agree with what I am explaining. They or their relatives went through the process of becoming citizens, and they feel just as cheated as we do by the present one-sided relationship.

Mexico is out of step with America, and we must stop the abuse! Of course we shouldn't expect a sovereign nation to jump at our every request, but we should expect them to comply with the variety of issues outlined above. For a number of reasons, Washington has not taken the threats from Mexico seriously. Yes, they are threats—and they are the very worst kind. These are the unspoken "we'll play dumb while we gain the upper hand" kind of threats. Sometimes a nation has to look to its allies and say, "Prove it." Enough with the rhetoric—show us actions. Now is that time, and Mexico is our partner who needs a trip to the woodshed. They can start by curtailing the river of illegals pouring across our borders and spend some time teaching their citizens about our virtues.

I still can't stop thinking about the idiots at the soccer game, the ones shouting the name "Osama! Osama!" as if he were some kind of god. No one bothered to explain the outlandish chants from the crowd; it wouldn't have mattered had they tried. This was inexcusable and should clearly send a strong signal to those of us who continue to reach out helping hands.

Had Americans shouted "Hitler! Hitler!" during World War II or "Iraqis Must Die" as we watched their athletes compete at the Olympic Games, or "Death to Iranians" during the hostage crisis of 1979, we would have caused a major international incident. In effect, that's what the Mexican fans did that day—but without the negative headlines, which, it seems, are reserved only for the United States. The video and pictures would have been displayed everywhere and around the clock. But what happens when insults are hurled at Americans? Most major papers buried the Guadalajara story with a paragraph or two, most television newscasts ignored it, and magazines decided it made interesting filler. How sad is that?

This new sport of anti-Americanism even comes with its own uniforms. One, a new "must-have" T-shirt found in the world's posh and hip locales, displays the phrase "I'm Afraid of Americans" on its front. Another reads, "I Can Tell By Your Smile—You Hate Americans Too." There are certain countries that are expected to treat us so outlandishly, but never should we expect it from a friend—an ally. Never. Friends are supposed to watch each other's backs, not rush for their knives.

7

. . . .

BLAME THE BOGEYMAN!

Don't find fault, find a remedy.

—HENRY FORD

CONGRESS WAS COMPELLED TO pass the Cheeseburger Bill and then voted to increase fines for obscenities on broadcast radio and television. The president forced a war on America. Democrats are out to ruin America. Conservatives don't care about the poor. Call it what you will, it all comes down to blaming someone else. Everyone wants to pin our problems on someone else, and even as we declare how tired we are of the whole mess, we have done very little to curb the desire to blame.

What has happened to this country? Why are we always looking for a bogeyman to blame for the things we screw up? Why can't we accept responsibility? There is freedom in taking responsibility. It's a more difficult path, but it's more rewarding too.

Instead of seeking solutions, we have become a nation of whiners who lobby for just one more rule—just one more law that we believe will put things in order. But it ain't gonna happen. Not here, not now, no way. If you want change, then accept some of the blame for the errors.

The Cheeseburger Bill is indicative of our lack of national character. I would call the whole thing a joke, except there is nothing humorous about it. With obesity looming as this nation's number-one health risk, Congress could see the gleam in the eyes of trial lawyers as they circled like vultures. Knowing something had to be done before the ravenous flock decided to swoop down on common sense, they hastily approved the legislation in March 2004. The bill's formal name is the Personal Responsibility in Food Consumption Act, and it is designed to block frivolous lawsuits against food manufacturers, sellers, and distributors.

WHAT WENT WRONG WITH AMERICA

I remember what it was like to have a moral compass in society, and we knew as we grew up what was right and what was wrong. Some say it was the age of innocence, but it was more an age of purpose and community. We cared about each other and about our families. We were proud of our country and what it stood for, something special and unique. We had journalists who sought out truth rather than promoted an agenda, politicians who talked about what was good about America, not what was good enough for reelection. We inspired and encouraged each other to do better rather than look for who we could blame for any misfortune that came our way. Maybe I'm looking at things with the rose-colored hue of memory, but it breaks my heart to see what is happening today. People suing restaurants because they are fat, as if the waitress held a gun to their head and made them eat. Politicians who spew hateful speech. News organizations that report "talking points" instead of investigating, that design polls to achieve a desired result and report the alleged findings as news to convince us how we should think. (Jacqui L.)

Though fast-food restaurants breathed a concerted sigh of relief and thanked their lobbyist gods, the legislation crosses that multi-billion-dollar line right into grocery stores, restaurants, and other food sectors. In a sentence, the House chose to act because they wanted to stave off the gathering storm of lawsuits that have been waiting to burst onto the scene.

How stupid are we? Here is the theory that pervades the world of fast-food (though it could be almost anything these days): "I am fat. I like to stuff my face. I eat at McDonald's. Therefore, it must be Ronald's fault that I can't see my feet and need two seats at the movie theater. Damn those golden arches! I'm suing!"

I'm going to go out on a limb here. I know this is a hard one to imagine, but is there any possibility that a person might just lose weight if they stop slamming down multiple Whoppers and choose instead a garden salad minus the ranch dressing?

I condemn entitlement programs on a regular basis because I recognize what they are doing to America, but their evils have more to do with us than social programs. They have helped to turn our nation into the land of selfish pigs, and that has nothing to do with our size. Pigs play in the mud, eat until they weigh hundreds of pounds, and consume almost anything. When they are plump and ready to slaughter, they wonder why the butcher comes for them instead of some other farm animal. And the difference between the oinking slabs of bacon and obese Americans would be . . . ?

For years, radio and television broadcasters pushed the limits until the line was fully crossed in 2002. That is when the F-word went uncensored during an awards program with little more than a peep by most. After that, the floodgates opened. "*Bulls—, d—head, a—hole,* and other words usually reserved for barroom brawls became staples on evening television and morning radio. Partial nudity, simulated sex acts, and raunchy jokes became the mundane, so naturally something had to be done, and as usual it involved government. Congress and the FCC joined forces to demand that media companies stop allowing such trash to seep into the mainstream fare. To be sure they were heard, the House voted overwhelmingly to increase fines for obscenities from $27,500 to as much at $500,000 per case and to revoke a company's license if the same offense happened three times.

I don't like bare breasts to be flashed during Super Bowl halftime entertainment, and I'm not particularly fond of foul language permeating the airwaves, but I also don't like the government tinkering with things they can't control. What is obscene? What is foul? I know, but do you? Does Congress? Perhaps I really don't either.

This is something I can control by changing channels, teaching my kids what to avoid, and contacting stations and sponsors myself. So why don't I? There is nothing stopping me from creating a coalition to help programmers know what families prefer and when to air the junk—if there is any reason to air it at all. Sure, it's nice to know new laws can be created and stiffer penalties imposed, and there is a time and a place for this, but by routinely taking this route, it becomes evident that we are simply too lazy to accept responsibility. The rallying cry of our past few generations sums it up: "Let politicians do it; I'm too busy." Say "so long" to another freedom.

The solution to our bogeyman problem is one of the simplest by far: just stop looking. I remember when I was a kid and afraid of the dark. If my parents didn't let me leave a light on, I was very specific in my sleep routine. I checked the closets, under the dirty clothes in the corner, behind the dresser, and then quickly poked my head under the bed, glanced around and then popped under the covers. Whew! Safe and sound and ready to close my eyes, but only for a moment because I still needed to squint every once in a while to be certain the shadow on the wall was nothing more than a shadow. Of course on nights when I wasn't really scared, I was still able to use it as an excuse to get out of bed about twenty times. Ah, childhood . . .

The United States can't afford a protracted adolescence; we have to grow up. Apparently, that's what happened to me, because after a while, my old routine ceased and a new one began: I climbed into bed, said my prayers, and closed my eyes. Did the bogeyman suddenly vanish, or did I just stop looking for him?

When we stop looking for someone or something to blame, when we make the decision to quit looking for a quick answer or an easy fix through lawsuits, then we too will have a chance to advance to the next level. The way it is now, our judicial system is taxed to dangerous levels, doctors are afraid to practice medicine, and people feel as if they need to fill out waivers before visiting friends for the evening meal because there is always the chance a hamburger may burn the inside of someone's mouth and an ambulance chaser will be knocking on our door.

> ## HOW TO FIX IT
>
> Take the blame and make a stand. Accountability is the key. I accept that I've failed my country, but I vow to do what's right. I will become anti-complacency. I will make my voice heard and encourage others to do the same. (Jerry W.)

Seriously, is the president really responsible for so many jobs leaving the country? Can budget deficits actually explode at the touch of just one set of hands? Do fast-food restaurants force sandwiches down our gullet?

A country where everyone else is to blame, yet no one is responsible, is a nation devoid of absolutes. Without absolutes, only chaos remains. Chaos leads to annihilation.

It's time to change our childish routine.

8

. . . .

THE SLOPE
TO DESTRUCTION

*It's the end of the world as we know it
and I feel fine.*

—R.E.M.

IT WAS 2:30 A.M. and my alarm clock had already gone off once, a telltale sign of an awaiting radio show. I usually don't stay in bed waiting for it to ring two or three more times, but this morning was different. A few more minutes would be okay. Besides, there was no way I wasn't going to hear how my wife's nightmare would end.

Laurie is typically a quiet sleeper, but as the night still enveloped the room, she was in a ferocious battle in her mind. Her legs and arms were twitching, and she was mumbling something. I leaned closer, trying to make out the words. "Run, Darrell. Run! They're coming for you! Run!" With those words she was done.

I could have stayed there another hour and it wouldn't have mattered; she was finished. As I analyzed what I had heard, a deep, sinking feeling washed over me. What if she was dreaming about an America in the not-too-distant future that rounds up anyone who dares to speak the truth and sound the alarm? What if her nightmare had government officials breaking through our front door while I dived out the back window?

I am not a "black helicopter," "aliens put something in my water" kind of guy. I have built a solid reputation as a straight shooter who is fairly balanced. But what I am about to describe still scares the heck out of me, and I am routinely exposed to it because of my research and radio discussions. Welcome to my slope.

The only way to steal a person's pride, patriotism, hope, or faith is to do it bit by bit. America lost its deeply held faith this way, and now we are on the verge of losing more than just our national identity: we are in danger of losing our soul.

I was talking with a friend, Katherine Albrecht, from Consumers Against Supermarket Privacy Invasion and Numbering (CASPIAN),[1] a group dedicated to privacy issues. As usual, we got caught up in a discussion about new technology and how retail businesses know everything there is to know about people these days. I try to stay up on the latest issues surrounding privacy, so we talked about Radio Frequency Identification (RFID) chips, grocery store cards, hidden cameras in shopping aisles, and even implanted GPS-type chips so parents can track their children.

"Darrell," Katherine said, "tests are already being conducted on a device that allows you to pay just by swiping your hand across a sensor." She was very matter-of-fact, as though there was little left to shock her anymore. Well, if she wasn't shaken, I certainly was. This was the stuff of Bible prophecy and sci-fi movies.

Several days prior, a lady called my radio show to discuss whatever the big topic of the morning was, and she dropped a little phrase that has stayed with me ever since. In an anxious tone, she said, "I feel like the country is disintegrating at a breakneck speed, and I can't do anything about it." I think the line resonated with me as it did because I feel the same way; our society is as out of control as it can be. The next step can only be chaos or anarchy. The best example I can imagine would be to have someone pour vegetable oil down a water park slide and then try to steer their little mat in a straight line. That's how a lot of people feel right now.

In one or two short generations our law, economy, and daily lives have been bombarded by "new and improved" everything. With each change have come new tradeoffs.

When I was a child, air conditioning was a luxury. If you wanted to cool down, you would head to the pond or stand in front of a fan for a few minutes. My memories are many of folks sitting on their front porches and talking with their neighbors and passersby while waving a handheld fan from the local funeral home, band, or church. Relationships developed, parents reprimanded others' kids, and neighbors became part of the family. Yards were big enough for full-fledged wiffle ball tournaments, water balloon wars, and bicycle stunts. Later, when the children turned into adults, they bought a house down the street or stayed in the general vicinity.

It was a simpler time. There were three television channels, mostly black-and-white broadcasts, and no remotes. Screen doors let friends announce their arrival before their cars even pulled into the driveway. And kitchens were made for home-cooked meals peppered with good conversation.

Now we have expensive home entertainment centers complete with surround sound and popcorn dispensers. Our air-conditioning systems ensure that we will be comfortable all day. Porches disappeared. And in most metropolitan areas an acre now handles five homes—minus any kind of a yard, of course. Every year 16 to 20 percent of us move; that's roughly forty-three million people.[2] Though the numbers are greatest in the Northeast, and a significant number stay in the same county, the statistics demonstrate how mobile our society is. When I move (and I have several times), it takes several weeks to say hello to my neighbors and months or years to blend into the community. If one out of every five move in or out at the same time, eventually we all end up feeling like an odd man out. By the time we get situated, we're making yet another call to the moving company.

> **WHAT WENT WRONG WITH AMERICA**
>
> Many problems face America today that did not exist during our parents' generation. The fast-paced lifestyles generated by the technological revolution have affected our family values. Televisions, computers, cells phones, etc., keep many Americans from communicating with their neighbors, family, and friends as done in the previous generations. What happened to the times when people sat on their porches in the evening and actually talked about their days and visited their neighbors to make sure of their well-being? (Bernard B.)

With the changes in lifestyle, or "cocooning," as a popular 1990s book describes it, we have lost touch with a key feature that made America the powerhouse it is: we lost our sense of community. These days, when people want to communicate they e-mail, text-message, or exchange voice mails. Seldom do we arrive at another's home unannounced, and all too often, when our kids have visitors over, we have no clue who their parents are. We have become an arm's-length society; that is, we'll say a friendly hello, but we really don't want to know one another—they will just vanish with the next job change anyway.

All of this is fertile soil for our destruction. If I don't know you and vice versa, how are we to form any lasting alliances for victory?

In the last twenty-five years our free country has put so many shackles on its hands and feet that it may never emerge from its torturous dungeon of slavery. If someone had suggested America would embrace even a few of our present societal ills, I would have bet the farm they were wrong—and I would have lost.

Just review this short list of changes. Each is problematic but can be explained away. It is when we put all the issues together, stacked one on top of the other, that the gravity of our country's predicament becomes painfully evident.

New in only a generation or two: Extreme feminism shoots its talons into all facets of daily life. No-fault divorce steals a couple's resolve to work through difficulties while destroying the sanctity of the institution. Legalized physician-assisted suicide. Cloned animals and plans for cloned humans. Legalized abortion (the *Los Angeles Times* now calls pro-family activists "anti-abortionists"). Prayer in schools and in public has been removed. And global-position satellites make it easy to track a citizen not just to the block on which he lives but right into his garage. When Big Brother makes full use of this technology, everything we do will be recorded in a database somewhere.

Doctors are ruled by drug companies and insurance companies. And teachers are forced to dumb down their lesson books so students' feelings won't get hurt. And the teacher had better know fluent Spanish if

> ## WHAT WENT WRONG WITH AMERICA
>
> Too much excess. Too much of a good thing. That goes for government, work, and families. With all our modern conveniences, it seems we work harder and longer, spend more for things we don't really need, and we have less time for families and friends. They took the front porch away, and now we don't know our neighbors. We have air conditioning, and we stay in more. When we are in, we have TV, video games, computers, etc. People don't visit as much. You would think with all our modern conveniences we would have more time to enjoy each other. People just don't seem as happy as they were in our time, even when things were rough. We bought into the modern age and kicked God out, or at least tried to. (Virginia L.)

she wants to keep her job (and about twenty-five other languages if she lives in some cities). Black boxes are being placed in new cars and in a substantial number of rental vehicles, allowing the car to be tracked or shut off and the driver's speeds and vehicle use to be graphed and charted. In many states, if you get into an argument with someone, you will be charged with assault—even if you were defending yourself. Say goodbye to gun ownership.

Kids are no longer required to respect authority and can have the adult in their lives fired with a simple insinuation. Foul language rules the school, sidewalk, and public airwaves. It has become hip to show simulated sex acts and push the limits of decency in what used to be called television's "family hour."

My parents were told that Social Security cards were a way to keep track of their payments into the system. Now, a few decades later, I can't use government programs, doctors' services, or drive a vehicle without providing my number, a number that was never meant to do anything but provide the benefit of account access.

Notice my deliberate use of the word *benefit*. When I need to give my dog a little medicine, I wrap the tablet in some bread or food so he wants to swallow it. Our government and a diabolical liberal front have sold us a bill of goods that we have blithely accepted because we believed we were getting something out of it. Well, yes, we were getting something out of it. It's called the shaft.

A controversy erupted in Alabama in 2003 after a sitting judge refused to remove a sculpture of the Ten Commandments from the courthouse. Judge Roy Moore cited several examples of case law that demonstrated the display of the commandments violated no law, but in the end both the statue and Judge Moore were gone. In the same year an atheist father sued so his daughter wouldn't have to recite the Pledge of Allegiance with the words "Under God" included. The infamously liberal Ninth Circuit Court of Appeals in San Francisco ruled in his favor. The father claimed it offended his little girl to make a pledge to something she didn't believe in. The one glaring problem came when the daughter later told the press she "liked" to recite the pledge and that she and her mommy were Christians. Once again the masses were steamrolled by the most minor of minorities, though the leftist loudmouths did their best to make mainstream America believe all the enlightened people surely agreed with the father.

In 2004 another very vocal group of mostly liberal citizens decided it was time to push for the legalization of gay marriages. The gay community used the backdrop of a fake domestic disturbance call so the men involved would be arrested. This Houston, Texas, case would force the courts to rule on the nature of gay couples. The case, *Lawrence v. Texas*,[3] made its way to the U.S. Supreme Court. After years of manipulation and strategizing, the homosexual community had maneuvered the prosecution into an indefensible position and set the stage for gay activists across the country to demand equal rights in marriage. The vulnerable state, they decided, was Massachusetts because the original charter and state constitution did not use the specific terms "man" and "woman" in defining marriage. The state's legislators fought for days during a constitutional convention after a judge ruled gays should be able to legally marry. Soon the wildfire began. The self-serving mayor of San Francisco, Gavin Newsom, started handing out marriage licenses to gays as fast as he could. Several other states followed suit and the offensive began.

A couple of decades ago credit was difficult to get, people struggled to save down-payment money for their homes, and if you couldn't afford the item you wanted, you could put it on layaway or go without. Now debt rules the nation at both the domestic and government levels. Homes can be purchased with no down payment and for 125 percent of the property value. This means homeowners are already upside down in their equity position before they ever take possession. I was talking to an automobile sales manager who explained that the majority of car loans carry fees from the buyer's last car or two. She said, "There is no equity to build up, and people go into a spiral they can never escape. One of the new loans is ninety-six months. There is no common sense involved in an eight-year loan," but people are snatching them up. The Bible reminds us, "The rich ruleth over the poor, and the borrower is servant to the lender" (Proverbs 22:7, KJV). By strapping so much debt to our backs, we are owned by the powerful and give up family and health to work ninety-hour weeks plus second and third jobs. At the same time, many countries' enormous debt allows lending nations to demand policy changes and special favors of the borrowing nations—unless the lending nation is the United States, in which case and depending on who's in the White House, such manipulations are publicized as indecent and immoral.

Select states are reviewing gun-control legislation while the courts decide if victims can sue gun manufacturers for making the weapon in the first place. Fast-food restaurants pay out huge settlements for spilled coffee and flimsy containers. A soldier sues his home state under "abuse" laws because he was injured in battle.

America's "victimized" citizens are heading for disaster.

At the beginning of this chapter I mixed social and legal issues with those from technology for a simple reason: this is how we will ultimately lose the battle unless we shore up support and strengthen our positions now. In addition to the black boxes, GPS tracking devices, and hidden cameras, we have some innocent-looking "benefits" that we are embracing without weighing the cost. We use those blasted grocery store cards every time we buy a box of cereal or package of rice because it's easier and allegedly saves us money. We pull into a gas station and pay with a credit or debit card and get our three-cent discount if we use the right card. In metropolitan areas we buy toll tags, which allow us to fly through the toll lines while a computer scans our passing. The government already owns as much information about us as it needs and can monitor our movements by tracking our Social Security number. Our driver's licenses now have magnetic strips on the back, pitched to us as an easy way for law enforcement to process our information. Our phones, utilities, computer connections, and bill payments all are attached to our credit or debit cards, and if we pay by check, our unique banking number follows us.

Those are just a few examples of how our movements are much more closely monitored than we could ever have imagined. Each innovation provides a nice little benefit; I mean, who doesn't want to blow through a long tollbooth line? But combine all these strings, and we are close to getting hanged.

I have mentioned the testing for RFID chips and the new payment scanning device that can be implanted in hands. Both offer great benefits, but in the wrong hands, they will erode another portion of our freedom. History demonstrates that one reason

WHAT WENT WRONG WITH AMERICA

Liberals have convinced us that we don't know how to take care of our children, vote, pray, or do much of anything without their immediate involvement. They have also convinced most of America that we have no right to be offended by others' behavior. Liberals want the government to control way too much of our lives while taking our money to pay for it all. (Sally R.)

Americans have been as successful and as free as we are is our ability to travel unhindered. That could change with a few simple mouse clicks.

This is what Katherine Albrecht of CASPIAN says about RFID technology: "A new consumer goods tracking system called RFID is poised to enter all of our lives, with profound implications for consumer privacy. RFID couples radio frequency (RF) identification technology with highly miniaturized computers that enable products to be identified and tracked at any point along the supply chain."[4]

The system could be applied to almost any physical item, from ballpoint pens to toothpaste, which would carry their own unique information in the form of an embedded chip.[5] The chip sends out an identification signal, allowing it to communicate with reader devices and other products embedded with similar chips.[6] Analysts envision a time when the system will be used to identify and track every item produced in the country.[7]

In-store tests for RFID chips have been under way since mid-2001 by some of the nation's largest manufacturers and retailers. The device is a little larger than a grain of sand and will be embedded in the items from food to clothes to the tires on our cars.[8] A half billion RFID chips were purchased by a company that makes shavers for early tracking consideration. After purchase, the chip sends a radio signal to a receiver at the register or store's exit for the benefit of better inventory control. Sounds like it will save big business a lot of money—dollars they will pass along to us by way of low prices, right?

What happens when the chips are in every product we buy? Since all products will have a distinctive identity number, everything we own can

HOW TO FIX IT

Write letters every day to your Representative and Senators. Stop buying products from the sponsors of trash TV. Stop going to the movies and watching smut. Stop buying magazines that promote porn. Stand up and shout from the rooftops that we will not take it anymore. Turn off the box and eat together, talk together, share dreams together, take vacations together, attend church together, pray together that God will heal our land. Stop disrespecting our leaders. Stop showing the world how to abuse free speech and demonstrate how we can support the leaders who lead without having to lie and cheat. Prove you have a vision for bettering the country and support those who share that vision with you. Enforce the rules. Enforce punishments. Love your children, your parents, your neighbors. Help the needy and the poor. Pray for our leaders. Pray for our troops. Pray for the sake of praying to the Most High. We can do it, but we have to want to do it. Stand up and never quit. Do you want it bad enough? I do.
(Hollie M.)

be tracked from creation to sale and all points in between.[9] It is not unrealistic to believe that someone will know what we own, what we eat, and where we sleep at any time.

Ponder the testimony of Jacki Snyder, manager of electronic payments for Supervalu Inc. and chair of Food Marketing Institute Electronic Payments Committee, to the U.S. House of Representatives: "Radio frequency is another technology that supermarkets are already using in a number of places throughout the store. We now envision a day where consumers will walk into a store, select products whose packages are embedded with small radio frequency UPC codes, and exit the store without ever going through a checkout line or signing their name on a dotted line."[10]

Europe may start placing a similar device in their money within the next couple of years, and the United States has hinted that it may do the same as authorities step up efforts to thwart counterfeiting. Once this happens, there will be no opportunities left for citizens to avoid the heavy hand of government and big business from measuring our every move.

So you're black and want to travel into an exclusive white neighborhood? Well, what if that community doesn't want you around them? Your gas supply will be stopped, toll roads closed to you, the police will be notified, and your engine will be shut off. Or what if you're one of those outlaw Christians—you know, the kind who keep causing trouble. You just won't shut your mouth about abortion, gay marriage, assisted suicide, pornography, and the Pledge of Allegiance, so someone decides to round you up and move you to a place where you will stop causing the country, the Liberal United States of America, any more trouble. You won't be able to use public transportation because your money can be tracked and your credit/debit cards have been canceled. No food for you because you can't pay for it, and even if you could, the machine will recognize that you aren't supposed to have it. Forget about walking anywhere; chips in the fabric of your shirts, pants, and shoes will reveal where you are and where you're going. In other words, you aren't going anywhere the authorities don't want you to go.

But if you wise up and follow your brothers and sisters of the Liberal United States of America, then you'll receive the wonderful benefit of your own under-the-skin payment device so you can operate effectively and efficiently. It will have your ID number embedded, and you will have the wonderful option of being fitted with a hand or forehead device to ensure easy scanning.

I can hear it now: "Ankarlo, you're spouting nonsense. Stop scaring the people." Nonsense, huh? If you are over fifty, think back to your days as a child. You never could have imagined microwave ovens, landings on Mars, debit cards, gas stations without attendants, computerized cars, cell phones, or GPS systems. You certainly would not have believed that your government would assist in the murders of more than thirty-eight million babies or that doctors would help their patients kill themselves or that a majority of this nation's citizens would side with a president who had an affair with an intern and then perjured himself.

Maybe my critics are right; perhaps this stuff is too far-fetched. I know all of the ills I have pointed to in this chapter sound like a warning siren, but maybe this stuff is nothing more than the kind of thing conspiracy theories are made of. Accept my apologies. I never should have frightened you. God knows that no government would ever round up, detain, or kill its citizens because of their lineage or beliefs. I don't know what came over me. If things ever get out of control here, and people chase me down like a bad dog because of my faith or conservative thoughts, I know I will be able to count on the courts and my liberal brothers and sisters to protect my rights.

Though I do wonder how many Jewish wives had nightmares just a few short decades ago, nightmares their husbands interpreted far too late and from which they never woke up.

> ## HOW TO FIX IT
>
> We all went wrong. As a people, we are consumed with ourselves. Look at all the stuff we have. And we go in debt getting more. We pay to watch TV in our homes. We have forgotten about our neighbors and our families. We work more and more, but if we are working, how can we raise our children? We don't take responsibility. It always seems to be someone else's fault. We don't stay married. It's not about what one can do for the other, but rather it's all about me. We don't go to church, because we are too tired to get up or because the people who go to church are at fault because they are hypocrites. We must win at all costs. We are afraid to stand up for what is good because we might offend someone, and that would be uncomfortable. (John C.)

RANT—DECENCY IS DEAD!

It is impossible for a man to be cheated by
anyone but himself.—RALPH WALDO EMERSON

It's a warm, windy Saturday in Texas. Fall arrived last week, so the clouds are bubbling, the trees are swaying, and life is good. So why am I seething? Why was I yelling only an hour ago as onlookers rifled through their pants and purses for their cell phones to dial 911?

As I strolled through the parking lot with my bride of a quarter century, she and I were laughing at the ridiculous movie we had just seen. We passed our car three times, because each time I looked at it, I was convinced it couldn't be ours—that dent wasn't there when we went in. Finally, Laurie rubbed her hands across the rear end of the sleek black BMW as she motioned for me to click the door lock. I was afraid to. What if it worked?

This is the third time in the last year that someone has hit one of my cars and left the scene without any kind of note under my windshield wiper. This is another example of how an advancing society evolved from purity to nothingness in less time than it would take me to get that perfect driving machine from zero to sixty.

I'm sure the idiot who put a crease in the left-side door had his monster-truck door get caught in the wind and lost control of it. I'm still optimistic (foolishly, I'm sure) to believe it was an accident. But then, after he did a thousand dollars' worth of damage to the car my friend had loaned me, the jerk probably laughed it off. "Look at what I did, Bob. I just wiped out a BMW!" And Bob replied, "Serves the rich SOB right. Now get in and let's get out of here."

Three months ago someone backed into my son's car and took out the entire headlight and passenger side assembly for the grille. It happened right in front of our house. Any note? Come on, what planet are you from? This is America. It was no doubt my dumb son's fault for parking the vehicle exactly where the law told him to. We're probably lucky we didn't get a call from the culprit's attorney claiming damages because part of my son's car rubbed off on his bumper when he hit it.

The third time, someone ran a key from front to back on another vehicle in a grocery store parking lot. Decency is gone in America, another tradeoff in our war for personal responsibility.

It should not be the long arm of the law or the fear of a baseball-bat-wielding wild-and-crazy white guy in his forties who is just aching to teach some jerk in a white truck a valuable lesson that determines the outcome of these stories. It should be the inner man who says, "I've made a mistake; I must correct it." Two hundred years ago a person would have waited hours to confess that it was his responsibility if he had damaged a neighbor's property. The same would have been true one hundred and even fifty years ago. An upright man wouldn't sleep through the night if he had harmed another.

In 2004 the perpetrator discounts his behavior: "They have insurance." "The wind caught my door. It's not my fault." "Why did he park it there if he didn't want the door to get hit?"

Missing from the pages of excuses is the one honorable, decent thing: own up to our mistakes. Decency once flourished. Now, may it rest in peace.

9

•••

ALL FED UP!
RED STATES—BLUE STATES

Gentlemen, Why don't you laugh? With the fearful strain
that is upon me night and day, if I did not laugh, I would die.

—ABRAHAM LINCOLN

I WAS SET TO share the stage with two military heroes, Congressman Sam Johnson and Col. Oliver North, when a gentleman approached. "Sir," he said, "I salute you for your great service to America." I politely thanked him but wanted him to know that I didn't share their rank; I never served in the military. "I know it is your son who is in the marines, and you must be honored, but that is not why I salute you." I was confused. "Darrell, if only the sheep of this country could hear the other side of the story that you present, we might have a fighting chance. I used to hear the news and read the paper, and that is how I formed my opinions. Man, was I lost."

After talking awhile, I thanked him for the kind words and started to move toward the other guests when he grabbed my arm. "People can say what they will about the crazy 'right' influences of our country's talk-show hosts, but at least they are telling the other side of the story. I'm fed up with the way this country is going; I almost feel like I have to apologize for believing in conservative values."

That line stuck with me; in fact, I recited it to myself several times during the evening. Fed up. This guy summed up in two words the feelings that I and others across America have been feeling for too long now. We are fed up with high taxes, politicians who manipulate, a government that exists to grow more bureaucratic, and a land of left-leaners who want to destroy everything this country was founded on and embraced as truth. My new friend is right; a lot of us are fed up.

It was the evening of March 19, 2003, and President George W. Bush addressed the nation. "Operations to disarm Iraq have begun," said the leader of the free world. "On my orders, coalition forces have begun striking selected targets of military importance to undermine Saddam Hussein's ability to wage war." Two F-117s from the Eighth Fighter Squadron, supported by navy EA-6B Prowlers, had begun an air assault over Baghdad only moments prior to the commander in chief's visit to America's living rooms. For months the president had been demanding that Hussein comply with U.S. and UN directives, something the serial killer had no intentions of doing. President Bush was tired of countless UN resolutions and idle threats; he too was fed up and had decided it was time to act.

WHAT WENT WRONG WITH AMERICA

Stand up for your beliefs in God and prayer. I want to see the government have less authority. I want the liberals to see that they are the minority. I cannot do that alone. It takes more than a village, county, or state to rectify. It takes every person standing up and taking charge of his lives and his vote. I plan to campaign against those who would destroy our country with their liberal views. Vote out of office those who listen to that garbage and control our lives. I plan to do whatever it takes to take back my life. (Sally R.)

America is at war, but it started before March 19, 2003, and it started before the attack of September 11, 2001. Our newest war has been festering for many years as our enemies have been slowly, stealthily stockpiling a sure-fire method of destruction. Unless we identify and rectify the problem, the history books will recount a great nation that once was the United States of America. This is not alarmist rhetoric; it is prophecy. Go to your calendar right now and look at the date. Circle it. Below the circle write these words: "The day Ankarlo warned that America would be destroyed; he admonished me to fight the fight." Don't be deceived. I am not a prophet, but as an observer of the obvious, it is my responsibility to ring the bell of freedom while it still has meaning.

On the eve of Operation Iraqi Freedom, the president also had specific words for the quarter million sailors, soldiers, airmen, and marines deployed to the Arabian Gulf region: "The peace of a troubled world and the hopes of an oppressed people now depend on you," he said. "That trust is well placed. The enemies you confront will soon know your skill and bravery. The people you liberate will witness the honorable and decent spirit of the American military." Those words could just as easily have been directed at every one of us as a rallying cry to defeat the enemies who have joined forces against us.

America has seen its share of wars, but never one like this. This time we are fighting two epic wars at the exact same time. The first is the external battle waged by terrorists and enemies of our country. The second comes from within—from liberal Americans who are putting us on a collision course toward destruction. Combined, they will cripple and destroy us. A proactive response is essential.

By now it should be clear to most citizens that many countries around the world despise us because of the things we most dearly cherish. Our poorest are among the world's most wealthy. Our freedoms are unsurpassed in the history of mankind. Our experiment as a representative republic has defined the term. As a result, we are on a hit list. Do you remember when, as a child, you received that shiny new bike? There was always one or two kids on the block who schemed to steal it from you. It was often your baseball teammate who slapped you on the back who, out of jealousy, plotted against you. It seems jealousy toward the United States of America can be found almost everywhere.

In today's world we have seen some of our greatest allies turn their backs on us. We have seen fence sitters openly protest us. It is bizarre for me to look at countries that readily accept our food, medicine, and military support as they distance themselves from us the moment things stabilize. Many of those are our friends.

This convergence of jealousy and anger toward the United States is a dangerous mixture. After September 11 this country was united for a brief period as we bathed ourselves in feelings of patriotism, camaraderie, and that thing called the American Dream. Remember how it felt? We mourned together, loved together, and defied all together. Now the attacks on New York City, Washington, D.C., and Pennsylvania have been consigned to textbooks as we return to our selfish ways.

While we work to perfect our apathy, and some of our allies prove their undependability, Islamic extremists have not minced their words. We are infidels and must die. It should be noted that the war cry from within the Muslim religion comes from a marginal but growing group of fanatics who must be stopped within their community. At the same time, growth in that community is in overdrive:

World Population	Christian v. Muslim Population Worldwide[1] Christian	Muslim
1900	26.9%	12.4%
1980	30%	16.5%
2000	29.9%	19.2%
2025 (PROJECTED)	25%	30%

In 1999 the Council on American-Islamic Relations (CAIR) estimated that there were more than 1.2 billion Muslims in the world. Using their stats, this means that Muslims represent between 19.2 and 22 percent of the world's population. Christianity remains steady at about 30 percent. Since America was founded on Christian beliefs that later became known as Judeo-Christian, we are watching as the foundation for conflict expands. The two religions, Christianity and Islam, have many similarities, but their differences are monumental. Chief among these is who is Lord and which group has the eternal answer. The fact that America is so closely aligned with Israel and Judaism only feeds the flame of hatred that many radical Muslims and Arabs harbor against us.

I want to understand the Muslim faith and the culture of its people. At the same time, to scrap a religion that has served America very well since our Founding Fathers put pen to paper while elevating others is mad. We will pay a price for it. Certainly, outside forces wage big and little wars against us but as they do, an equally impressive foe battles from within.

At the same time, look closely at the liberals, city dwellers, socialists, Democrats, or whatever you want to call them. You will see that there is a concentrated effort to push through political agendas and social change that will only disintegrate more of our foundation. At almost every turn it seems the Christian God is relegated to second-class status in town squares, schoolrooms, and in society in general, while our country's leaders embrace other religions on the basis of diversity to show the world how "open" our nation has become. Personally, I am fed up as I watch America's heritage being raped before my very eyes.

It shouldn't be ignored that former vice president and Democratic presidential candidate Al Gore had his highest concentration of votes from those who rarely or never attended a church service. Evident is the fact that those responsible for turning the tide toward a godless America do so because they have lost touch with the reason this country was formed in the first place.

Review the great religious divide as illustrated by this chart showing how a citizen's church attendance helps decide where the vote goes:

U.S. Church Attendance & the 2000 Presidential Candidates[2]

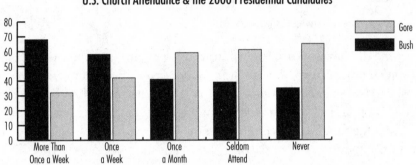

The O'Leary Report/Zogby International poll of Red States (citizens who voted for George W. Bush in 2000) and Blue States (Al Gore supporters) reveals a nation deeply divided by party, ideology, and values. As history will recount, George W. Bush had a nail biter of a victory after weeks of nationwide bickering and Supreme Court action. It is true that Gore walked away with an excess of a half-million more votes than Bush, but further examination of the numbers tells a tale of a nation at odds. Bush won 1,759 more counties than Gore and walked away with victories in thirty states, compared to Gore's twenty-one (including Washington, D.C.), but left-leaning liberals in the biggest cities continue to claim that the election was "stolen." Big cities have histories of liberal voting records and further illustrate the war from within (see the chart on page 100).

How does it feel to see the country's biggest cities flex their muscles for a liberal candidate though they are in the minority? Or to be informed by nonchurchgoers that the president who led us through the greatest act of terrorism this country has ever known is a thief who stole his election? Does it feel like a punch in the gut to watch as your nation's mainstream religion is systematically swept from existence while others

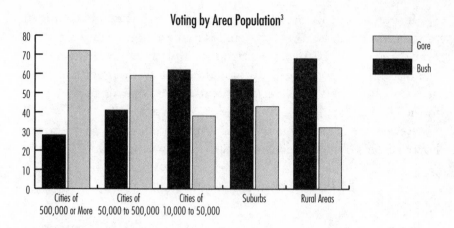

Voting by Area Population[3]

become the flavor-of-the-month to those who are far cooler than you? Don't complain. If you love country, God, and family, then you are supposed to be ashamed of yourself—or at least that's the feeling I get when the Left opens its "know all–be all" mouth.

Just for fun, look at the map below showing how the ballots were cast on a county-by-county basis. The tight race wasn't as close as first thought. Take particular satisfaction if you are conservative and God-fearing, because you are not alone; in fact, you are the majority! On the other hand, the map also serves as a graphic image of the divide in America that tears through the heartland.

Election 2000 County-by-County Map[4]

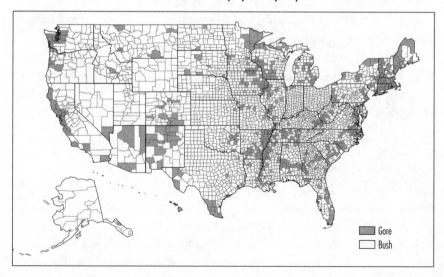

I had a liberal listener call my radio show as I was discussing President Bush's win: "So what if he won the red states?! Who would want them? Those people are just uneducated Bible-thumpers. Bush can have them all." He was obviously a Yankee transplant to Texas, an undisputed red state. This guy's call served a purpose, and another caller picked up on it: "Conservatives in this country are like battered wives." As most know, battered woman syndrome is a very real and bitter problem in America defined by women who are so belittled and beaten down (physically and emotionally) by their husbands and boyfriends that they eventually conclude that they deserve what they get. They recite a negative mantra in their minds that tells them they aren't any good anyway, and the bully beating them must be right. Soon the will to fight back is buried so deep, some never return to the real person they once were. It's only after the woman breaks free that she sees how deceived she was. As conservatives, we must not let the thugs terrorize us from our moment of greatness. We are each called to make a difference—to have an impact.

Further examination shows what should have been a landslide for George W. Bush:

Counties won by Bush	2436
Counties won by Gore	677
Population of counties won by Bush	143 Million
Population of counties won by Gore	127 Million
Square miles of country won by Bush	2,427,000
Square miles of country won by Gore	580,000[5]

Fed up? Employees don't walk off the job, spouses don't abandon relationships, and citizens don't revolt until they become fed up. Such emotions are good because change naturally follows feelings of discontent. We are a nation under attack from allies, foreign foes, and domestic enemies. The time to wage a counterstrike is now.

Before you're ready to do battle, you have to get outraged. If you are satisfied with your existence, and all systems seem to be working fine to you, then you will remain passive. If you think the task is too daunting because of a world population of more than six billion or a U.S. population pushing three hundred million, then you will give yourself another excuse to remain uninvolved. This isn't a personal attack against you, because we all have done it. We've all made excuses for nonaction.

God knows, those population statistics alone would make the heartiest warrior tremble. The object is to affect change right where you are—in your home, church, school, and community. If we all take our small bites, we can make a difference.

> ## HOW TO FIX IT
>
> All Americans who consider themselves Christian and who believe in morals and values need to get off their duffs on election day and turn out to vote good, decent, God-fearing people into office. We need godly persons to preside over our courts and pass legislation that will put God back in the classroom, end abortion, and return morality to our culture. (David W.)

In the end there is one certainty: we will all die someday. Look at some pictures of yourself from childhood days. Try to remember the dreams, plans, goals, and desires you had then. Which ones came true? Now look in the mirror. Which ones do you still want to come true? Finally, imagine yourself as an elderly person. What regrets do you think you will hold on to when you realize you allowed yourself to be ruled, dominated, and talked down to as a second-class citizen when all the while you held the key to change in your very heart and soul?

Become fed up.

10

· ·

SPECIAL INTERESTS AND AMERICA'S CULTURE WAR

There's a cultural war going on. The religious right is winning. We're losing.

—SHOCK JOCK HOWARD STERN

STATES BATTLE OVER GAY marriage rights, radio and television indecency, gun control, and higher taxes. Every day our headlines remind us of the war that is under way for the soul of America, and every day we look to our elected leaders for solutions. Something tells me we will be waiting for quite a long time—especially if lobbyists and special-interest groups have anything to say about it.

Special-interest groups exercise too much control over our government and our culture and our leaders. Both sides of the aisle are so caught up in the game that many have lost the desire to fight.

Politics. It seems like such a simple thing. You want to lend your voice to a cause for change, or you get drafted by well-meaning friends and business associates who believe you have the charisma, quality, and leadership skills to make a difference. So after you discuss it with your family and test the waters a little, you decide to go for it. If you are like most that get into the ring, you run as a Republican or Democrat, and as soon as you enlist your first volunteer, your party is there to provide feedback and support. It is right here, at the beginning, that the push begins, as you are provided with suggested protocols to follow and warned to avoid this person or that issue. It all makes sense. The process is time-honored. But you still feel manipulated. *It's okay*, you think, *I'm new at all of this. As soon as I get situated I will be able to take more control.*

Somehow, as if by miracle, you are taken seriously and become a contender. You really have a shot. Almost as if on cue, invitations begin arriving for speeches, dinners, and coffee soirees where contributions start accumulating. And with each check someone puts in your hand you feel a mixture of emotions. On the one hand, you are touched by the generosity of average citizens; on the other, you wonder what it will cost you—what do they want in return? Some of the more substantial gifts come with the hearty handshake that firmly implies a return favor is expected. Another bit of your soul slips away. If the race is close and the money is tight, the implication may be much more than that. The giver may give you a very clear indication of what's expected. You need the cash. You want to win. The people are counting on you. The sellout has begun.

The headlines announce your victory on the morning after your win, complete with acceptance speech and the customary concession call from your opponent. Soon you arrive in Washington and once again are reminded of your position in life as you are relegated to the farthest, worst, and warmest-in-summer/coldest-in-winter office in the Capitol. If an elder statesman steps in to help with your plight, you owe him one.

After you have been around for a while, you begin to make some sense of the system. Every vote, lunch, and committee comes with a price. Sometimes people owe you. Sometimes you owe. That's politics. It starts to feel natural. Another piece of your soul hangs in the balance. Will this city destroy you?

As your assistant comes in with the schedule of the day, you are prepared to meet with fellow leaders and constituents, which you do, but you can't help but notice the number of calls, e-mails, and meeting requests coming from the world of special-interest and lobbying groups. These groups will argue that they have every right to your time because they represent many voters; thus your time is actually better served with them. They will also remind you that they have the right to spend money to help or hinder you because their money can actually be termed as votes, many votes. They will claim that the dollars and opinions they throw around are sacred, inherent with freedom of speech.

Soon the dinners, golf outings, and special trips dot numerous pages on your schedule. And politics is a system of owing and being owed. You head back to your rented apartment a few blocks from the Capitol—the one you share with other freshmen Congressmen—and after picking up a picture of your spouse and family, you look in the mirror and wonder who is really in control. The person looking back is staring a hole right through you. "Am I doing any good?" you ask yourself. "Am I making a difference? Is it worth it?" Some days you are fully confident and on others you question everything about the political process in America.

Reelection time rolls around, and here you go again, but this time you have some power players and their money in your pocket. Your virgin flight into politics years earlier was full of passion and conviction. This time around, you say the right words and use inflections to sell your point, but you yourself aren't totally sold. You can't be. A lobbyist or big-time supporter may be offended, and you can't afford that. So you waffle. It's only a little at first, but that will change with time.

WHAT WENT WRONG WITH AMERICA

The liberal takeover that started in the 1960s crept up on us, and we ignored it. Now, forty years later, God has been expelled from school, deviant sexual behavior is regarded as "alternative," the sacred institution of marriage is under attack, murdering terrorists are called freedom fighters, Hollywood turns out mindless filth that gives Muslim countries a good reason to despise our culture, yet they turn it around and blame the hate on our "outdated conservative values," and the farce of separation of church and state threatens to secularize all of America and turn us into a copy of that most miserable of socialist nations, France. As the quote goes, "All that is required for evil to prevail is for good men to do nothing." We did nothing for forty years, and now we are reaping what we have sown. (Joseph M.)

You win another term in a landslide. After spending time with your family, you catch a limo for the airport. Your spouse used to drive you so you could spend a few more minutes before the grind of D.C., but that has become too disruptive to everyone. Once you get back to your apartment, with a lot of additional clout due to the win, you head back to the mirror—the soul-searching mirror. That person staring back doesn't have as many questions as before. In fact, it isn't really a stare. It's more like a glancing gaze. No big deal. And you're off to yet another meeting with new friends, the special-interest groups. Over time you accumulate all the power essential to a long-lasting career as a politician.

And this is what is wrong with our nation. Career politicians and special-interest groups who exist for one reason—to continue existing. It is one big, bad, nasty cycle, and it has destroyed more than a few good men and women.

In America today there is a major culture war, one like never before. And we are losing—badly. When Janet Jackson exposes a breast during a halftime Super Bowl game, the country starts crying about the loss of morality, and there is no doubt that we should cry long and hard, but it didn't start there. Where are those tears of anger when prime-time network television shows nudity and shouts profanity on a nightly basis? When music stars obscenely and erotically gyrate while they extol the virtues of killing cops, beating wives, having sex with children, shooting "the man," and enjoying illicit drugs, something tells me we are a little late in arriving for battle.

Our government is buried so far in debt that we will never see daylight again, even as liberals tell us the answer is in higher taxes. We have a record number of jobs being outsourced to foreign countries. Drug costs have skyrocketed, forcing our elderly to decide between pain and groceries, while they are warned not to buy cheaper drugs from Canada. A doctor can foul up a surgical procedure because he was a little drunk, but the patient has limited recourse. These stories are all too familiar, and they represent only a few of the thousands of issues nipping at our heels. As we career out of control, please remember to thank three important groups for their failure to take the culture war seriously: special-interest groups, weak politicians, and "We The People."

The tide is sucking us out to sea because only a few have dared to wage a war and stand in the gap for consistent and realistic change. Take any one of the issues listed above, work it through the system,

HOW TO FIX IT

We've struggled for centuries to become civilized. Today's culture, however, seems to celebrate the coarse, crude, and ignorant. Our society could jump leaps and bounds over others if our schools and parents would teach the Three E's: ethics, etiquette, and elocution. Think of all the problems in society today. Through ethics and etiquette we would have fewer lawsuits. We would learn to work out or problems on our own. Elocution is more than the science of speaking; in a classical sense, it is also learning to be civilized. Practically no one today critiques himself or herself. Ready to criticize others, we do very little to improve or civilize ourselves. (Paula D.)

and you will find special-interest groups who win because they have the money while politicians fail us because they need the money. Those are beasts that have long dwelt in our midst. There is no good excuse, but at least we know them by their actions. What can be our excuse? What lets us off the hook for turning our backs when the country needs us most?

There is a sad part to any representative government, and that is when citizens become complacent, due in large part to a belief that their elected officials are being paid to handle problems. This is some of the most backward thinking we could ever hear, but it is true. We don't take time to learn about pending legislation, changing policies, or any of the other devices that impact us because we believe we have men and woman who are fully competent of getting the job done.

If you win the lottery later today, will you give all your winnings over to your attorney, whom you've hired to administrate your affairs, without ever looking at a bank record or checking a spreadsheet? If you are like me, you will be making regular trips to that bank just to look at your loot—or at least review the financial records. Why is it that we know how we would treat our money, but when it comes to our lives and our children's futures, a majority of us have zero idea how to get involved or how to keep an eye on the people we have entrusted with the job.

Part of the reason is laziness. Part of it is a lack of education about the system. And most assuredly, a big part of it is a direct result of the daunting size of government. The portions are so large, most of us simply have no clue how to jump in. As an example, just look at these numbers: our current budget deficit is about $480 billion. According to the Treasury Department, our national debt is a little over seven trillion dollars, and it is increasing at a rate of $2.03 billion per day. What average Joe could ever get his arms around something like that?

That, I believe, is exactly what the special-interest organizations love to see: if the system can be made as unresponsive and complicated as possible, then the gravy train rolls on while John Q. Public takes graduate courses just to figure out what's going on.

I believe there are answers to our cultural decline and the money that creates a climate for it to continue:

1. All politicians should account for every penny they receive, who gave it, and how it was spent. Fancy accounting would be grounds for immediate impeachment, as would gifts and contributions that exceed

set limits. By being openly accountable, we can source the influences on our laws, government, and culture.

2. All politicians should adopt at least one issue that is affecting our cultural decline and dedicate no less than 10 percent of their time to finding solutions. The issue would be openly promoted as belonging to the politician, and his/her abilities to succeed in solving the issue would be fair game during reelection.

3. Media companies should self-govern the amount of sex, violence, profanity, and questionable lifestyle choices they present. A maximum amount of each could be published, and if the media companies consistently violate the limit, their licenses could be revoked.

4. Major policy change cannot come from inside the Beltway alone. There are too many lobbyists, lawyers, bureaucrats, and politicians who live off the redistribution of the fruits of our labor. Real change comes only when Americans rise up and demand it of their government. The Founding Fathers always knew that a representative republic was a process that required the full participation of passionate and patriotic citizens. Thomas Jefferson said it best: "The People are the only sure reliance for the preservation of our Liberty."

5. Schools and parents must work together to create an open line of communication. If a student is enrolled, then parents and teachers should be required to update each other at least once every two weeks via e-mail, phone, letter, or personal consultation.

6. Churches and religious organizations should spearhead national PR campaigns to teach the population that it's okay to avoid things that destroy us personally, spiritually, and culturally.

7. Families must stop hoping that someone else will do their jobs. Ultimately it is our personal responsibility.

Imagine what could happen if a series of checks and balances could be developed encompassing special-interest/lobby money, politicians, media companies, schools, churches, and citizens. Our government has existed for more than two hundred years because we have relied on this kind of system. Isn't it about time we extend it to a culture that is bankrupt?

I described the loss of direction that faces our politicians when undue pressure is placed on them by special interests. A similar pressure hangs over all people who impact our culture. It is a war that can be won, but we have to first agree who the enemy is and what weapons we should use to win. I have given you a few of my ideas; what are yours?

II

• •

OH, THE HYPOCRISY!

They deem him their worst enemy
who tells them the truth.

—PLATO

THERE IS A REASON countries around the world hate the United States of America, and though I could point to our foreign policy, economic decisions, or a thousand other issues, the answer really boils down to a single word at the root of it all: hypocrisy. We are a land of hypocrites, and the world despises us for it.

A few years ago in Italy, I found myself in an interesting conversation about our national duplicity. The exchange was actually quite pleasant at first, as I attempted to imitate the accent of the dark-haired Italian but only butchered the dialect. While the man dragged his hand through his thick locks, he made light of my prematurely graying hair. In broken English he suggested that my faded hair was a result of my stress-filled life. I laughed. He didn't.

"You Americans are all too serious," he said. "You want the world to think you are carefree, but we all know you are not. You lie about a lot of things."

I was on vacation; I could have avoided the confrontation. But how does a guy go about getting great stories if he runs from them?

"We lie?" I queried. "That's an incredibly loaded thing to say to a man about his people. Can you back that up?"

"Bakk eet upp?" he asked.

"Yes, 'back it up.' It means explain or prove it." I was sure this would be an hourlong conversation because of the language barrier, but I had misread him. The well-dressed man must have been practicing his next several lines for a lifetime.

"You are all hypocrites. You wage war in countries that don't want you. You complain about the immoral acts of your president though you openly joke about doing the same things. You act like the USA has all the answers but you have poor people living in the streets. I know; I have visited."

His tirade lasted twenty-five minutes as we sipped coffee outside a bistro in the chill of a February afternoon. We politely argued about so many things, my mind was preoccupied with the conversation for the rest of the day. I took both points of view and fought the issues to completion in the solitude of my hotel room. In the end there was no escaping it. In many ways we do live a two-faced existence.

Look at our well-respected companies. During an eighteen-month period some of the mightiest fell. Enron sold for $84 a share in 2000 and plummeted to $1 a share less than a year later and went bankrupt shortly thereafter. Twenty thousand employees lost their jobs. The Justice Department stepped in.

One of the world's largest conglomerates, Tyco, saw its stock nosedive from $60 a share to less than $10 as its CEO, Dennis Kozlowski, was forced to resign and was later arraigned on charges of tax evasion. The Justice Department alleged that he stole more than $600 million from the publicly traded company.

Within a six-month period Adelphia Communications Corp., one of America's largest cable television providers, went from a value of approximately $12 billion to bankruptcy. Indictments followed for CEO John Rigas for making off-balance loans of almost $2.5 billion to himself and other family members. The company's stock went from a high of $42 to a low of $.70.

Global Crossing filed for bankruptcy as its stock lost 99.9 percent of its value. Also losing more than 99 percent of its value was WorldCom, a huge telecommunications company that hyped earnings and hid costs—until the government caught up with them.

American corporate greed. The rest of the world looks askance at us when we say "play fair" while our highest-paid leaders lie and cajole anyone who will listen, much like the carnival barker of days gone by.

Iran, North Korea, India, Pakistan, and other countries have nuclear weapons or are in the process of developing a program to acquire them. Several powerful countries, including the USA,[1] placed each nation on notice, explaining that the development of such weapons cannot be tolerated. The world asks who put America in charge of deciding such things.

During Operation Iraqi Freedom, America demanded that Arab television cease its propaganda war by halting continued efforts to show the bodies of dead U.S. servicemen being dragged through some streets. When our news broadcasts showed dead or dying Iraqi servicemen and women, we claimed it was in the best interest of our citizens to show our advancements.

In America we decry cruel and unusual punishment and then lock a criminal away for a hundred years. We vote to overhaul campaign finance laws but create enough loopholes to allow the system to go unchanged. America views pornography as counterproductive and then funds it with tax dollars through the National Endowment for the Arts. We claim to be a compassionate country but allow the pharmaceutical industry to flash cash around Washington, D.C., so the purchase of prescription drugs from Canada at half the price is illegal. Senior citizens miss the compassion in that decision.

The FCC increased obscenity fines from $27,500 to $500,000, due in equal parts to public pressure and a presidential election year. They aim for radio broadcasts in particular. Meanwhile, some of the sleaziest programs in the nation's history play during the family hour on television sets from coast to coast. Apparently fake laughter, applause, and actually seeing the person have sex somehow makes it okay.

I haven't touched on the environment, nation building, a country that turns its back to the ills of an evil dictator because he helps us in a region, or the countless others. I don't have to. We know we are a people who have been blessed more than any other in history. We get what we want when we want it. And if you are in the way, we can get you too. Many of these events happen in ways that we can't comprehend. Backroom strategy sessions and international conference calls usually get the balls rolling, and we hear a sanitized version on the evening news, usually so late in the process that we couldn't do anything about it if we wanted to.

I love America and respect our system, but as long as mankind is in the mix, there will be graft, greed, and corruption. It goes with the fallen nature we are born into. At the same time, if we fail to recognize our failures and continue to ask others to fix them when we should also be rolling up our sleeves, then we too hold the chisel in hand as the epitaph is slowly etched into the nation's gravestone.

We cannot expect the rest of the world to follow us or love us if we require more of them than we do of ourselves. They want to see how our honest, representative process works for all persons before they will commit to respecting us.

One of my brothers, Orville, is president and part owner of a multi-million-dollar corporation in New York. With his position comes great clout. He can eat anywhere he wants, fly first-class, and enjoy all the other enormous perks of his industry. He rarely does any of that. If only our government and corporate leaders would follow his management style. "It has everything to do with integrity," he said. "I don't want to demand that people follow a select set of rules that I impose, while they watch me live a high-and-mighty life. We all work together to win as a company."

We are a kind, generous, and caring people, but still we confuse the world with the difference between what we say and what we do. All anyone has ever asked of a leader is that those at the top openly demonstrate integrity and stay off the high horse that somehow elevates them above all others—at least in their own minds.

We can tell the world in only so many ways that we are a morally upright land before they look us in the eyes and demand that we back it up. Right now we would fail that test because our leadership, on both sides of the aisle, needs new blood. There has to be a shakeout in management, just as was required in some of those top companies that have recently collapsed. I nominate you, and shortly I'll give you the tools to fix it.

When the Italian gentleman and I parted, we shook hands. "You are a good man," he said. "I think I could like you. I want to like America. It will take time." I hope he realized he would love real Americans—if only we could show them to him and the rest of the world.

12

· ·

DOES "THE STAR-SPANGLED BANNER" STILL MAKE YOU CRY?

A thoughtful mind, when it sees a Nation's flag, sees not the flag only, but the Nation itself; and whatever may be its symbols, its insignia, he reads chiefly in the flag the Government, the principles, the truths, the history which belongs to the Nation that sets it forth.

—HENRY WARD BEECHER

AMERICA. EAGLE'S PRIDE. Peace. World Trade Center. Freedom. Veterans' Remembrance. After September 11, these words became more than just symbols, they became shrines to lost innocence and newfound hope. Each also became the name of a school somewhere in the USA.

Patriotism became the "in" thing for a time, with flags and banners flown on cars, houses, boats, and anything else we could find. The mad dash was to show pride in everything American. We were a hurt people, a grieving people, and we wanted to stand in solidarity with one another.

I can't recall how many times I saluted or waved to a passing person with the Stars and Stripes proudly displayed. We let people take parking spaces, cut in line at ball games, and drive way too slowly in our lane of traffic. Heck, for a while we actually went out into our yards and talked to our neighbors. We had to. We needed to.

It was more than just emotions that we were trying to understand; many were also trying to get a handle on the explosion of patriotism that overwhelmed them. It makes sense. This wound was inflicted not just on our people but on our country too. It reminds me of the old line: "I'll

113

yell at my wife if I want to; but if you yell at her I'll take your head off."
Not too many felt like tearing down the psyche of America, at least not
right after the tragedy.

Besides citizens, big business found a new sense of pride in their
country. Car companies offered 0 percent financing, complete with the
slogan "Keep America Moving." A national toy store told parents to
bring in their children to color a flag. A jeans company featured a doll
wearing their pants and a Band-Aid on his arm with a Red Cross sticker
that said, "I gave blood." An airline ran a commercial showing a fire-
fighter boarding one of their planes. Once the crew realized who he was,
they bumped him to first class while the captain explained to the rest of
cabin, "There's a hero on board." A beer company even told us to drink
their brand to help the victims of 9/11. Thousands of similar images
were everywhere. And we loved it.

But almost as suddenly as the patriotic atmosphere arrived so too
came the backlash. The *Boston Globe* was one of the first to bemoan the
sugary sweet love of country. "For some people [i.e., our editors], the
sudden glut of American flags is reminiscent of the hoopla that precedes
Homecoming Week at college." The *Los Angeles Times* told the story of a
first-grade teacher in Wisconsin who wanted nothing to do with an attitude akin to Nazi Germany and refused to lead her children in the
Pledge of Allegiance, stating, "Mandating patriotism is a really scary
thing. It leads to nationalism and ultimately, to fascism."

The backlash against patriotism started as a whisper campaign of
sorts but was soon everywhere. Some people even called my radio show
or sent me e-mail to let me know that I, and people like me, would
"probably follow Adolf Hitler if he were alive." No. Sorry. Not a chance.
Just because I love my country and the symbols that represent it does not
make me a mass murderer. The suggestion is slanderous.

Why is it that people who lean left and get backed into a corner have
no better retort than to go back to a deep black hole in history and
somehow try to shut us down with comparisons that are ridiculously
nonsensical? I can be proud of my country and maintain my dignity and
individuality. Just because I want to recite a pledge or wave a flag doesn't
mean I'm a crazy right-wing wacko but may in fact simply suggest that I
feel like demonstrating my thankfulness for being born here. What is so
wrong with that? By the luck of the draw I could have been born in the
throes of another country's civil war, famine, or murderous regime. I

could have been born into third-world poverty or in a country like Iraq under a dictator.

I am blessed and want to show it. Somehow that became wrong to a strong group of liberals desperately in search of a cause.

Meanwhile, while I am supposed to remain quiet for fear of becoming a Hitlerite, teachers like the one in Wisconsin are free to indoctrinate and kidnap the minds of our children. They're free to slip condoms onto bananas and explain how my distant relative was a monkey.

In 1943 the U.S. Supreme Court ruled in the landmark case *West Virginia State Board of Education v. Barnette*[1] that students can't be forced to recite the pledge. Once again we get another example of incrementalism in action. Interestingly it was the PTA, the Boy Scouts, parents, and educators who fought the requirement to salute the flag and say the pledge chiefly because a child who refused would be expelled on charges of insubordination. Some religious groups said that to engage in a ceremony with the flag and the pledge would be tantamount to worshiping idols, and they wanted no part in that. So instead of meeting in the middle, most schools slowly did away with the exercise.

> ### WHAT WENT WRONG WITH AMERICA
>
> America has lost her moral compass. In the weeks that followed September 11, 2001, it seemed as though we regained some of what was lost in the past, but those days have ended. Our courts are fighting over whether the Ten Commandments can be publicly displayed, whether "In God We Trust" should remain on our currency, whether "Under God" should be deleted from our national pledge, and whether the holy institution of marriage should include same sexes, multipersons, or out of species for that matter. (Michael L.)

How difficult would it have been to continue the lessons on patriotism by letting the objectors remain silent with hands to their sides during the brief moment? At least our young people would have been exposed to two of our most beloved symbols.

The operative word is *symbols*. The flag reminds me of all the things that are great about America, but it is not America. The same holds true for the pledge. When a country loses its identity, it loses its sense of national pride. Finally, it forgets what sets it apart from all other countries.

Connecticut Republican F. Philip Prelli supports a law requiring schools to set aside time daily to recite the pledge. "I was surprised to find that some of the schools were not saying it on a voluntary basis," he said. "I can't force patriotism, but if I never teach patriotism, I can't build the base for it." How right he is. "We were getting away from patriotism in this country. For generations we all said the Pledge of Allegiance. We should be doing that for our children now."

A bill proposed in Colorado would require students in every grade to take a unit of patriotism. Sold as a way to complement other studies in civics and history, the state senate said it was too restrictive and changed the language to "encouraged, not mandated classroom experience."

We have become a country of milquetoast citizens who are afraid to take even the simplest of stands. Come on! A class on patriotism—how much more of a no-brainer decision can there be?

HOW TO FIX IT

We need to return to a belief that there is absolute truth. We've become a society where everyone sets their own selfish standard for what is true and beneficial to themselves. America's history was founded by those who were focused on the good of everyone and not on their own selfish self-interests. We need to stop looking at everyone as a protected class—African Americans, Hispanics, homosexuals, women, etc.—and start considering everyone as an American. In every situation the question to be asked should be, "What is best for the United States of America?"—with an emphasis on the word United. (Valerie A.)

After 9/11 news reporters and anchors on stations from coast to coast wore flag pins, tie tacks, and red-white-and-blue ribbons. But that show of support for the nation was short-lived as more and more news managers were told that journalistic integrity and independence were compromised by allowing anchors to wear such symbols. Are we to assume that citizens would be angry because their evening news reader dared to sport a flag lapel pin? Perhaps the "freedom of choice, oh, you offended me" crowd of liberals among us might be, but anyone with any sense of pride would understand the sentiment, especially after such an epic attack on U.S. soil in 2001.

Remember when Dan Rather cried on the David Letterman show? This veteran, albeit liberal, newsman with fifty years' experience was ridiculed and made the butt of jokes. Personally, I thought it was refreshing to see one of our "show no emotion" broadcasters give us a glimpse of his humanity. That was not a national embarrassment; it was national pride.

At a St. Louis TV station run by faculty and students at the University of Missouri, on-air news employees were instructed not to wear anything to show support for a specific cause. This included flags or patriotic ribbons. When a legislator found out about it, he shot off a memo to the university: "If this is what you are teaching the next generation of journalists, I question whether the taxpayers of this state will support it." That representative deserves to be voted back into office!

In another case, the city editor of the *Texas City Sun* was fired after writing an editorial that President Bush's actions on the day of the attacks needed to be investigated. In this case, the paper's publisher made a personal apology to his readers as he dismissed the man. "Censorship due to nationalism," cried journalists. There was only one problem: it wasn't a rampant censorship issue based on the belief that management's patriotism had gone too far. It was merely a young journalist who asked a tough question at the wrong time. That would be like asking a new widow if she could put her dead husband on ice and take a romp on a beach. The romp may be the perfect thing—later. The reporter's column may have been fine—later. The timing was wrong, but as is all too often the case, this kind of story was used by the Left to demonstrate how fanatical Americans can be. That argument didn't apply to this story.

> ### HOW TO FIX IT
>
> The need or good of the many must outweigh the need or good of the few. We as a nation need to make laws that will benefit America as a whole, not just minorities or special-interest groups. We are being torn as a nation by those who are demanding their rights. In the pursuit of their rights, they take away the rights and freedoms of other Americans. (Linda B.)

Having emotions for your country does not make you weak and incapable of asking tough questions of leaders or a partisan hack. I don't know why we continue this exercise in the absurd. Back off. A little love of country goes a long way.

Oh, I can hear the label maker coming out already. *Click, click, click* goes the machine, and out pops a handy little label for this thing I've been describing: nationalism. Before you wear it as a badge of honor, it is important to note that it is hurled as a vitriolic insult. Again we hearken back to Hitler, swastikas, and concentration camps. Or so we are told. If you can be put into such a small, defined box, then you will quietly succumb to the practices of a few who wish to see this country disappear into oblivion.

The dictionary defines *nationalism* as "loyalty and devotion to a nation" or "excessive fanatical devotion to a nation." I proudly proclaim to be a nationalist in accordance with the first definition; I am proud. I am not fanatical or wild-eyed. But I do appreciate the symbols and processions that remind me of the greatness of America.

One of my most enjoyable moments comes when I attend a sporting event and it's time for the national anthem. Anyone who knows me will tell you that I will request that you either remain quiet or sing along; no eating, drinking, or talking allowed. Off-key. Loud. Countrified. Operatic. It doesn't matter. In my mind there are few things better than the voices of fifty to sixty thousand people sharing a common thread of patriotism. For a brief moment or two we pause to remember. We pause to be unified.

We shall always remember—at least until the lesson has finally been erased by a very vocal minority.

13

WHAT COULD HAPPEN IF CONSERVATIVES THROW IN THE TOWEL

Americans never quit.

—GEN. DOUGLAS MACARTHUR

WHAT DO YOU THINK would happen to our nation if liberals controlled all facets of our society and, ultimately, the world? The easy answer finds a culture that is totally dependent on big government and leaders who pimp away its better qualities. The tougher and more ominous response leads to the eventual end of our species as we know it. I know that last line seems far-fetched, but I will make a case for its plausibility later.

The liberal concept is not necessarily a bad thing on its surface. Essentially it says we must take care of all levels of humanity; something that goes to the soul of a person and a nation. The problem with the liberal plan becomes evident when its purveyors attach the growth of social programs and government offerings in order to participate. The American system of government was never meant to create and train generations of citizens to become consumers.

Conservatives like the old adage, "Give a man a fish; you have fed him for today. Teach a man to fish, and you have fed him for a lifetime." We want people to take responsibility for their own lives. It's not that we don't believe in lending a helping hand; indeed, we do. Instead, it has to do with our intense desire to see people take control of their own destinies. When liberals tie aid to government, they create an infrastructure of imprisonment. How odd is it that their freedom, help, and opportunity is really nothing more than a Ponzi scheme that will keep receivers behind bars of entitlement, affirmative action, and long lines of handouts—rarely finding a way out.

Partakers of the programs live with a creed that is opposite of the rest of society's. Their new credo says, "It is better to receive than to give," and therein lies the significant problem. Once a proven formula has been altered, all bets are off as to the expected outcome.

There comes a moment when a baby feeding at his mother's breast must be weaned. The process is natural, and both mother and child know when the time arrives. Junior seems disinterested, preoccupied, and eats in shorter bursts. Something inside that baby says it is time to grow to a new level. When solid food is introduced, the child begins a regimen that will stay with him for the rest of his life.

The same principle applies to suckling citizens and big government. The longer they remain connected, the less likely they are to fully develop. Feelings of guilt and helplessness manifest themselves in the hearts and minds of the receivers, and they eventually give up. I heard someone down on their luck use the phrase, "Since I gave up hope, I feel a lot better" to describe his coping skills. The vast majority of citizens want to work; they want to contribute.

The broadcasting business is not known as the bastion of security; in fact, most of us put a few bucks aside because we know the day is coming when work will cease. When a media person is "on the beach," as we like to call it, he may get picked up by a station within hours or he may flop on the shore for months. It depends on a variety of factors and usually doesn't reflect on his abilities. I remember the first time I lost a job in the radio industry. I was out of work for a few months, and the hardest thing to do was wake up each morning because I had to look at my wife and kids and know our income would remain scarce a while longer.

I remember walking into the employment office to register for work and unemployment benefits. Since I paid into the system, I felt I had the same rights to that money as anyone else did. Even after preparing mentally with that mindset, I can still feel the sense of embarrassment I had. It swept over me nauseously. I felt like I was worthless. I hung my head, hoping people wouldn't recognize me as the high-profile radio personality who was now standing in lines in search of a check.

The greatest motivating factor for me to find employment was the walk to the mailbox on Tuesdays because I knew a small disbursement would be waiting for me. Once a month I would go to the labor office to show that I was still alive and kicking and looking for work. I abhorred proving my need for yet another week's payment so much that I dedicated myself to job searches and résumé preparation no less than ten to twelve hours a day, seven days a week. No one promised to fix my problem and find me work. If I wanted it, I had to go out and get it. The lines, checks, and weekly employment forms taught me great respect for people who work in employment sectors where job loss hangs like a gallows noose. Either they too will hang, or they will devise a plan to escape their prison.

Big government wants us on the dole because it needs a reason to exist. Too often government leaders remind me of the mother in a Munchausen-syndrome-by-proxy case. She claims to love her child but does things to make him sick so she can care for him, thus receiving a hero's anointing. She whispers, "Oh, my baby needs me," as the whimpering child fights the poison she slipped into his bottle. If big government can keep enough sick people in the machine, then a need for greater tax dollars and more social programs is validated and a career in politics is ensured. It's insane.

In the American system we believe in checks and balances. A liberal, by definition, is one who freely gives. A conservative provides the counterbalance, willing to give but always asking for proof of the necessity. It is better if a man gives away his treasure carefully because he will have it

---

WHAT WENT WRONG WITH AMERICA

America is a great country. So young, so strong. But we've been invaded by a faceless enemy. Liberalism. We've somehow exchanged our outgoing and "do anything" attitude for political correctness. We fear to show our own flag because it might offend someone. What happened to the 1776 America? Where did men like George Washington go? Nowhere, really. They're within the hearts of all real Americans, but they are constantly being quieted because of pride. Liberalism doesn't want real Americans to conquer and change this country back to the way it was in its earliest years—the time when you could show a flag and not be looked down on. We've lost all we are, our patriotism, because if we aren't proud of our country, we would hardly be a country at all. Just a place where people live. (Karyssa)

longer and have better control of its destiny. To give it all away leaves no room for error. But the liberal begs and browbeats, "I'm out of resources because I gave them away. Give me some more." Once the spigot is turned on, it is difficult to turn it off again.

I could have gone the route that so many have taken before me by looking at the short-term results of deep-seated liberal philosophy. Things like higher taxes, bigger government programs, and more agencies looking over my shoulder would have been easy to track and outline. Since those are givens, let's look at the system and see where it ultimately leads.

Following the predictable direction of liberal causes, my conclusions may be less convoluted than they first appear. The liberals in our midst believe in abortion, gay marriage, government reliance, cloning, endless second chances for cold-blooded killers, hedonistic lifestyles, and federal judges who play with our Constitution. Excess is a liberal's middle name.

Every one of those issues has volumes written about it and is so burdensome that most Americans throw their hands up in surrender. We just cannot keep track of it all. The debates are too long, the fights too dirty, and the process too complicated. On top of that, the other side doesn't play fair. Liberals will engage in personal attacks the moment you espouse any conservative values or an opinion that differs from theirs. This alone is enough to quit the fight, but quit you can't. The battle is too important. Meanwhile, our population can be divided into four sectors; some are still fighting while others have already succumbed to the enemy.

If we follow a liberal agenda, countless millions will remain propped up by big government, and millions more will follow. Their addiction is the weekly or monthly stipend. And should any of them criticize big

---

WHAT WENT WRONG WITH AMERICA

Liberals have robbed our culture of its moral fiber, and we, the God-loving majority, have turned a blind eye to it and let it happen. Some of it was even kind of enticing. We have been entertained by what we have seen and heard in our culture. It catches our eyes when a sexy woman sells us this beer or that car. We have complacently allowed the media to push the envelope to the very edge and beyond. After all, it's a victimless crime, that lust thing—right? Well, we've bought into that lie, and let human nature convince us that one exception won't hurt anything. It's okay for the kids to watch the R-rated movies and listen to their dirty lyrics in our popular music too. (David W.)

government's approach is tantamount to biting the hand that feeds them. So these masses will hardly dispute anything promulgated by the liberal leadership. Thus one sector of the population is out of the way.

Next are the taxpayers who shoulder the burden of society's freebies. They are so busy working to pay inordinate taxes, they don't have the time to engage in policy debates. Instead, they quietly slink through life. Another population sector disabled.

Group three is comprised of the people who believe in taking care of numero uno and no one else. I call them the I-me-mine generation. To rely on them is risky and unpredictable. Some may be willing to fight for what is right, but one never knows until the first shots are fired. Count this group as doubtful.

The fourth and final group is made up of God-loving, patriotic, involved Americans. They have opinions about the direction of the nation and aren't afraid to share them. They write letters to the editor and contact their congresspersons when the issue is crucial. Simply put, they care. They represent the majority, but many have bought into the lie that says they are the minority and should remain silent. Because the battle for the future of this country is so daunting, many of them are complacent. Yet I believe they can be awakened in time.

Now fast-forward fifty to a hundred years. How many remained steadfast and ready to fight against a bureaucratic machine that demands to be fed continually? If history says it will be a faithful few, then don't bother to read the rest of this book because we will have lost the war. Unless *We The People*, average Americans, lock arms and fight now, the debris we will find on an old, almost-forgotten battlefield will be most oppressive.

In this fast-forward scenario, big government has grown into a slogging behemoth that exists only to be fed. Your neighbors, brothers, and friends are on its payroll and complaining only a little about forgoing several meals a week. They won't complain too loudly because they know how lucky they are to be earning a wage that was once reserved for third-world countries. If any complaints are reported, these workers will be tossed aside—too many people wait in long lines to replace them.

Big government tried to handle all the diseases that came as a result of cloning errors and inbreeding experiments, but it didn't react in time. Many years earlier the nation put its okay on all facets of cloning because each was sold to the public as having a legitimate reason to exist and go forward. It started with embryonic cloning. Resistance to the concept was reasoned away because it was life in its earliest stages. Society approved. It escalated to the creation and cloning of body parts and finally complete humans. Since the process came in small waves initially, only a few protested. When all the protections of law were made available to these soulless wonders and their masters, it was too late to do anything. The masses remained quiet much too long. When a human host needed a body part

> ## HOW TO FIX IT
>
> We have to discipline ourselves. We must speak out against those who would drag us into the sewer. We must grow a backbone, re-instill a self-pride and a pride in our wonderful country. Require all youths to give at least two years of service to the country, be it in the military or another type of community service like sweeping streets, working in hospitals or anywhere else that will strengthen our moral fiber. (Earl F.)

or a lifesaving organ, they were able to resort to their clone. But that stopped once the ACLU stepped in to lobby for full human rights for the cloned humans. Since these scientific creations had all rights and benefits of naturally born humans, they became a swift drain on governmental programs and society in general.

The need for mass-produced clones became evident when the humanity went berserk. It started with gay liberation and led to gay marriages and adoptions. Once this lifestyle was embraced by society, other fringe groups demanded inclusion and formed alliances. It took a few decades and billions of dollars in mind-changing ad campaigns, but when television, radio, newspapers, and Hollywood jumped in, passage of equal rights for all groups was unavoidable. Soon men with nine-year-old wives wanted children, which led to escalating levels of birth defects and other medical issues. Sex and marriage between humans and animals was overwhelmingly approved, though pregnancy between the species took scientists a while to figure out. AIDS was replaced by another disease that had similar effects, except the afflicted didn't die from it. Since the disease was highly contagious, medical camps popped up from coast to coast. But they went bankrupt after the economy imploded.

New species of humans roamed the country, the result of the human-animal relationships. Schools could no longer teach because no common language was prevalent. Food was scarce, and law and order ceased because the new species lacked a conscience or any understanding of right and wrong.

Soon, mankind was no more.

Is this fodder for a sci-fi novel? Perhaps. Is it far-fetched? Maybe. Can it happen? Well . . .

How many people fifty years ago believed a woman could become pregnant without sexual intercourse with a man? (In fact, just before Mother's Day 2004, scientists unveiled a procedure where mice were created with two genetic mothers but no father. No dad was needed in any part of the process. How much longer before this moves to the human stage?) Who thought gays would be joined in civil unions or marriages when they were still hiding in closets? Would you have believed it if you read the newspaper headline about "Dolly the Cloned Lamb"? Would you have accepted it if someone showed you a statistic that proved dollars generated from pornography were greater than the combined income from professional football, baseball, basketball, soccer, and hockey? If someone showed you what looked like a grain of rice but explained that it was computer technology, you would have been sure they were making up sci-fi stuff, especially since the average computer took up an entire building.

WHAT WENT WRONG WITH AMERICA

America took the first wrong turn in the road when women were sold the bill of goods that we could "bring home the bacon, fry it up in the pan, and never ever let him forget he's a man." From that point on, despite what anyone may say, children took a back seat to a paycheck, and in many cases became "backseat drivers." The family came to depend on the extra income, never realizing that "hearth and home" was the outgo. The end result became store-bought cookies, fast-food dinners, chubby-faced kids, and disposable cash. The plasma TV became the ultimate after-school babysitter, and completed homework a thing of the past.

Every right we wanted, we took, and if anyone yelled foul, we screamed "discrimination" or "abuse" ten times louder. Forty hours became eighty, and fatigue made the bed for complacency. Those with an eye for power stepped up to the plate and hit a home run every time the welfare ball was thrown. We loved it, and we wanted more of it. It was sweet, and it was f-r-e-e—as the first line of coke from the dealer. We began to use credit to excess because the second income now bought "necessities," but the "laborsaving" devices we purchased never yielded any leisure time. Convenience branded us, now Big Brother watches us, and the saying was never truer: "What one generation tolerates the next embraces." How catastrophic it would be for us to realize, too late, that the federally funded fork in the road we are traveling down has only "No U-turn" signs posted from here to there. (Teresa L.)

A word to the wise: Most conservative Americans believe in God and a soul. We throw up roadblocks when we see the cliff's edge in sight, though we are ridiculed when we do. When we question if groups grown out of unnatural or morally bankrupt roots should have the same rights and equalities as others, we are labeled "uncompassionate." We are troublemakers when we oppose the systematic murder of millions of children, and we are close-minded when we speak out against the evils of cloning or embryonic research. If we dare suggest that government is too big and offers too many hand-outs, we are condemned as uneducated idiots.

Liberals, on the other hand, are "enlightened" in all things, or so we are told.

The term "throw in the towel," which I used in this chapter's title, is derived from the sport of boxing. If one fighter's corner sees that their man (or woman!) is getting creamed and may suffer serious injury, they wave a towel and then toss it into the ring, signifying that the fight is over. The referee immediately steps in to stop the beating. As a society, we may be on the ropes, but conservatives cannot throw in the towel—this fight is too important.

WHAT WENT WRONG WITH AMERICA

After World War II the country was full of patriotic dreams and the glory of victory. Love is in the air for all the welcomed-home GIs, and new families were started. My parents left the farm and moved to the big city looking for a better way of life to start a family. And they did so in 1948. As the 1960s roared in on us rather stealthily, many of the baby boomers who had a "better life" given to them wanted to experience life apart from Mom and Dad's politics and decency—to expand our minds. And so we did. We wanted to believe what the university professors taught us because, naturally, we were the first generation to go to college, let alone graduate from high school. We protested wars, politicians, bras, and any other thing that would get us noticed, for we were the new thinkers. Not willing to step back and think that perhaps Mom and Dad were right all along, stubborn, foolish pride led the way down the path to any and all "enlightenment." (Margaret)

RANT—JUST A ROOM MOTHER

The very essence of leadership is that you have to have vision.
You can't blow an uncertain trumpet.
—THEODORE M. HESBURGH

Lorraine Brock couldn't believe it in January 2004 when her two boys came home from Stinson Elementary in Plano, Texas. Their heads hung low as they explained they would not be allowed to hand out Valentine's Day cards at school. In fact, none of the children would be allowed to hand out any cards. It seems the school district decided that Valentine cards could be offensive for some children, even though this has been a time-honored tradition throughout America.

What may have set off the district's action was a child who dared to take candy canes to class during the Christmas season. The candy canes had little notes explaining the Christian tradition behind the treats. Apparently some parents were outraged to hear that the colors in the candy represented the purity and forgiveness of Christ. Since it was Christmastime, a time celebrating the birth of Jesus, the child's parents felt the gift and explanation were acceptable. Remember, schools in America have no trouble sharing the backgrounds on other religions as well as the man-made holiday of Kwanzaa. But if someone has the nerve to mention the Christian tradition behind a holiday, all hell breaks loose. There was a major furor over the distribution of the candy, and ultimately the school said never again.

To be certain that none of these elementary school deviants hatched another lawbreaking idea, Valentine's Day cards and candy were banned. If students child wanted to put cards on their desks so other kids could come by and pick one up, that would be okay. How stupid is that? What about the outcast student? You know, the ones who are overweight, pimply, nerdy, or—Christian? What happens when no one drops by to grab a card from their desks?

Lorraine Brock was livid when I spoke to her. She was preparing a full frontal assault on the school administrators. I asked her if she was an activist. "I'm just a mom," she answered. "I have been given the privilege to serve as a room mom, but I'm terribly concerned. Our culture is thus that everyone has to learn discernment about many issues that we face daily. By not allowing our children to share their own traditions, I believe we are putting padded walls around our children and not preparing them for the real world. These stories are harmless and are only meant with the greatest love for one another." So Lorraine decided she had to act; she had to get involved.

First, she made calls to other parents to find out if they shared her concerns. When she discovered how many other parents felt the same way, she was emboldened to move forward. Remember, when we feel isolated, more often than not, we are afraid to act. When we feel like others are pulling for us, we are willing to take risks.

Her next mission was a well-thought-out letter to all parents with children at the school. It was not combative nor overtly aggressive. It was, however, to the point and full of details. Remember, people will join your cause if you provide full disclosure and sources for follow-up. The letter was distributed via e-mail, and then a few select copies were sent to media types like me. Important: It is not wise to mass distribute a letter or campaign to all media outlets at the beginning of a boycott, challenge, or protest, because those that are not with you on the issue can spin the story from the very beginning, effectively hurting your support. In this case I was a sure choice to see the letter because of my handling of similar topics on my radio show.

Lorraine's next move was to ask for the help from the other parents to apply pressure. Again, no threats were made, but those people who get paid by the public are usually swift to respond if they see a strong representation of citizens who can take their jobs away in the not-too-distant future. As a result, school administrators said they would look into the matter. This is doublespeak for, "Silly room mom doesn't have enough to do in her life, nor do those other moms, so we'll placate them."

But Lorraine didn't stop there. She knew the media would respond if the story had a little juice, a little tabloid appeal. So she compared the Valentine's Day card story to the candy cane outrage, and the community was abuzz. Excellent move. In less than twenty-four hours, her story was featured on the television news, in the newspapers, and on the radio. Now instead of a few hundred angry parents, she had thousands backing her. The school district relented and agreed to discuss ways to fix the problem. A couple of days later, the children were told they could distribute the cards with personalized notes.

Lorraine Brock, a quiet room mom, was triumphant. So victorious was she that a few weeks later the school district announced plans to hold a "random acts of kindness day" to let the children honor one another. Give it time; I'm sure someone will decide that too is offensive. Hopefully, Lorraine Brock will be ready to spring into action again.

14

THE HEARTLAND
RESPONDS

You say you want a revolution. Well, you know we all want to change the world.

—JOHN LENNON AND PAUL McCARTNEY

REVOLUTION REQUIRES A TRANSFORMATION of the human spirit from a place of rest and contentment to outrage and action. It is a difficult decision for a person to embrace and an equally tough chasm to cross in our souls, but once the journey begins, rarely do we stop. Look at protests like the Boston Tea Party, the civil rights movement with Martin Luther King Jr., and the convening of a group of men huddled in a sealed-off meetinghouse in Philadelphia two hundred years ago. Then you can begin to see the enormity of it all.

Most of us find it easier to comply or conform rather than fight. That is why we may let a smoker send his fumes in our direction or allow a line cutter to make his way to the front of the pack. We may be incredulous, but almost all fighting still takes place in our heads. Action can be too risky.

Explosives and guns need triggers to take them from inert devices to instruments that can kill. Sometimes the trigger is nothing more than a few moments that push us over the edge, but usually it is a culmination of "too much, too long" that prepares us to move beyond our comfort

zone. With the wrong mindset, this brings disaster. With properly chan-
neled actions, we get revolution.

After the Boston Tea Party, King George declared, "The colonies
must either submit or triumph." He knew that the actions in a harbor
town were not isolated to a few malcontents but the beginning of a wave
that had already started to spread throughout the colonies. He knew the
American colonists had had enough.

I believe if King George were alive today, he would recognize the
same indicators he saw in 1773 and wonder aloud if America was on the
verge of another revolution. We are tired of high taxes, disappearing
rights, patronizing lawmakers, excessive laws, and an imploding federal
budget. Our system of government is one of the greatest ever devised in
the history of mankind, but we know that it is broken. We know it needs
an overhaul. And we are just coming to terms with what to do by way of
a massive course correction.

Leaders recognize that the more complicated an answer is, the more
likely we are to become complacent. For instance, look at the U.S. tax
laws, regulations, and IRS rulings. They totaled four hundred pages in
1913. In 2002 that same information spanned more than fifty thousand
pages. Most of us are a long way from believing this is just an evolution-
ary process. It is like a deficit in the hundreds of billions of dollars and a
budget in the trillions—too hard to comprehend. No, many Americans
are beginning to feel just like their cousins in Boston so long ago. The
whisper always starts out soft: "It's just not fair."

Revolution is a process. It takes time. The signs of its beginning are
becoming evident, and that gives me hope. For as nonreactionary and
jaded as our masses have become, there is something stirring. Citizens
are becoming emboldened by some of the victories they have experienced as of late and may be on the verge of taking their wins to the next
level. I can only hope.

Here are just a few of the victories that may create the foundation
for change:

The obscene dance at the halftime show of the Super Bowl played
out before tens of millions of viewers, and no matter what anybody says,
it was no accident that Janet Jackson exposed herself. Her career had
stalled. She was set to release a new CD. And she needed publicity. She
had hinted in advance that she would do something outrageous. Her exposed breast took less than a second of television time, which is just

about how long it took for God-fearing family-oriented citizens to crack. Someone was definitely going to hear about this one.

Within days, more than 200,000 complaints blew into the Federal Communications Commission—surpassing the old record by about 120,000. Congress called for hearings with the broadcast industry leaders and demanded answers. Though many of the politicians were grandstanding in an election year, the public kept the heat on. As a result, new rules were proposed and some passed, which increased obscenity fines from less than thirty thousand dollars to as much as a half million dollars—per incident—and if the act happened during a network or syndicated show, all stations could be fined. When the FCC hinted that it might tie radio and television license approval to a company's track record of compliance, things went from grins to serious overnight. Suddenly, the industry that once laughed at a $27,500 fine as "the cost of publicity" was taking precautions for self-protection. Shock jocks were fired, demoted, and brought under control

> ## WHAT WENT WRONG WITH AMERICA
>
> We've lost our backbone and the courage of our convictions. What do other countries see when they look at America? Do they see a nation of love that truly embraces peace and justice for all, or a nation of rich, selfish, indignant individuals with their hands dug deep in each other's pockets? They see us through the eyes of an ungodly media and the arrogant opulence of Hollywood. They see a past president who committed adultery with a young intern. Was he kicked out of that office? No. Instead, his wife became a senator. They see a country that has embraced the idea that it's okay to ignore the dignity of human life, whether in the womb or old and neglected in a nursing home. They see a country that is dependent on its government's welfare programs instead of encouraging individuals toward a strong work ethic and education. They see a country more concerned with giving children condoms at school than speaking English well or learning their multiplication tables. (Susan G.)

as stations issued zero-tolerance policy manuals about broadcast content. Though some of the politicians' efforts were far-reaching, citizens were seeing the fruits of their outrage—and they liked it.

As early as 2002 word was circulating that Academy Award–winning actor/director Mel Gibson was planning a movie about the last hours of the life of Jesus Christ. Hollywood was buzzing; they wanted to know if Gibson had lost his mind. What would compel the superstar box-office generator to self-destruct like this? After investors pulled out of the project, he invested almost $30 million of his own money to get the movie made. During the filming, prominent industry pundits declared that the project would be Gibson's undoing, which subsequently killed his search for a distributor. He plodded along. He set up screenings for ministers and civic groups. He went on talk shows. He took his story to the people. Granted, some of his positioning was nothing less than Hollywood hype, but there was genuineness to his story. There was another *Rocky*

HOW TO FIX IT

We can responsibly exercise our constitutional right to vote. Vote for the right person to lead us. Change the laws to serve and protect a free country. Stop letting the minority think for the majority. Speak up out of love for this country and for the rights of those who cannot speak, especially for those who have made the ultimate sacrifice and can no longer speak. Be an American first. Respect our many cultures and beliefs, but be Americans first. United, we can do it. (Dave P.)

coming out, and we wanted to help him. Add to the mix the strength of a normally noncommittal, usually disorganized group known as Christians, and Gibson was about to see a miracle.

The publicity he generated landed a distributor, and the sheer numbers of advance tickets purchased within the Christian community prompted theaters across America to give the film priority status. The end result? In a little less than a month, the film *The Passion of the Christ* became the tenth highest-grossing movie of all time with almost $500 million in ticket sales. And by early July 2004 it was ranked as the fifth highest-grossing film in history, bringing in more than $1 billion worldwide. Not bad for a little film that no one wanted.

Suddenly, instead of finding their typical place as the punch line of a foulmouthed comic's joke, Christians were starting to sense that they had more clout than anyone imagined. After all, this is the same group that helped a former evangelist-turned-preacher realize more than $40 million in sales of a Revelation-laden thriller set of books called The Left Behind series. Are Christians waking from their long slumber?

In October 2003 CBS announced plans for a miniseries on the life of President Ronald Reagan, featuring James Brolin in the starring role. Brolin's marriage to superliberal Barbara Streisand caused conservatives to wonder what the biopic was going to cover. When portions of the script started to make it to talk radio and circulate via the Internet, their worst fears were realized. This was going to be a hatchet job on an American legend and icon, a man who was then still alive and suffering from Alzheimer's disease. Citizens went on the offensive to expose the underhanded plans of the movie's producers and CBS. After concerned citizens stepped in with boycott plans and negative publicity, the network pulled the plug, sending the movie directly to cable. Citizens began believing, "I'm just one person, but I can make a difference."

In 1990 Terri Schindler-Schiavo, a strong young woman with no major medical problems, was walking down the hall in her home when, without warning, she collapsed into a motionless bundle of humanity. She was rushed to a hospital in a coma, and when she emerged she was in a "locked-in state," which meant she had limited abilities to communicate or move. She is responsive to stimuli but is no doubt disabled, requiring ongoing therapy and gastric feeding and hydration tubes.

In 1998 Terri's husband petitioned the courts of Pinellas County, Florida, to end her life by removing her life support, and in 2003 the courts agreed. According to doctors, once the feeding and hydration tubes were removed, she would die within approximately two weeks.

Many Americans, including me, were outraged. How could a court decide that food and water should be taken from a patient when it knew the outcome would be death? Personally, I have a living will that includes specific instructions about what should happen to me if I am ever incapacitated like this. I hope my family will abide by my wishes, but to stop my food and water would be nothing short of murder.

I remember the first time I invited Terri's dad, Robert, onto the show. He was in a critical "help me save my child" mode and was taking his story to the country via whatever media outlets he could find. His voice was shaky and drained, but he was battling with all of his might. I wanted to help but felt useless. The battle was being fought in Florida and involved years of testimony, medical records, and activist judges. But just as Robert was booked for a return engagement, he heard the bad news: the court had agreed to let Terri's husband remove her life support. I spoke to him moments after he learned the verdict, but instead of giving up, he had an air of victory. I could tell he was determined to fight, though doctors moved immediately to implement the wishes of Terri's husband.

I gave out all the necessary phone numbers and issued a bulletin to my newsletter subscribers explaining the time-sensitive issue. "Please call and write Florida Governor Jeb Bush," I pleaded. "And contact his brother, the president." I then gave out his personal fax number. I was not alone. In retrospect, I am sure I was just a little player in the whole affair as people from coast to coast were taking up Terri's case as well. Switchboards blazed and phone banks were overwhelmed as the clock ticked away. For six grueling days Terri received no nutrition or fluids, and her body started to shut down. But in the middle of it all, Governor Bush got the message and intervened to stop the execution. Florida's legislature soon passed Terri's Law, legislation aimed at saving Terri's life and the lives of others like her.

Today Terri is in a hospice facility and requires care, but she is very much alive.

Do I want a revolution? Yes, I believe I do. I want it to happen in hearts, minds, and souls first, because the only other possibility for revolutionary change would be of the violent variety—the kind that starts civil wars and kills hundreds of thousands if not millions. No, I don't want bloodshed, but I do want change. There is no reason for a failed system to continue for generations to come. I don't believe our form of government could sustain things the way they are now anyway.

The next step is for the masses to wake from their slumber and demand accountability. Up to this point we have just gone along because that's what everyone does—that's what our parents did—conform. I have said many times: if workers across America were given their full paychecks without any deductions on Friday and then required to hand back real cash for taxes and other related payroll deductions on the same day, we would have a bona fide revolution by Saturday.

> ## HOW TO FIX IT
>
> Act like it's September 12, 2001, all over again, all the time. We were so united, so determined to not let terrorism, or anything else, bring us down. September 11 was a day of sadness, but September 12 was a day of strength, unity, and victory. I was only eleven years old then, but I could tell we got our 1776 attitude back. Nothing could take us down, and no one could tell us to hide our flag. We need to band together, stir up our patriotism, and not hold back no matter what the PC police might say. (Karyssa)

The heartland is inching closer to the realization that we are being manipulated into submission while our rights fade, taxes increase, and opportunities dwindle. But until we finally get to that level of understanding, the big and small victories will serve us very well as our own private revolutionary boot camp.

15

. . . .

YOU WORK FOR ME!

Ninety percent of the politicians give the other 10 percent a bad reputation.

—SECRETARY OF STATE HENRY KISSINGER

ROCK STARS. FOR REASONS unknown to me, some politicians think they are rock stars, when in fact, they are usually just a paycheck away from my decision to fire their sorry butts. At some point these self-appointed celebrities forgot about the "citizen politician" concept our forefathers believed in. Though many of our original leaders served in politics for more than a year or two, they almost always served in one role for a specific time and then changed to another. Others made their investment and then returned to private life, which often meant cleaning out stables and tilling the back forty. The citizen politician practice ensured new blood and fresh ideas and kept swelled heads to a controllable few. They were no better than us because they were us. We threw that concept to the wind the day we allowed our elected representatives to become professional politicians.

In the late 1990s I covered the impeachment hearings of Bill Clinton. While I was in Washington, I decided to drop in a friend in the House of Representatives. After we hooked up, he wanted to take me to the inner sanctums of the Capitol, which required us to use an elevator. There were two banks of elevators. One on the left and another on the right. (How appropriate!) Pages, citizens, businesspersons, and others used the elevators on the right. As we waited for the doors to open, some doors across the hall opened, so I grabbed the congressman by the arm to indicate that we had our chance. Before I could say a word, three senators, including one that would later run for president, stepped in and punched the buttons. I was on my way to join them when my friend stopped me. "Sorry. The Senate likes to use those elevators. We'll have to wait."

I was taken aback. "You're an elected representative."

"It doesn't matter. That's theirs," he said.

"What would happen if you and I jumped in?" I said, only half joking.

"Oh, we can get on but it may be very uncomfortable, and I'll probably hear about it later," he whispered, motioning that our elevator had finally arrived.

I looked at those senators and noticed something else about them and a lot of other politicians I encountered or interviewed that week. Seldom did they like to look directly at people. I know the behavior. I've seen it before. Big-time television performers, movie stars, and music celebrities play that game. By avoiding eye contact, they create a psychological barrier that says, "I'm important. Don't bug me."

That incident has stayed with me all these years because it is such a perfect example of the haughty attitude many of our elected leaders, from both chambers and both sides of the aisle, carry with them. I am a firm believer that we should respect the men and women who serve in Congress, because it can be the greatest calling a person may ever answer. However, my respect wanes greatly when they take on rock-star personas.

On more than one occasion I've had to remind a politician, "Buddy, you work for me."

I am not the kind of person who calls, e-mails, or stalks my elected leaders. I reserve my contact for two important situations. The first is to congratulate them when things are going well. Every once in a while, it's nice to catch a politician doing something right. My college psychology professor called that positive reinforcement.

The other reason for contact is to explain my position on a particular matter and to ask for representation. I believe most Americans are just as clear-cut; just do the job you campaigned to do and we're happy.

On the other hand, when I feel that I have a leader who bamboozled his way into office and won't respond to my concerns, then I have no problem hammering him (or her). I do not believe in making threats or exaggerated comments, but I have no problem with expressing my anger when I am impassioned. Granted, a staff member usually gets the brunt of the communiqué, but if enough of us send the same message, it is most certainly passed along.

As an aside, when I say I don't make threats, what I mean is that I don't make personal threats against the officeholder. Not only is it a low thing to do, but in today's climate, it can bring the law to your door. With this said, I don't have a problem informing a politician that I will do everything in my power to see him removed from office. As a citizen, that is not just one of my patriotic rights—it is a patriotic duty.

I fully realize that the people I help to place in office cannot always vote as I want them to, but what I don't understand is the concept of a servant overruling a master. Don't let me catch them giving me lip service—if they acknowledge me at all—only to follow the directive of a special lobbying pal or a politically correct vote. If they don't have the moxie to stand up to such simple pressure, how can they ever be expected to boldly take a stand when solid issues hang in the balance?

> ## WHAT WENT WRONG WITH AMERICA
>
> Greedy career politicians are not making decisions in the best interest of the country. Rather they focus on what will get them more votes in the next election, or worse—what will benefit their political party. A glaring example is our porous borders. Do our borders need to be protected in this new era of terrorism? Do we need to screen all foreign nationals who come to this country? Absolutely. Our politicians will not pass laws to protect our borders, because that decision may insult or anger a particular voting bloc such as the Hispanic or Middle Eastern. Politicians are putting their own greed to remain in power above the safety and security of Americans. (Karen A.)

If you feel you are not getting the representation you need or your community demands after letters and calls have failed to work, consider the following acts of recourse:

1. Go to the politician's office. It's best to do this at his district or state office. This way he gets the full impact of the fact that you are a local constituent. Of course, if you're visiting D.C. you can ask for a meeting there too, though it's a bit more difficult to get past his office staff. Either way, be willing to wait in the outer offices until you get a few

minutes to make your case. Obviously, it's a smart idea to call first to make sure he is in town. An appointment is always the best idea, but a cold call sometimes serves a very valuable purpose.

2. If the lack of leadership continues, a call to your state's party offices is not a bad idea. You will want to be sure that others who feel as you do also make similar calls so the party knows you're serious and trouble may be brewing. When the party applies a little pressure, your representative knows you understand the system.

> ### HOW TO FIX IT
>
> Our republic started with the idea that our government would be composed of a sampling of the people being governed. All three branches have been saturated with career lawyers. This has effectively destroyed the checks and balances between the three branches. As a result, our government no longer represents the common man. (Jim G.)

3. If representation is sorely lacking, letters to the editor and tips to radio and television newspeople can go far—especially if they see you have done your homework about the matter and that others share the same opinion. Now it is not just pressure from a few, but it can become pressure from the whole district, state, or nation. I try to reserve this approach as a last resort and only after all personal contact has failed. Why turn the heat to a full boil when a small flame will work as well?

4. Register to run for the position. Sometimes the only way to teach someone a lesson is to take their job. Even if you don't win, you will have effectively put the issues front and center.

There are other ways to communicate with your elected leaders, and I will go into greater detail later in the Making a Difference section.

Remember, this is *your* country, they are *your* elected representatives, and you should never be made to feel as though you are a lesser person or citizen than they are.

They work for you!

16

· ·

TALK RADIO SAVED
DEMOCRACY—SORT OF

*The best defense against usurpatory government is an
assertive citizenry.*

—WILLIAM F. BUCKLEY JR.

As a child I remember going into the living room during the early evening hours to find my father in his favorite chair and watching the national news. If he was in that serene dozing-off stage that most dads enjoy in front of the television, I would start to change the channel and immediately hear his low mumble.

"Don't change that dial."

"But Dad," I would argue, "it's just the news. No one cares about the news. I want to watch cartoons."

"I have to know what's going on in the world, son," he'd say. "I have to keep up on things." Then his gaze returned to the screen.

For most Americans this scene is played out millions of times a day, even today. For some reason we believe the lie that the local and evening news channels are giving us a healthy dose of honest reporting. They are not. Instead, we are manipulated with slight nuances and twists of words to believe information that isn't completely accurate.

Do I believe most reporters are out to change their stories to fit a particular agenda? No. Do I believe they try to do their best in getting the details right? Yes. Do I believe that people at the top of the news food chain have agendas? Absolutely. And that is a problem. Send reporters into the streets to gather the facts, and if they already have a worldview that borders on liberalism or if they're already anti-administration or anti-American, the story will always convey that slant. If a reporter lacks those biases, the top dog in the newsroom will shape his stories to make sure the party line is followed and reinforced. It doesn't matter if the newman is a cub reporter or a longtime pro.

But things are starting to change.

Critics will say what they will about the power of talk radio in America, but there is one point that cannot be overruled by anyone anywhere: talk radio has helped to inform and equip citizens like never before. It may indeed be a contributing factor to the salvation of this country and our democracy. This is no exaggeration. It is a dead-serious truth.

How many times have you heard someone say, "Well, that's not what I heard on the news. They said the president made it all up." She spoke to you with such conviction because she was convinced she had heard the outright truth via the news broadcast. But what she heard was a slant on the truth, and for a few decades that half-hour broadcast has slowly indoctrinated us to believe the negative, to fester doubts about our country, and to take a wait-and-see attitude as our way of life passes away in front of our eyes.

In August 1988 a light bulb went on. Dramatic changes didn't happen overnight, and the solution wasn't evidenced on that day alone. It needed time for germination and growth. But then, as if a sonic boom had just swept over the land, people started tuning in to a daily dose of "talent on loan from God." Rush Limbaugh, a name synonymous with conservative thought in America, hit the airwaves. Before long he revolutionized AM radio, talk radio, and the radio industry in general, and he did it in the purest way possible: he empowered the masses to believe that they were the major players in the democratic processes of their government. That's all there was to it. He empowered us to believe that we mattered. We didn't know it at the time, but we had been waiting for this phenomenon for a very long time.

Talk radio is one of the most dramatic examples of media upheaval and changes in power distribution we will ever witness. In no time, regular people were listening to Limbaugh's show, hearing more details to national stories, and scratching their heads when this included information that the news media had excluded or interpreted differently. Something wasn't adding up. As a result, people started to question the stream of information from the television and other news sources.

This is what President Ronald Reagan wrote to Limbaugh in December 1992, a month after Bill Clinton defeated George Bush:

> Thanks for all you're doing to promote Republican and conservative principles. Now that I've retired from active politics, I don't mind that you have become the Number One voice for conservatism in our Country.
>
> I know the liberals call you "the most dangerous man in America," but don't worry about it, they used to say the same thing about me. Keep up the good work. America needs to hear the way things ought to be.[1]

I was talking to a very distinguished gentleman the other day, and somehow we started to discuss Limbaugh. As we did, the man's entire countenance changed. I could tell that he was not just a fan, he was a "ditto head." I asked, "What made Rush so great? What made you listen?" His answer was to the point: "Finally, after years of feeling alone and helpless, I heard this guy on the radio saying exactly what I had been thinking. Suddenly, I felt validated and powerful. I wasn't alone."

Truth does that. It sets you free. I'm not suggesting that Rush Limbaugh is the purveyor of all truth; God knows he's made his share of mistakes. We all have. But the truth issue comes into play as Americans see how the media game works to easily lead us down the wrong path if we are not hearing both sides of a story.

In my home I honor the old tradition my dad passed on by watching my evening news in my lounger. But that's where the similarities end. I am never alone. My wife and at least one of the kids always seem to be in the room at the same time, and if you walk by our house you would certainly believe we must be watching the end of a hotly contested sporting event. We are yelling, debating, and occasionally jumping up and down because we recognize just how much a news reader is slanting his stories. At times we are so outraged we have to sit still and shut up for a few minutes. Though these days we are not as shocked by the stories, we've come to expect them. After a while we're back into a pleasant family mode. And as a father passing along his own traditions, I am glad to know my children see that in life there are always at least two sides to every issue.

Talk radio is largely responsible for this change. One guy who became a mentor to hundreds of other broadcasters came up with a plan—and it worked. I get thousands of letters a month from people who repeat what my friend said about Rush Limbaugh. They write to tell me of problems at their school, in their neighborhood, or with politics. They write and call radio shows like mine because they no longer feel isolated or imprisoned in the dungeons of mediocrity. They want their stories to be heard, but most important, they want to get involved in the process of positive change.

One of the most popular cable news channels in the country is Fox News. I was hosting a syndicated radio show for Sony Networks in New York City when a friend in one of the other offices described the fledgling idea. The cable operation, as I remember it, was begun as an entertainment channel with a focus on America and conservative values. In 1996 it morphed into a news operation and came into its own during the 2000 presidential elections, just like CNN became a dominant player in the world during the first Gulf War.

Fox News is a ratings winner because of talk radio. Owner Rupert Murdoch is not dumb. First, he snagged news great Roger Ailes as his head of news, and together they assessed the popularity and influence of talk show hosts, and knew that Fox could tap into it. Murdoch and Ailes quickly determined that the quiet majority needed more than a voice. What talk radio had accomplished in liberating their hearing, Fox News would do to change their viewing habits.

Retired ad salesman Bob Spratlin was so impressed with Fox News that he invested about three thousand dollars in a billboard to say, "Thank God for the Fox News Channel." The seventy-year-old said, "I wanted to wake people up. I wanted to say, 'Wake up, America! Wake up, you young people!'" Spratlin added, "[Fox News] gets to the meat of it, and they give you both sides and let you make up your own mind. I don't always agree, but I like it when I hear it from them."

Media analysts say that Fox News has mirrored personality-driven talk radio and coupled it with news that doesn't mind reflecting a pro-America attitude. "They've really struck a chord with people frustrated with the mainstream media," said Jeff McCall, a broadcast journalism professor at DePauw University. "A lot of people say the media aren't as patriotic as they should be. Fox is sort of a news network where people aren't afraid to say, 'We're American.'"

I was talking to Bill O'Reilly, a talk-radio colleague and television commentator on Fox, and he echoed what many conservatives have been feeling. Then I asked if he had thought about running for office. "I have more influence right now than anyone in politics except the president. Why would I let that go?" he answered. "If there came a time when the two parties left a door open for a third-party candidate to run and win, then perhaps I would consider it." O'Reilly gets it. This tall Boston University–educated journalist started out by painting homes and teaching history, but his big breaks into broadcasting came in Scranton, Pennsylvania, and Dallas, Texas. His conviction in strengthening America is strong because he has never forgotten his upbringing, his humble beginnings. People relate to that.

Because of talk radio, a "Contract with America" was signed in the mid-1990s, both houses of Congress have strong conservative representation, and the fiasco of the 2000 election was properly debated. Because of talk radio, the problems in rebuilding Iraq haven't been transformed turned into a hate-filled sellout like Vietnam—though the mainstream media constantly try to take it there.

Sure, some talk hosts do what they do because they see it as show biz. Others want the money. Many just spout off because they can. But We The People can spot them from two cities away. Most talk radio hosts, though, are people with a conviction to research and relay their findings to the public, because if they don't, only a part of the story will be told.

Glenn Beck, a pal of mine, started that way. He was a burned-out disc jockey who was quitting the business. But he went to his father for advice. His dad told him that God had given him a talent, and it wasn't time to let it go. Beck, with a family of his own to worry about, told his dad that he had passionate issues he wanted to discuss, but he

HOW TO FIX IT

It's time for us to become activists. We've let the fringe elements take center stage. Maybe it's time for average Americans to take some time to organize within their community, talk about what's going on, and do something about what is wrong. Boycott news programs when you find out they are not being fair; write letters to their sponsors. Support candidates and get out and vote for those we support, not just sit on our butts and complain about them. I myself have become a letter writer. I write to everyone...in the news...in the government...in entertainment if I think they are out of line. And I encourage others to do the same. When we stand together and make ourselves heard, people listen and respond. (Jacqui L.)

didn't know how to start. Eventually, he took a shot at talk radio, and when he cracked the mike, people swarmed to hear more. Why? Because he is an average American who, with the help of a major radio network, has the ability to help all of us recognize ourselves in a story and come to a conclusion about the choices we should make.

Talk radio does that. We want people who have picked up a scar or two along the way and managed to survive to be willing to lead. We want leaders, journalists, and talk-show hosts who shoot straight with us. We now know what it is like to be spoon-fed, and we don't like the way it leaves us feeling.

Talk radio may not have single-handedly saved our democracy, but it has provided a large forum for people to hear and air complaints and solutions. And that powerful instrument absolutely serves as a catalyst for positive change. There is nothing wrong with having faith in God, enjoying our families, and declaring our patriotism. No one understands this like the hosts, producers, listeners, and callers of talk radio.

PART 3

· ·

RECLAIM AMERICA

How to Fix It!

17

THE GOVERNOR'S GONE MAD!

THE BEGINNING OF THE TENNESSEE TAX REVOLT

Who dares, wins.
—MOTTO OF THE BRITISH SPECIAL AIR SERVICES

FOUR HOURS. THAT'S ABOUT how much time my producer and I take to research and prepare for each hour of my radio show. So for a typical morning show we have about sixteen hours of work behind the scenes. Day in and day out, this is how we operate. Though we have to remain fairly fluid in order to handle breaking stories, it is a rare thing to completely throw out an already-planned program, primarily because I hate backtracking and my producers despise canceling sought-after guests.

It was November 1999, early evening, when I heard rumblings about something happening at the Tennessee State Capitol, but no one knew exactly what it was. I made a few calls to some contacts, but nobody knew any details. Then the phone rang. It was a state senator and she was hot. She had just been informed that the governor had called a special session of the legislature with an express desire to strong-arm an income tax onto the books. Up to that point the Volunteer State had never been subjected to the thievery of an income tax. "Darrell, we can't let this happen," said the exasperated senator. "We have to fight it!"

The next call was tough to make because I would soon be telling my producer that we had to scrap the plans for the next show because I had decided to broadcast from the steps of the Capitol so my fellow citizens would know of the clandestine plans of a newly reelected leader. It can be broadcasting suicide to scrap a planned show based on conjecture and a few calls, but my instincts said it was the right thing to do.

As we spoke, the picture starting coming into focus. Drop this . . . Call him . . . Handle that . . . Meanwhile, I was chasing down clearances at the Legislative Plaza, checking on equipment and engineering requirements, and following up with contacts.

My producer called back in a panic. "We may not be able to get the equipment; it's being used later for the sports guys—" I interrupted, "We can't make one of the most important radio broadcasts in the history of this state because the equipment is going to be used by the sports department? Call back and reserve it, and if they say 'no' then let them know I will rent it from our competitors across town and give them full on-air credit."

Moments later my boss was on the line, trying to figure out what I was up to. "This is not about a morning show going out on location just for the fun of it," I said. "This is our obligation." After a few more moments of explanation, he conceded, and the equipment was mine.

Don Sundquist was a fairly popular governor who handily won re-election on a promise of no new taxes. He was an affable man—kind of plain and to the point—so when he made promises like that, Tennesseans believed him. For the record, a few weeks earlier my wife and I enjoyed attending the Governor's Ball with a direct invitation from his office. Now I was caught in the dubious position of uncertainty. "How can a leader make a promise knowing that other plans were already in the works?"

We worked late into the night to confirm as many details as we could. Our plans put us at the steps of the Capitol by 4:00 a.m. It was cold and frosty. My breath hung in the air. I remember shifting from foot to foot because the marble slabs had sucked in the cool of the evening. Waiting for the sun to come up was demanding because my feet were numb and my legs felt the cutting wind as it blew through my jeans. In addition to the elements, I wasn't sure if listeners would understand how desperate this tax situation was.

The kind of show I did in Nashville relied on a smooth opening, so the first twenty minutes each day featured lighthearted fare to get the day up and running. That would not happen on this day. This day was about lies, manipulation, and challenging people you once thought were on your side, people you had once believed in.

The sun wouldn't come up for another two and a half hours, and my engineer gestured to me with that "You're on the air" finger. "Friends," I began, "I am broadcasting live from the Capitol where in just a few hours, your governor plans to hit you with an income tax." The more I thought about what I was doing, the more fervent I became. Everyone knew the state was having budget problems. We had certainly talked about it enough on the various radio and TV shows in town.

"We have to face reality; either Sundquist is a liar or he was too dumb to see these financial problems coming. Perhaps it's both. Personally, I believe he has deliberately misled us. Right now, it doesn't matter what his game is. All I know is that right now we must stop him."

And the battle was on. In the darkness of that nippy autumn morning, I laid out the information we had gathered. I was adamant, high-pitched, and slammed the story from every angle.

Talk-show hosts quickly learn not to judge how well a show is going based on calls or visitors, because a majority of the audience will never pick up the phone. They just listen. Even though we are not supposed to make those kinds of judgments, there are still times when it does happen. After almost an hour, only a few calls had come in. For a moment I was alarmed. *What if this isn't a big deal to voters? What if they don't care? What should I do next?* All of those thoughts bombarded my brain. I hadn't come with any other material—no jokes, no personal stories, no other headlines to expound. I kept going because there was no other recourse.

While the calls picked up, my confidence did not. The issue just didn't have the kind of power or presence I expected. In the dis-

> ### WHAT WENT WRONG WITH AMERICA
>
> Government no longer responds to the needs and desires of the people. It responds to the wants and desires of its major campaign contributors and special-interest money. How can we be so naive to believe we really matter to either party? We are only gullible pawns who believe election-year promises and never complain when we are disappointed again and again. (Ray H.)

tance I saw a lone truck approaching. The driver circled the Capitol area and then screamed out his window, "Don't let them do this, Darrell! You go get 'em." He was gone as quickly as he had arrived. That gave me a shot of adrenaline and a little more spine, but I still felt like I was howling at the wind—and a very chilly wind at that.

0

From around the corner I saw her. She was a young woman in her late twenties or early thirties, and she was pushing a baby stroller. That struck me as very odd. I wondered what mother would be walking her child downtown so early in the morning. As I talked, I watched. She walked from one end of Seventh Avenue to the other and then turned repeated the process. What was she was doing? On her next pass, during a commercial break, I approached her. I didn't have the chance to ask question because this young mother didn't give me a chance: "We are here to stop the income tax. I am not going to let this happen to my son; it is his future. If you don't mind, I am going to keep marching back and forth to show support for what you are doing."

I had felt that spine-tingling sensation before. It was there with me in Springfield, Missouri, when our town took on 2 Live Crew. The baby steps I learned to take in that Ozarks town had prepared me for this fight, but the energy that comes when common folks join an effort is something that will stop even the most seasoned broadcaster every time. An emotional surge jolted me back into the game. This mom had pulled her baby from a warm crib, bundled him up, and pushed him into the middle of the battlefield. She was exactly what this lone broadcaster needed. I was supercharged.

As the morning progressed so did the will of the people. Soon others were marching with the mother and her stroller. One single mom had turned into five families. Then it was ten. Next it was a hundred and then hundreds. Cars and trucks drove by and honked their horns. Listeners were calling in to ask what they could do. And state representatives rushed to join the cause with answers at the ready.

The special session was set to begin an hour after my show was to conclude, so I called the station's program director to get permission to continue. "I've been listening, Darrell. You know what it feels like out there—[you] call it," he said. We stayed on.

The crowd grew and homemade protest signs were everywhere. These people were not going to roll over and take whatever the gover-

> **HOW TO FIX IT**
>
> The problem with America is that it is a nation in transition. Our identity is being blurred by the Left. The lazy, selfish Left want a world without consequences. Liberals do not know the pleasure and value of hard work. What are the incentives in a socialist system? If the idea progresses and everyone becomes enabled by the state, who will do the work, who will pay taxes, who will there be to take from? (Kenneth K.)

nor decided to dish out. I learned later that Governor Sundquist had viewed the gathering crowd from his office window, and he exploded in anger. He certainly had not anticipated something like this, but he also wasn't sure what he could do. This is where he made a very crucial mistake: he postponed the vote until the following day. I'll bet he wishes he hadn't prolonged the matter, because his tactical error allowed this grass-roots movement to regroup and form a plan.

Throughout the day the governor attempted damage control, and every time he outlined another part of his plan to a roomful of incensed legislators, one of them would pick up a phone and call me. The citizens knew everything going on every step of the way, and they weren't happy.

Other broadcasters had been discussing the issue as long as I had, and they stepped up their

> ## WHAT WENT WRONG WITH AMERICA
>
> We can begin by not reelecting any congressperson. We need new blood in Washington. Most of the problems dogging America today lie at the feet of our legislative branch. We need term limits on Congress similar to the restriction on the executive branch. Our government functions fine with a president serving no more than two full terms and would function fine with Congress being similarly restricted. One does not have to be a lifetime politician to do a good job in Congress. (Ray H.)

involvement. Dave Ramsey, whose syndicated show aired a few hours after mine, joined me at the plaza and covered the historic event in his show, as did two competitors from another station, Phil Valentine and Steve Gill. Each had been talking about the possible income tax, but now they were standing by my side. And I'm sure the politicians pushing for the legislation knew they were in for a lot of trouble.

Only a few nights before, our station had coordinated an information rally at the Grand Ole Opry—a mainstay of Nashville and a property that belonged to the same company that owned us. That evening more than a thousand people showed up to hear the facts about the state's budget woes and to rally for victory. We invited representatives from both sides of the issue. I moderated. When it was time for questions and answers from the audience, two lines quickly formed and trailed out the back door. The typical, normal, everyday people wanted a piece of someone's hide, and they were going to get it. Emotions increased. And startled politicians could do nothing but listen; they were trapped.

Out of the corner of my eye I noticed some activity on the left side of the building. People were shifting and making way for someone. Finally, as the person on the right wrapped up, a tiny woman came to the other microphone on the left. As she adjusted the stand and brushed back her hair, I could see she was ready to do business. Her deep green eyes were on fire with a sense of passion. The auditorium hushed.

At first, her words were hard to hear and understand. She paused to take a breath and calm her nerves. Then she began again. Tatyana Merryman spoke perfect English with a Russian accent. This is a paraphrase of what she said: "I came to America from Russia. We were owned by the government. We couldn't do anything without the government's knowledge and permission. I fought to get here and to be an American citizen and this is how my elected leaders treat me? I am ashamed of you. I am embarrassed for you. I will help to defeat you now and when you come up for reelection."

The audience burst into applause. Her disdain for the underhanded plans of the governor became the spark needed to defeat the income tax. If people would catch that enthusiasm and be empowered to take a stand, then the governor would lose.

The next morning I was out at the Capitol again. This time other radio and television stations were there too.[1] It became a frenzy of sorts because all of us were vying for the perfect spot to get our story and live feed. My engineer had arrived a couple of hours before the rest of my team and had to fight for the spot from which we had broadcast the morning before, where everything was so still and cold just twenty-four hours earlier.

I was champing at the bit as I waited for the hour when my show was to hit the air. I had details, inside information, guests, listeners, and Tatyana Merryman. I told the audience the day before that we would honk horns and sound the alarm, and I continued with that on this day. And my audience responded. Where it took more than an hour to get people up and running and focused on the issue the previous day, they were ready to go when the sun came up on this day. Our phone lines were jammed as soon as the show started, and about a dozen listeners were already standing beside us at the Capitol. This was going to be a very good day.

As the morning progressed, the crowd increased. Thousands appeared at Legislative Plaza, and drivers honked and blared their horns as they circled the Capitol. The circling stream of traffic was constant. Protest signs, bullhorns, folks dressed as patriotic figures, and whole families stretched in every direction. Yet while the crowd was responding, something amiss was afoot. There was a feeling in the air that I did not like; something didn't feel right.

Halfway through the broadcast, during a commercial break, I pinpointed the problem. There were so many media people trying to claim this as their story that a competitive frenzy was starting to detract from the cause. This wasn't my event; it wasn't any one person's or station's. This protest belonged to the people, and suddenly they were being pulled in a variety of directions. So I came up with a plan.

During an extended newsbreak I went to the other broadcasters and suggested we join together as one unified front. We would share time on each other's stations, and at a predetermined time we would ask each of our listening bases to honk their horns for a full minute no matter where they were in the state. My station was a popular and powerful signal that covered at least half of Tennessee. In concert with all the other stations represented at the plaza, we felt we would blanket the state as far as Memphis to the west and Knoxville to the east.

> ## WHAT WENT WRONG WITH AMERICA
>
> Our system started to nosedive when legislators learned that they could get reelected if they brought more and more pork home to their districts. The decline continued when more and more people came to expect the government to do absolutely everything for them. Some people believe the government can simply pull benefits out of a hat at no cost to the people. And politicians perpetuate this idea by trying to do exactly that. No one stops to think of the long-term consequences. (Mignon SV)

At the predetermined time, a countdown ended with horns blowing in every part of the state. Downtown Nashville was so loud with the echo off the buildings that no one could speak. They couldn't be heard if they tried. Bank transactions, phone calls, board meetings, and anything else dependent on the spoken word simply ceased. Thousands of everyday folks were going on record.

People later told me that they wept in their cars as they sat at traffic lights, tried to park, or inched through drive-time traffic. Said one, "Suddenly, I did not feel alone anymore. Other people felt the same feelings that I did. I laid on that horn. I really laid on it."

One gentleman wrote me that he was listening to the show while fishing at his favorite hole about a hundred miles from Nashville in a sparsely populated area when, from out of nowhere, came the sound of a honking horn. He said it lasted for a single minute, and when it was done, the driver screamed at the top of his lungs. "Yee haw" skimmed the surface of the lake and traveled forever. "At that moment, I was one of the proudest Americans ever," he said.

Governor Sundquist continued with the session later that day, but he knew it would lead to nothing. He was one or two votes from victory the day before, but soon he realized his support had vanished. A lot of politicians may be dumb, but they can count pretty well. And I believe they calculated the length of time people honked their horns and multiplied it by the number of cars and knew very well that those were votes going somewhere else.

After a variety of meetings, hearings, and gatherings, the governor declared, "The tax issue is dead." Tennessee voters rejoiced. Government did what the voters demanded.

Voters were empowered. Regular citizens suddenly realized they could lead as well as the next guy. In the next election, many threw their names into the mix for state house and senate seats, and many won. Others ran for school boards, planning commissions, and other elected posts. Leadership no longer belonged to only the high and the mighty.

Apparently a slow learner, the governor took another run at the tax the following June. But the systems and the citizens were already in place to do battle. We would not be defeated. I left Tennessee shortly after that, and though Governor Sundquist tried a few more times to revive the income tax issue, each time, new leaders stood at the Capitol and dared him to try. In July 2001 the income tax protests had become a routine event as citizens refused to be forced into accepting something they clearly did not want.

Fox News reported it this way: "Just minutes before the Senate vote, state police locked the doors to the Capitol after hundreds of protesters got out of control—banging on the doors of the chamber, breaking office windows, and accosting lawmakers as they made their way down the statehouse hallways with police escorts."[2]

Donald Sundquist spent his last days as governor as a lame duck, forever branded as the man who tried to take government away from the people.

18

RECLAIMING THE POWER

> *What the statesman is most anxious to produce is a certain moral character in his fellow citizens, namely a disposition to virtue and the performance of virtuous actions.*
>
> —ARISTOTLE

AMERICA IS MORE A state of mind than it is a geographic location. When you ask Europeans, Asians, Arabs, and Africans what they think about America or Americans, their reactions are usually swift and hopeful. They have heard a lot about us, and we offer them a promising potential beyond anything they might know in their native country. Or at least that was the way it once was. Once upon a time, people clambered aboard whatever transportation they could find just to get a shot at the American Dream. This was the Promised Land, and they wanted to share our way of life as much as they did our bounty. People still beg to come to America, but it seems their attitude has changed over the last half century. They don't want to assimilate; they want to take what they can and silently slip through the cracks.

We have lost our prominence, position, and moral power. But don't overlook why these are lost: it is our fault. Too many of us know better, we privately hold on to our deepest love for this nation but remain ineffective because we don't turn our internal passion into an outward expression for transformation. These days we know that reactions abroad aren't as positive as they once were, and though we recognize it, we spend more time snacking than we do looking for ways to change America for the better. Sometimes this is no more than laziness, but most often it can be traced to a lack of knowledge. A person starting a new job is limited in productivity until someone explains the machinery to him.

155

Then it's a race for advancement, bonus money, and a white-collar job. Knowledge creates an atmosphere for change.

In this section I will sketch out the basic details of getting involved in the work to change our nation in a positive wat. This is not all about political affiliation, because there are almost limitless ways to make a difference without running for office or working in a campaign office. We all have gifts, talents, and desires that are uniquely ours. You know in your heart if you are a leader or a follower. Go with your strengths instead of trying to be someone you are not. You know what gives you the greatest sense of satisfaction. Find a cause!

Take a look at your computer across the room. Assume that you and your group want to issue a paper on the dangers of drinking and driving. For many, the greatest delight will be found in quietly keying a three-thousand-word essay while another tends to graphics. Some want to open the computer to make it work faster and better, and others love nothing better than to research statistics. As the project grows, a team member will want to present the information to the public. And while you may get butterflies and sweaty palms from such a thought, this person is thrilled at the opportunity.

America will wither and die unless we reclaim our power—now! Seek out your passion. Get in tune with the one or two things about this nation that get you worked up. Does the political process appeal to you? How about media or volunteering or working behind the scenes?

Perhaps you feel better suited for a slot on the school board, a citizens action council, or as a helping hand at the voting polls. It doesn't matter. Discover what turns you on, make a few calls to figure out the process, and get involved.

In the following pages you will find many ways described in which you can participate in the process of impacting America. There are thousands of opportunities for all of us, but I will focus on two of the most important and historical methods: politics and volunteerism. If you choose to get involved in just a small part in either one, you will most likely find a place that will change someone else's life, the country's history, and your inborn drive to give something back. It all starts with your conscious decision to get involved!

Don't walk away from this book without making a decision to affect the process. Find what you like to do and then do it well. Everyone has a role to play in America's future. What is yours?

Right: The Springfield, Missouri, newspaper announced that 2Live-Crew vowed never to return to the city after 8,000 people joined me for a Stand Up for Standards event. This gathering helped me to understand just how powerful the voice of the people can be.

Below: In November 1999 I was caught up with a few protesters in Nashville—and right in the middle of things. For days protesters surrounded the Tennessee Capitol to voice their objection to a new state income tax.

Above: The Tennessee Tax Revolt may have started with me on a cold November morning in 1999, but it quickly became a grass-roots fight of and by the people. Thousands of people marched around the capitol with signs, and others circled the area and honked their horns to get the attention of their legislators.

Below: Protests continued through June 2000. Earlier the streets were impassable. Crowds filled the roadways and sidewalks in every direction. What struck me about each no-income-tax rally we held was how willing average citizens were to get involved once they had the facts. I was keenly aware that this event belonged to the people and was touched by the homemade signs and the traffic jams and the presence of complete families. They understood the problem and refused to sit back and let their politicians steamroll them!

Right: The guy with the sign (back left) understood exactly what some not-so-up-front politicians were attempting to do: steal our money!

At the first Texas United rally the sound system was barely functional, so I grabbed a bullhorn to communicate with the 3,500 Texans who joined me on that rainy, windswept night in February 2003. This event became a national phenomenon. The two kids on the left (holding the God Bless America sign) are two of our four children: Ben and Katie.

People came to Texas United with homemade signs, flags, umbrellas, and a love of country that I had never experienced before.

Passion swept over me as I announced that my second son, Adam, had just joined the Marine Corps. He is directly to my right in this picture.

Since the first rally was a huge success, the Dallas Cowboys organization joined with us to promote another. Dubbed Texas United 2, more than 14,000 people packed Reunion Arena on April 6, 2003, to pay tribute to America's finest.

On Armed Forces Day in 2004 I decided the time was right for another pro-America demonstration. We called it Operation Enduring Support and focused our appreciation on the men and women in the armed forces.

With Texas United 2, the crowd took a little more of a hands-on approach!

Left: A listener (Michael, next to me) had giant thank-you banners printed. Even after they were full of signatures, people still stood in line to find a little space to sign their name. The other gentlemen with the banner is Jason, who had just returned from the war front.

Right: A rally participant's sign said it all.

Below: Toward the conclusion of Operation Enduring Support, I asked the participants to "plant a flag" in honor of one of our servicemen and women. Later I asked everyone to pick up someone else's flag and to remember and pray for the name penciled in on the flagstaff.

19

• •

THE POLITICS
OF IT ALL

DICTIONARIES DESCRIBE POLITICS IN several ways, though in the end it boils down to two popular definitions: (1) "The theory and practice of forming and running organizations connected with government," and (2) "The totality of interrelationships in a particular area of life involving power, authority, or influence, and capable of manipulation."

We all engage in political activities every day, though we may not be aware of it. We see politics in our families, in the workplace, in church, and even in the weekend softball league. We either want something someone else has or we want to see a friend elevated in stature, and we play a game of politics to get it done.

Say what you will about the recent spate of reality shows on prime-time television, but one thing is certain: we tune in not just to see who will win but also so we can relate to the strategies and maneuvers. We see the participants manipulate a person or situation, and privately we consider the steps we would have taken. That's politics: a combination of power, influence, and competition. The better we are at achieving our goals, the more we want to involve ourselves. Some of us are quite content in indulging at a small and local level, but others aspire to go for the brass ring in Washington.

The challenge in harnessing the explosive possibilities of the American political process is not to get caught up in the process just to know the conclusion—who wins and who loses. The stakes are too high

157

for such elementary thinking, and too many great causes have been crippled by such nonsense. Don't run for office just to play the game. Run to effect change in some positive way. Winning is the tool that helps you get the job done; it is not the be all/end all. When you win, savor the victory for a moment. One has to win in order to do anything in politics, but as soon as winning becomes the goal, the only thing, the victor has sold out.

Since the beginning of civilization, people have had the intense desire to be recognized, not just as part of a group, but as individuals who have every right to be heard. Over time and culture, when the right to be heard has been available to all, it has been a powerful agent for advancement. When the right to be heard has been ignored or quashed, it has produced uncountable moments of shame, such as the period of slavery in this country when African Americans were considered little more than property.

Equality is what individuals have striven for over the centuries. Civil wars and cultural upheavals have focused on the right of a person to be validated by and contribute to a society. But in the third American century, we have grown so accustomed to the right that we now take it for granted.

Look at the polling percentages to see how far we have stumbled as a group that once valued individuals as represented by a single vote. During the 1998 non–presidential election year, voter turnout was abysmal. The lowest percentage of individuals making it to the polls came from Tennessee (only 23.7 percent). Minnesota had the highest percentage of voters that year (60 percent, but even that statistic points to the 40 percent who stayed home). On a national average, only 36.4 percent pulled a lever, touched a screen, or punched a chad. Sure it was an "off year," as some would call it, but if we are not willing to get involved at the local level, where we see the most immediate impact, then why should we care about a national election? These numbers show how much work is ahead for those of us who still have hope. Not only do we need to effect change, but we have to get the fence sitters back into the process.

The first thing to recognize is that we are Americans. We are proud, honorable, work-oriented, and very protective of our freedoms. Most of us will get involved if we just know how. Do you have a political affiliation? Are you a registered voter? Do you vote? Let's start with the voting aspect.

VOTING

The right to vote is a great equalizer. For that brief moment when you step into a voting booth, it doesn't matter if you are black, white, Hispanic, female, evangelical, rich, or poor. For the time it takes you to mark your ballot, you matter. Your clothes may be old and your shoes worn, but you matter. Life may have hit you hard a few times and your faith may be lost, but you matter. That is the power of the vote.

I don't know how many times I have had people tell me that the voting process is just too difficult. Either they don't know the rules, can't get registered, or don't know where to go to vote. In other words, they look for any excuse *not* to do the one thing that sets this nation apart from most others. How unbelievable is it that we possess such a valuable right, such a rare opportunity to participate in our government, and yet so many look for ways to avoid it.

Here are the easy particulars, and though there may be slight nuances from state to state, these are good rules to use.

To vote in America, you must be:

> a U.S. citizen
> a resident of the county
> at least eighteen years of age on election day
> not declared mentally disabled by a court of law
> not in jail or incarcerated

After you register to vote the first time, you remain registered as long as you remain at your current address and renew your registration every two years when you receive a new voter registration certificate in the mail. If there are errors on the renewal certificate, call or write the local voter registration office and explain. (The contact information is usually included with the renewal certificate.) If you move, simply re-register.

Out of the twenty-one established democracies of the world, America places twentieth[1] in voter turnout. That statistic should embarrass all of us. What a joke we have become. Turnout for presidential elections in other democratic nations runs between 75 percent and 80 percent, but in the USA we are lucky to see polling data in the mid-50 percent range. What has happened to the vision that set America off, like a shining city on a hill?

Yet it is not enough for you to head to a school, church, or library to cast a ballot and then go home. I don't know how many times people have told me they voted for a particular candidate because "I think I recognized his name," "His name sounded American," or "I saw a poll that said he was going to win." That kind of voting is not voting. Rather it is akin to buying a quick-pick lottery ticket and then dreaming about how you will spend your newfound riches. The difference is that when the wealth doesn't come your way, you just return to your daily routine. When the wrong person gets into office because you failed to do your homework, you are partially responsible for the errors that follow his election.

Voting requires a commitment on your part. It begs you to know the participants. What are their positions? What have they accomplished in the past? What do they bring to the table? If you had $10 million in the bank and were looking for someone to handle it for you—to be your representative—with whom would you trust it? Why are we willing to let people represent us in aspects of our society—in matters of taxes, medicine, and law—without investing the time to make a knowledgeable decision?

I can hear someone comment: "You're too idealistic. The system is too corrupt. There is not real choice, so my vote doesn't count." Too cynical. This is what the Federal Election Commission reported concerning outcomes determined by a single vote:

In the 1829 election for the U.S. House of Representatives in Kentucky's Second District, Jackson Democrat Nicholas Coleman defeated National Republican Adam Beatty 2,520 to 2,519.

In the 1854 election for the U.S. House of Representatives in the Seventh District of Illinois, Democratic candidate James C. Allen bested Republican William B. Archer 8,452 to 8,451.

In the 1882 election for U.S. House of Representatives in the First District of Virginia, Readjuster Robert M. Mayo defeated Democrat George T. Garrison 10,505 to 10,504.

Recent examples in nonfederal elections include the following:

In 1977 Vermont State Representative Sydney Nixon was seated as an apparent one-vote winner, 570 to 569, but Nixon resigned when the state house determined, after a recount, that he had lost to Robert Emond, 572 to 571.

In 1994 Republican Randall Luthi and Independent Larry Call tied for the seat in the Wyoming House of Representatives from the Jackson

Hole area, with 1,941 votes each. A recount produced the same result. Luthi was finally declared the winner when, in a drawing before the State Canvassing Board, a Ping-Pong ball bearing his name was pulled from the cowboy hat of Democratic Governor Mike Sullivan.

In 1997 South Dakota Democrat John McIntyre led Republican Hal Wick 4,195 to 4,191 for the second seat in Legislative District 12 on election night. A subsequent recount showed Wick the winner at 4,192 to 4,191. The state supreme court, however, ruled that one ballot counted for Wick was invalid due to an overvote. This left the race a tie. After hearing arguments from both sides, the state legislature voted to seat Wick 46-20.[2]

That mindset of "Why vote? Mine won't count anyway" is exactly what is slowly putting us in a stalemate. You bet there is corruption, and we all know liars abound in politics. The machine itself spits people out just for the pleasure of it. I don't discount any of that. We have a monumental task ahead of us, but if good, solid, and capable people stay out of the process, then where is the hope?

REGISTERING TO VOTE

IN MANY nations the government tracks down its citizens to register and participate in the voting process. In America we would be ripe for a fight if that happened because we cherish our freedom of privacy so dearly. The chief problem with having these freedoms is our inability to do what needs to be done to spend a few short minutes securing our opportunity to vote.

An application to register is available at numerous public buildings in your area:

> county offices
> libraries
> Department of Public Safety
> county courthouse

You can also register to vote by mail. Check with your local voter registration office or call the Secretary of State: Elections Division in your state. Reclaim your right to be heard and to be included and exercise your right to vote.

Citizens can now register to vote online via their national or state political parties or at one of several bona fide websites created for the purpose. However, pursuant to the Help America Vote Act of 2002, if you register to vote by mail, and it is the first time you have registered to vote in your jurisdiction, you must submit a current, valid photo identification or a copy of a current utility bill, bank statement, government check, paycheck, or other government document that shows your name and address with this application or present it to the appropriate state or local election official the first time you vote in a federal election.[3] If you want to register by mail, the process gets a little more complicated if you have recently moved to the area where you will vote, because you will need to vote in person in the first election in which you participate. There are a few exceptions, which your clerk can explain. Your local clerk's office or your secretary of state's website will have all the forms and information you need to complete the process.

The simplest way to register is at the time you renew your driver's license. Eligible drivers receive a voter registration application in the mail with their driver's license renewal information. The only way the process could be easier is if someone came to your house and filled out the forms and mailed them in for you. The concept of motor/voter registration came about in 1994 when Congress passed the National Voter Registration Act (known as the Motor Voter Act).

FREQUENTLY ASKED QUESTIONS ABOUT VOTER REGISTRATION AND VOTING[2]

Q: Where is my polling place?

A: Polling place locations in each community are determined by local election officials. For the address or location of your specific polling place, please contact a county election official, who may be either the county/municipal clerk, supervisor of elections, or board/commission of elections.

Q: Why are federal elections held on the Tuesday after the first Monday in November?

A: The Tuesday after the first Monday in November was initially established in 1845 (3 U.S.C. 1) for the appointment of presidential electors in every fourth year. 2 U.S.C. 7 established this date for electing representatives in every even-numbered year in 1875. Finally, , 2 U.S.C. 1 established this date as the time for electing U.S. senators in 1914.

Q: Why early November?

A: For much of our history, we were an agrarian society. Lawmakers took into account that November was perhaps the most convenient month for farmers and rural workers to be able to travel to the polls. The fall harvest was over (spring was planting time, and summer was taken up with working the fields and tending the crops), but in the majority of the nation the weather was still mild enough to permit travel over unimproved roads.

Q: Why Tuesday?

A: Most residents of rural America had to travel a significant distance to the county seat to vote. Monday was not considered reasonable since many people would need to begin their travel on Sunday. This would have conflicted with traditional Sunday activities.

Q: Why the first Tuesday after the first Monday?

A: Lawmakers wanted to prevent election day from falling on the first of November for two reasons. First, November 1 is All Saints' Day, a holy day for Roman Catholics. Second, most merchants were in the habit of doing their books from the preceding month on the first. Congress was apparently worried that the economic success or failure of the previous month might prove an undue influence on the vote.

Q: When can I vote?

A: The polls in most states open at 6:00 a.m. or 7:00 a.m. and close at around 7:00 p.m. or 8:00 p.m.

Q: When is the last day I can register to vote in the next election?

A: Find your state in the list below to view the last day on which you can register to vote.

REGISTRATION DEADLINES FOR ALL ELECTIONS

ALABAMA	10 days before an election
ALASKA	30 days before an election
ARIZONA	29 days before an election
ARKANSAS	30 days before an election
CALIFORNIA	29 days before an election
COLORADO	29 days before an election (If the application is received in the mail without a postmark, it must be received within 5 days of the close of registration.)
CONNECTICUT	14 days before an election
DELAWARE	20 days prior to a general election and 21 days prior to a primary election
D.C.	30 days before an election
FLORIDA	29 days before an election
GEORGIA	The fifth Monday before a general primary, general election, or presidential preference primary; the fifth day after the date of the call for all other special primaries and special elections
HAWAII	30 days before an election
IDAHO	25 days before an election if registering by mail; 24 days if registering in person; or election day at the polls
ILLINOIS	29 days before primary; 28 days before a general election
INDIANA	29 days before an election
IOWA	Delivered by 5:00 p.m. 10 days before a state primary or general election; 11 days before all others; a postmark 15 or more days before an election is considered on time
KANSAS	Delivered 15 days before an election
KENTUCKY	28 days before an election
LOUISIANA	24 days before an election
MAINE	10 business days before an election or delivered in person up to and including election day
MARYLAND	9:00 p.m. on the fifth Monday before an election
MASSACHUSETTS	20 days before an election
MICHIGAN	30 days before an election
MINNESOTA	Delivered by 5:00 p.m. 21 days before an election, but election-day registration is available at polling places
MISSISSIPPI	30 days before an election

MISSOURI	28 days before an election
MONTANA	30 days before an election
NEBRASKA	The fourth Tuesday before an election or delivered by 6:00 p.m. on the second Friday before an election
NEVADA	9:00 p.m. on the fifth Saturday before any primary or general election; 9:00 p.m. on the third Saturday before any recall or special election unless held on the same day as a primary or general election (in which case the deadline remains the fifth Saturday)
NEW HAMPSHIRE	Must be received by city or town clerk 10 days before an election or register at the polls on election day
NEW JERSEY	29 days before an election
NEW MEXICO	28 days before an election
NEW YORK	25 days before an election
NORTH CAROLINA	Postmarked 25 days before an election or received in the elections office or designated voter registration agency by 5:00 p.m.
NORTH DAKOTA	North Dakota does not have voter registration
OHIO	30 days before an election
OKLAHOMA	25 days before an election
OREGON	21 days before an election; there is no deadline for applications for change of name, change of address, or to register with a party
PENNSYLVANIA	30 days before an election
RHODE ISLAND	30 days before an election, but check Saturday hours
SOUTH CAROLINA	30 days before an election
SOUTH DAKOTA	Delivered 15 days before an election
TENNESSEE	30 days before an election
TEXAS	30 days before an election
UTAH	20 days before an election
VERMONT	Delivered to the town clerk before noon, postmarked or submitted to DMV on the second Saturday before an election
VIRGINIA	Delivered 29 days before an election
WASHINGTON	30 days before an election or delivered in person up to 15 days before an election at a location designated by the county elections officer (usually the county courthouse)
WEST VIRGINIA	30 days before an election
WISCONSIN	13 days before an election or completed in the local voter registration office 1 day before an election or completed at the polling place on election day
WYOMING	30 days before an election or register at the polling place on election day

20

. . . .

A CITIZEN POLITICIAN

AN INTERVIEW WITH CONGRESSMAN MICHAEL BURGESS FROM TEXAS'S TWENTY-SIXTH DISTRICT

D.A.: You were a doctor with an established practice, and yet you decided to run for Congress. Why?

M.B.: It wasn't like I had always been thinking about running for office. But over several years of changes in organized medicine I found myself asking, "How did they let it get like this?" I realized I could be involved in the Texas Medical Association (TMA) and American Medical Association (AMA) but would need to be in a different position to have a really positive impact on medicine. In 2001 Congress cut Medicare reimbursements and that's when I knew I had to take a shot at the House. It was late 2001 and Dick Armey was retiring after eighteen years, so I decided to put my hat in the ring. His vacancy created an open seat, which meant anyone could run, so I thought, *Why not me?*

D.A.: How did you proceed?

M.B.: In 2001 Texas had gone through redistricting, and though I was aware of things going on politically, I wasn't engulfed in it. I didn't really know how my district looked after all the changes, so I did some Internet research. I went to the secretary of state site and pulled a form—a petition to file—and filled it out and sent it in. It wasn't that hard to find; a person really doesn't even need help to complete it. In Texas you can gather the necessary signatures or pay a filing fee. Since I was deciding to run so late in the race, I paid the fee. It would have taken time to get the signatures, and if some are not accepted, a candidate can be tossed off the ballot on a technicality. I didn't want that to be a possibility. I wanted to focus my energies on winning. After I decided what to do, I told my wife. Laura was incredulous at first because we had never discussed the possibility of my running for office. I went to the TMA/AMA and asked what they thought, and they said I had a single-digit chance to win—not very encouraging. But when I went to my state senator with the idea, she was very encouraging and gave me the name of a consultant. Here I was, a doctor with a crazy notion to run for office, sitting in a campaign consultant's office. It was surreal. He looked at me and said, "If you don't plan to invest at least $200,000 in a campaign, no one is going to take you seriously. If you don't have the money, I hope you are willing to get out and raise it yourself." I spent a little over $100,000 on my election and raised almost all of that in less than four months. That was my campaign, and thank God we won. There were other candidates for the office, and I'm sure they spent nowhere near the kind of money I did and probably didn't hire campaign consultants. Everyone has to know what kind of race they what to run.

D.A.: What kind of support system does a candidate need?

M.B.: You need great people around you; people you trust. I talked to my wife, the kids, friends, and physician partners to make sure they were squarely with me. Everyone was very encouraging, but I'm sure many of them thought there was no way I could win. Most family arguments center on money, and leaving a prosperous medical practice that I had built up over twenty years for a major pay cut in Congress is not something to be decided alone. Had Laura said "no," I would have pulled out immediately. A candidate has to have people around him or her who will speak honestly because it will only hurt everyone in the end if they don't.

D.A.: Most people are afraid to run because of the cost involved in campaigning. Where does a candidate get the money? Running for office seems like it could bankrupt you. How much pocket money is involved? Does a candidate ever get all of his investment back? If not, wouldn't this be enough to keep most people from even thinking about running?

M.B.: You can either "gift" your investment in your campaign or you can "loan" it, and though I'm not an accountant, the basic difference is that when you loan it to yourself, you can repay yourself from campaign contributions if you win. Once you declare and file all the correct forms, you can begin to raise money for your election. Some folks have the funds and can just pay for it all out of their own pocket; that's why many "gift" the money. For most of us it doesn't work that way. We have a little money to put in, but with the help of a little more money from a lot of people, we have the cash to run for office. Donations are meant to be an extension of the voice of the people. They are voting with their money, so use the money wisely in your efforts. With strong support people around you, people who can help you keep track of your finances, a person should not think his campaign will bankrupt him.

D.A.: How important is it for a candidate to connect with his party? What does the party offer?

M.B.: When you're running in the primaries, it's every man for himself. The party, at least in my case, didn't jump in for anyone, though it did give a few hints here and there, but that's what parties do. The primary is all about getting the word out and letting people decide if they want to support you. I consider primaries to be the choice of the people. Once you win the primary, you are the candidate for the party ticket on which you ran. In my case that was the Republican Party. After you get congratulatory calls from congressmen in your state and across the country, a party representative calls to offer assistance. The party wants to know how much debt you are carrying, how your organization looks, what your overall plan or strategy is, etc. The party will make sure you know it's on your side. There is a little "Good job winning the primary, now we're going to help you so you don't screw up the election" help and guidance. The party may help out with money, but usually the party makes sure you're able to raise your own money. The party does a great job increasing your visibility and awareness. If it's a tough race, this is when the party will have senators, congressmen, and senior elected officials show support.

D.A.: Are you treated differently by friends and family now that you hold office? Do you have to maintain some distance from people so you can do your job adequately?

M.B.: No. Everyone still basically treats me the same. The one thing that surprised me most was how many people come to me every day to ensure that their program or funding issue isn't changed because of a budget adjustment. I was really surprised at that. Some days there are so many people lined up in my office, I can give each one no more than fifteen minutes to state their purpose and push their agenda, even if the economy ebbs and cutbacks are mandated. I was kind of shocked to see how many people, companies, and programs have a direct link to federal funding.

D.A.: What's the best way for a constituent to contact you? How can we be assured that you are getting our messages?

M.B.: E-mail, phone, U.S. mail. Don't send stuff to D.C., though. Send it to my district headquarters. After the ricin-anthrax-terrorism scares involving the mail, things got a little funky. Security people have taken mail from me in the past and warned me that I may never see it again. On the other hand, if it goes to my district, the odds of my knowing about it are much better. I can't read and respond to all of the mail—I had more than thirty thousand pieces this past year. If an officeholder tried to answer all his mail, it would be a full-time job and he wouldn't have time to legislate, vote, or take care of his district. When I get a major outpouring of mail, it's a clear indicator how the people feel and it helps me act accordingly. I was voted to represent a particular area, so I feel like I already have a keen sense of what my constituents want, but personal communication helps. Letters definitely make me study the issue at hand. At the same time, if I get mass-marketed pieces, like from a special-interest group, I still weigh the issue, but I keep in mind that there's a campaign involved. In the end, I am an elected representative, so yes, I want to hear from my constituents, and yes, your input can impact my decisions.

D.A.: What is the one thing you wish you would have known before tossing your hat in the ring?

M.B.: I can't say there has been anything that so overwhelmed me that I would reconsider running. The job's tough, but it's just too rewarding to complain about. It's satisfying to know that I am helping.

D.A.: You are up for reelection. How does your schedule change to compensate for the extra attention that demands? Does remaining in office weigh heavily on a politician's mind?

M.B.: You spend a bit more time to make sure your campaign systems are working well. You attend a few more events and shake a few extra hands. Where you see the changes in a reelection year is when it is a presidential election year too. Suddenly, every speech is important. All appearances are important. All sides ratchet up the competition, and you don't let the other parties get away with anything because you can't afford to. This is when we all feel the weight of a reelection year.

D.A.: What kind of feeling do you have when you walk the halls where our greatest leaders have convened, knowing that you are now in their ranks?

M.B.: A lot of people think the swearing-in ceremony is emotional, and I guess it is, but you have worked and prepared so painstakingly to get there that it's almost a routine you go through. For me, the one thing that has been very moving on more than one occasion is when I have worked hard for my area and have stayed in my office into the night. Then you look up and realize you are the last person in the building. You wonder, *How many others have done this?*

I CONCLUDED the interview by asking Congressman Burgess for a favorite quote. He laughed and said, "It's from Davey Crockett after he lost his reelection bid from Tennessee: 'You all can all go to hell, I'm going to Texas.' I have that on a coffee mug." While he was quoting Crockett, I heard a buzzer in the background and asked the congressman if that was his call to the floor. "Yes. It's time for me to cast a vote." He hung up the phone and returned to the "people's business."

SO YOU WANNA RUN FOR OFFICE?

The future of this republic is in the hands of the
American voter.——DWIGHT D. EISENHOWER

There is something deeply alluring about seeking political office. Overnight you are catapulted to a different level with the people you have known all of your life, and strangers in the community now drop your name as if you have been best friends forever. Suddenly there is a newfound sense of validation; after all, you ran and won. But before you get ahead of yourself, and compose that heartfelt acceptance speech, it is probably a good idea to get a sense of what the upcoming weeks and months are going to be like. Stacey Cordeiro of the Massachusetts Green Party prepared an outline of the things candidates need to consider before jumping into the battle.* Although her outline (reproduced below) is specifically geared toward Green Party candidates, her insights apply to almost anyone seeking office.

QUESTIONS TO ASK YOURSELF

What are the specific changes you want to make in your community? Is running for this office the best way to make these changes? What powers does a person in this office have to create these changes? How else could you work toward your objective? Are you the best person for the job? Is yours the face you want on your local...party? Is it the face the local [party] wants for itself? Do you really want the job? Are you absolutely healthy and sane? (You will be under tremendous pressure.) Does your partner think it's a fantastic idea? (Don't even think about running if the answer to this is not "yes.")

FORMING YOUR EXPLORATORY COMMITTEE

You are not going to run for office alone. You will be relying heavily on the people around you. So don't decide to run for office alone but involve those people in the decision who will be working on your campaign. The first thing a prospective candidate usually does is to host a small gathering in their home to pitch the idea and see what kind of support might be available. It's very important to get the right people at this meeting. Don't just invite your friends. Invite those people who will be critical of the idea. Make sure that someone present has managed a campaign before.

What You're Listening For

If they want you to run, the people at your exploratory committee meeting should ask you very tough questions, be very impressed with your answers, and express their enthusiasm about your campaign without hesitation. As the prospective candidate, you will want to hear this. Be very careful

---

*See Stacey Cordeiro, "How to Run a Political Campaign," June 3, 2001, http://www.gp.org/organize/howtorun_mass.pdf.

not to convince yourself that you hear this if you don't. Ask someone you trust if they are hearing the same things you are.

What You Will More Likely Hear

The people in the room like you. If they've come to the meeting, it's because they care enough about you to give a little of their time. They don't want to hurt your feelings. So when they voice concerns, assume that their reservations are even bigger than they say. Listen for hesitation and doubt in people's voices. What they might want to say is that they don't think you should run.

What You Might Also Hear

People will feel flattered to have been invited to this kind of "inner-circle" meeting. People like to feel important. Some people will advise you to run because it will make them feel important to be part of your campaign. The kind of support you want is the kind that comes from a shared commitment to the goals of the campaign, not someone's glory—not yours, and not anyone else's on your campaign.

Who Comes to the Meeting

If someone doesn't come to the meeting, it's probably safe to say they don't think your candidacy is worth their while. But don't assume that if people come they do support you. Good attendance at an exploratory committee meeting is not the same as support.

The Final Word

Before they leave, ask people if they think you should run. Ask for a yes or no answer. Also, ask if they are willing to make a significant commitment to your campaign.

What to Expect from People

A rule of organizing is that only about half of the people that commit to something will actually come through. This is true for your close friends and advisers, too. Things happen in people's lives, and people that you are counting on will drop off the campaign. Make sure you aren't relying on too few people to get this big job done.

WRITING THE CAMPAIGN PLAN

Having a written campaign plan is one of the most important, but most neglected, aspects of most campaigns. Writing a campaign plan will spare you a lot of anxiety and wasted effort. You should have a written plan before you do *anything else*! Here are the elements of a campaign plan:

How Many Votes

People will tell you that you'll win this race on one issue, or with the support of one person, constituency, or neighborhood. The reality is, the *only thing* that will win the race is enough votes. You will need to go to your town hall's elections department to find the following numbers.

Number of people registered to vote: An accurate number won't be available until a few weeks before the election. Until then, estimate this number by looking at the trend in this number over the last eight years or so (it varies in four-year cycles). For a more accurate estimate, look at the trend in the number of residents eligible to vote, and the trend in the *percentage* of those who are registered to vote.

Percentage of registered voters expected to turn out: To estimate this number, again look at historical data (eight years back should be plenty). Make sure you're comparing your race with a comparable election year. Consider soft factors like the number of candidates in the race, and whether there are any hot issues on the ballot.

Percentage of votes needed to win the election: In a two-way race, this is a pretty easy formula—half the votes plus one (actually, you should shoot for 51 to 54 percent to be safe). But many races have more than one seat, and more than two candidates. Look at past races that are similar to yours in the number of candidates and number of seats. Consider soft factors such as the extent to which the race is dominated by one or a few candidates, and consider how strong your competition's support is. You will have to come up with a target percentage that you think will win you the election, which is more art than science. Once you've settled on a number, pad it by a few percentage points to be safe.

The number of votes you need is the estimated number of registered voters times the percentage turnout expected times the percentage you need to win. As the election gets closer, many factors will change. You may need to revisit these numbers periodically over the campaign.

Where will they come from? You will want to know how many votes to shoot for in every ward and precinct in your district. To estimate these, find a candidate that was like you in ideology. It doesn't matter if the candidate won or not, but it helps if they didn't totally bomb. More recent candidates are also better....For your comparison candidate or question, calculate what percentage of the vote total came from each precinct. Then, take these percentages and apply them to your overall vote goal to get vote goals for each precinct.

How Much Money Will It Take?

Sometimes people make rough estimates about how much a campaign will cost. Usually, the suggestion is $1 to $2 per household in your district, or even as much as $5. You should put together a more detailed budget as soon as possible, using real estimates of costs from vendors. Set a fundraising goal and meet it.

What's My Message?

There are a few hard truths in campaigns, and one of them is that people only have so much attention for what you have to say. Therefore, you have to be able to let people know why they should vote for you in *just a few words.* Your message should differentiate you from your opponents in a meaningful way. While you should be able to discuss relevant issues intelligently and in detail, you should also be able to discuss them in about a quarter of the time that you'd like! You should have pitches ready in thirty-second, three-minute, and ten-minute versions. You should get used to the idea of saying the same thing over and over and over again.

When Does It All Happen?

Despite long campaign seasons, the majority of voters don't make up their minds until the last couple of weeks of the campaign. This is especially true for local elections, when a fairly large group of voters (about 15 percent) go to the polls undecided! While most of your work persuading and turning out voters will go on in the last couple of weeks to one month before the election, there is a lot of work to do to prepare for the campaign. Much of this can be done well in advance, such as planning, fundraising, message development, volunteer recruitment, etc. The better prepared you are, the smoother things will go during the crucial period at the end.

CAMPAIGN STRUCTURE

The Candidate

Once the candidate has hired a manager, it's her/his job to sound and look good and stay on-message (say the same things over and over again), making it sound fresh each time.

The Kitchen Cabinet

These are advisers to the candidate, like family and personal friends. They do *not* oversee the campaign.

The Treasurer and Assistant Treasurer

The treasurer of the campaign is legally responsible for any financial irregularities. She/he is also responsible for making sure that campaign finance reports are filed correctly and on time, which can be extremely challenging. But because the treasurer's name appears on all pieces of campaign literature, some campaigns would rather have a well-known person than someone who knows how to do these things as treasurer. In this case, they sometimes appoint an assistant treasurer to actually do the work.

The Campaign Manager

A great campaign manager is someone who works well under pressure, who knows how to delegate responsibility, and who can keep focused on the goal in the face of interminable distractions.

The Steering Committee

Some campaigns have a "Steering Committee," which should really be called a list of high-profile endorsers. They do not necessarily do any work on the campaign, just lend their good names.

The Advisory Committee

This is what your exploratory committee will eventually become. An advisory board is a low-profile group of people with experience running campaigns. They are the ones who decide on direction and strategy.

The Campaign Chair

This is basically the chairperson of the board (the Advisory Board, above). This should be a fairly well-known person, but also someone who will put in significant work on the campaign, particularly in networking.

The Spokesperson

This can be the same person as the campaign chair. The spokesperson is the first person the media go to.

The Campaign Committee

- **Field Manager:** This is the person responsible for the voter ID and election day Get-Out-the-Vote activity.
- **Fundraiser:** The fundraiser does the follow up with pledges, events, and house parties.
- **Volunteer Coordinator:** This person recruits volunteers to do phone calls, door knocking, and literature dropping, and makes sure enough volunteers show up for each activity.
- **Media Coordinator:** This is the person who sends out press releases to local media, welcomes media to your events, and keeps up with what the media are saying about the race.
- **Scheduler:** You will need someone to handle all the requests you get for the candidate to appear at events. The scheduler is the one who determines which events are worth going to and arranges for a trustworthy volunteer to drive and accompany the candidate there.

- **Constituency Organizer:** You should have constituency organizers for every constituency that's important to the campaign. Constituencies can be based on ethnicity, identity (e.g., GLBT, elderly), or affiliation (e.g., unions, students). The job of these people is to identify important issues, get the candidate's message into the community, recruit volunteers, and collect voter ID's.
- **Administrator:** This person runs the office.
- **Research and Writing Coordinator:** This person gathers together all the experts who will help the candidate write position papers and supervises the production of well-written campaign materials.

FUNDRAISING

Fundraising doesn't have to be scary or horrible if you plan well and set achievable goals. You'll raise enough money to run the campaign and get it off your mind, and avoid sending yourself to the poorhouse as well.

Candidate Calls

By far the very best way to raise money is for *the candidate* to go through all available lists, pull the people she/he knows even vaguely, decide how much money to ask each person for, call them up and ask them for a commitment in a specific amount. Being successful at candidate calls is all about the follow-up. You should send a confirmation letter to the donor right away with an envelope for them to send the check. You should then follow up the pledge every two weeks until you get it. Depending on how comfortable your candidate is with this, this is far and away the most money you will make for the investment of time and money required.

Fundraising Team

Everyone is more likely to give if they are asked personally by a friend. Because your candidate knows only so many people, a fundraising team broadens the number of people who can be asked on a personal level. Good candidates for your fundraising team are those who believe deeply in the campaign, who have an extensive contact network, particularly one that doesn't overlap substantially with your candidate, and who are likely to do what they say they'll do. The flake factor applies here as well as everywhere else; 30 percent to 50 percent of the people who make commitments to you will not come through. And 30 percent to 50 percent of those who make commitments to your fundraising team members will also not come through, so plan accordingly! Make sure your fundraising team has all the materials it will need (campaign literature, your bio or résumé, etc.) and check in with them often! It's the job of the fundraising team member to secure the *pledge* of a contribution, and the job of the campaign to follow up on it.

House Parties

House parties are small events hosted by campaign supporters who invite people from their own contact networks to meet the candidate. The host of the party must tell the guests ahead of time that they will be asked to contribute money and volunteer time to the campaign, then make a pitch after the candidate has given a very brief speech and answered questions. House parties are very time-intensive because the campaign has to follow up very closely with people who agree to host house parties. Of course, the flake factor applies here as well. But at least the cost of food and invitations is usually borne by the host. Hosting a house party is a good way for someone who is not ready to commit to the fundraising team to help with the fundraising. House parties also can create positive voter ID's, identify new volunteers, and create lists of names for the candidate to call personally later for larger donations.

Events

Large events, or benefits, are probably the biggest time and money suck in the fundraising world. Events hardly make any money for the effort, but since they're so visible, people think of them as the primary fundraising mechanism. Events can lose money as easily as they can make it. However, events can serve a useful purpose, such as punctuating a fundraising drive (a celebration of meeting your goal) or putting on a good show for the media or your supporters. Events should be farmed out to a highly trusted volunteer or even a paid consultant to avoid taking up too much of the campaign's focus. If an event looks like it's going to bomb, it's better to cancel ("postpone") it. It looks a lot worse to have a poorly attended event than to reschedule one.

Direct Mail

Direct mail is mostly used by very large campaigns with a lot of money, by professional mailing houses to lists of prospective voters. Usually, the first mailing loses money or breaks even. Then the mailing house will send another fundraising piece to those who responded to the first one, and that's how they make money. On smaller campaigns, you might periodically send fundraising solicitations to people on your own campaign list of volunteers, supporters, and voter ID's. Fundraising letters are much more effective if followed up in a timely manner with a phone call. People who send in small donations are likely to send larger donations if asked for them, so the candidate should give small donors a call.

THE MEAT OF THE MATTER

The purpose of a campaign is this: to identify *by name* enough voters to win the election, and to turn these people out on election day. The way to do this is to contact voters and ask them if they support your candidate. Assign numbers to names: Yeses are 1, Maybes are 2, and Nos are 3. Your job is to identify enough 1's to win—actually, you should identify 130 percent of the 1's you need, because 30 percent will probably "flake" on you.

How to Identify Voters

1. Word of mouth: Ask your supporters to find you ten voter ID's each.

2. Phone banking: Get lists of voters from your city or town. Look up the phone numbers, call people, and ask them if they support your candidate. Don't ask more than one question in a phone call.

3. Door knocking: During the course of persuading voters, you will also make some ID's.

How to Affect Turnout

On election day you should have the names and phone numbers of the people who said they'd vote for your candidate. One to three days before the election, call all these people and remind them to vote, and ask whether they'll need assistance getting to the polls. On the day of the election, a campaign volunteer sits at each polling place all day with a list of ID's from that precinct. As voters come in and tell the election official their name, your volunteer looks for that name on his/her list and crosses off the name. Two hours before the polls close, your poll workers call in or deliver these lists. The people who have not shown up to vote must be called and reminded to go to the poll. If necessary, someone must be ready to pick them up and drive them there.

How to Persuade Voters

When you know who your 2's are, you can go to work turning them into 1's. One good way to do this is by mailing them literature designed to sway them your way, or leaving it on their doorsteps (*not* in their mailboxes). Another good way to turn a 2 into a 1 is to get a visit from the candidate. Door knocking is very time-intensive, so you shouldn't waste it on people who are already with you (1's) or people who are already against you (3's). In addition to these very precise persuasion methods (called "high-quality" contacts), you can use the media to persuade voters your way. Because you have much less control over the message and who receives it this way, media attention is called "low-quality" contact. Other types of low-quality contacts are advertisements and radio spots. A popular estimate is that it takes three to eight contacts to persuade a voter.

Laying It on the Map

Now go back to your comparable candidate and categorize the precincts by their support for that candidate (high, medium, low) and by the turnout in the last election (high, medium, low). This will help you decide where your efforts can make the most difference. Don't waste your time trying to persuade voters in low-support precincts, and don't try to squeak a few more ID's out of high-support precincts. Stick to your persuadable voters in medium-support precincts.

Another good way to target persuasion efforts is to concentrate on repeat voters. A review of the voting lists in the past few elections will help you identify these people. Likewise, trying to increase turnout in high-turnout precincts isn't going to give you much result for your work. Instead, concentrate on low- and medium-turnout precincts. In precincts with very low support, any campaigning you do can activate people to go out and vote against you. These are good places to collect voter ID's by word of mouth. Don't forget absentee voters—these are the most likely to turn out! Your town hall can give you a list of people who have requested absentee ballots.

WHAT'S NOT MEAT

Campaigns face considerable pressure to focus too much on visibility efforts such as candidate appearances, lawn signs and bumper stickers, and groups of supporters standing at traffic circles with signs. These are necessary evils, most useful for giving your existing supporters confidence in your campaign. But they persuade only a few people, if any, and do not provide *any* positive voter ID's. Don't concentrate on these. Voter registration is a worthwhile effort, but is not the best campaign strategy unless it's clear that you can't win without it. The reason is, the more votes you add to the mix, the more you dilute the effect of each vote. So persuading a likely voter is a much more valuable campaign activity than adding a new voter to the mix.

WHAT TO DO AFTER YOU DECIDE TO RUN

You have gone through the all the pluses and minuses of running for office and are convinced you are the right person at the right time for the right position. You know that you can make a difference, and you're ready to dive in. What are some of the rules and regulations associated with a political campaign? The following is derived from a Guide for Candidates posted on the website for the state of Rhode Island.* Call or write to your secretary of state or local election offices to be learn the specific requirements of your state or municipality.

Q: How old does a candidate have to be?

A: If you want to run for the U.S. Senate, you must be at least thirty years old and a registered voter. The U.S. House of Representatives requires a person to be at least twenty-five, and most states prefer a candidate to be at least eighteen for most local and state races, though we all have heard of a sixteen- or seventeen-year-old mayor or city council member.

DECLARING YOUR CANDIDACY

To run for office, you must "declare" that you are a candidate and must name the office you seek. If you are a member of a political party, you must make this information known, and if you plan to run unaffiliated or as an independent, this information also must be made public.

Q: Is there a declaration of candidacy form?

A: Yes. If you wish to start the process of becoming a candidate for any office on the ballot, you must file a declaration of candidacy. If you wish to run for U.S. Senate, U.S. House, or independent presidential elector, you should contact your secretary of state, Elections Division, for the appropriate forms. If you are seeking state or local office, you may still contact your secretary of state, though they will most likely refer you to a different state or local division. It may take a call or two to get to the appropriate person, but consider this practice. When you run for office, you are entering the black hole of bureaucracy. Get used to it.

Q: Can a person declare for more than one office?

A: Usually, yes. But you may not run for the same office under different parties. For instance, you may not be listed on a ballot as a Republican candidate for U.S. Senate and as a Democrat too. You cannot run for one office as a member of one party while trying to win a separate office

*"How to Run for Political Office in Rhode Island: A Guide for Candidates," State of Rhode Island and Providence Plantations Office of the Secretary of State, State House, Providence, RI, http://www.corps.state.ri.us/elections/manuals/2000%20 how%20to%20run%20guide%20web.pdf

under a different party's header. On the other hand, if you want to run for city manager and state senate, you may do so as long as rules do not prohibit your service in more than one elected office. Before you entertain the idea, ask.

Q: Can a person switch parties?

A: Yes. It happens more often than you would expect. The procedure is known as disaffiliation and usually has a specific time period during which it must be done before an election. The process is simple because you are merely swapping parties. Again, states vary on requirements, but it is usually as easy as obtaining a form from your local board of canvassers or election offices approximately ninety days before you file your declaration of candidacy.

Q: What is an endorsement?

A: This is the system party officials use to declare that a particular candidate represents their party. This is usually the prized jewel in a campaign because a candidate with a party endorsement typically gains manpower and financial support while a fringe or second-tier candidate may not.

Q: Who endorses whom?

A: This is an example from the state of Rhode Island:

Endorsement Made By:	For Office Of:
State Committee	U.S. Senator and U.S. Representative
Senatorial District Committee	State Senator and Senatorial District Committee Member
Representative District Committee	State Representative and Representative District Committee Member
City/Town Committee	Local Offices and City/Town Committee Member
Ward Committee	Ward Committee Member

Q: What happens if I am not endorsed and I want to run as a party candidate for public office?

A: You will first have to obtain nomination papers and once again, the Office of Secretary of State is the best starting point. Once you receive your papers, you will need to qualify by collecting a specific number of signatures; this will put you on the ballot. If there is no primary for the office you seek, your name will appear on the ballot for the general election, but you will still have to collect the required number of signatures.

Q: What are nomination papers?

A: So that ballots are not loaded with hundreds of names for every position, a candidate must collect a specific number of citizen signatures on forms known as nomination papers. Each state and
   position has different numbers, so check with your state for full details. The number is usually
   easily obtainable for a bona fide candidate. For example, Rhode Island asks for 50 names if you
   are running for state representative, 100 names for state senator, 500 for U.S. representative,
   and 1,000 for U.S. senator. The signatures do not have to be from a particular party. For example, if you are running as a Republican, you may collect a signature from a Democrat who would
   like to see you run.

   There are a few other requirements involving nomination papers, so be sure to check with
   your Office of the Secretary of State or local election offices to cover your bases.

Q: Is it really possible for me to get on a ballot without a primary?

A: Yes. The reason for a primary usually involves more than one candidate seeking the same office
   at the same time. You won't have a primary if (a) no one else filed a valid declaration of candidacy; (b) the other candidate(s) withdrew from the race; or (c) no other candidates filed their
   nomination papers in a timely manner. There are other rules which pertain but these are the ba-
   sics.

Q: How does a candidate know where his name will be listed on the primary ballot?

A: The rules typically state that a party's "endorsed" candidate be directly under the party name and
   that the candidate will have an asterisk(*) preceding his or her name. Unendorsed candidates for
   federal and state offices are listed in the order they were chosen in a lottery. Unendorsed candidates for local offices appear alphabetically under the endorsed candidate's name.

Q: How is my ballot placement determined if I am a candidate in the general election?

A: A lottery is conducted by the secretary of state.

Q: What are the political parties in the United States?

A: A better question might be "What is not a political party in America?" There are hundreds,
   maybe thousands, of fringe parties that solicit votes, funds, and attention ranging from the Pan-
   sexual Peace Party to the Marijuana Party, from the Internet Party to the Knight's Party (the latter
   is an offshoot of the Ku Klux Klan). Listed below are several parties that may be worth investigating because of their stance or size or both.

REPUBLICAN PARTY

Republican National Committee
310 First Street, SE
Washington, DC 20003
Phone: 202-863-8500
Fax: 202-863-8820
Website: http://www.rnc.org/
Major conservative party
  Affiliated groups include:*
    National Republican Congressional
      Committee (NRCC)
    Speaker of the House and House
      Republican Conference
    National Republican Senatorial Committee
      (NRSC)
    Senate Majority Leader's Office
    Republican Governors Association (RGA)
    Republican Mayors & Local Officials
    National Federation of Republican Women
      (NFRW)
    Young Republican National Federation
      (YRs)
    College Republican National Committee
      (CRNC)
    National Teen Age Republicans (TARs)

REFORM PARTY OF THE USA

420½ South 22nd Avenue
Hattiesburg, MS 39401
Phone: 877-467-3367
Fax: 601-544-1424
Website: http://www.reformparty.org/
  cgi-bin/hcgmain.cgi
Fiscally conservative party formed by Ross
  Perot when he ran for president in 1992.

DEMOCRATIC PARTY

Democratic National Committee
430 S. Capitol Street, SE
Washington, DC 20003
Phone: 202-863-8000
Website: http://www.democrats.org/
Major liberal party
  Affiliated groups include:*
    Democratic Congressional Campaign
      Committee (DCCC)
    House Democratic Leader's Office
    Democratic Senatorial Campaign
      Committee (DSCC)
    DSCC #2
    Senate Minority Leader's Office
    Democratic Governors Association (DGA)
    Democratic Legislative Campaign Committee
    Young Democrats of America (YDs)
    College Democrats of America ("College
      Dems")

GREEN PARTY OF THE UNITED STATES

P.O. Box 57065
Washington, DC 20037
Phone: 202-319-7191 or toll-free (U.S.): 866-
  41GREEN
Website: http://www.gp.org/
Informal left-leaning group that hit big when
  Ralph Nader ran for president under their
  auspices.

LIBERTARIAN PARTY

2600 Virginia Avenue, NW
Suite 100
Washington, DC 20037

*Per http://www.politics1.com.

Phone: 202-333-0008
Website: http://www.lp.org/
Believes in total individual freedoms and is the
    third largest party.

NEW PARTY

88 Third Avenue
Suite 313
Brooklyn, NY 11217
Phone: 1-800-200-1294
Website: http://www.newparty.org/index.html
Socialist/left/labor-oriented party

AMERICA FIRST PARTY

1630 A 30th Street
#111
Boulder, CO 80301
Phone: 866-SOS-USA1
Fax: 303-265-9230
Website: http://www.americafirstparty.org/
Revitalize the great American experiment of
    Founding Fathers.

AMERICAN HERITAGE PARTY

P.O. Box 241
Leavenworth, WA 98826-0241
Phone: 1-888-396-6247
Website:
    http://www.americanheritageparty.org/
Small and Christian-focused.

CONSTITUTION PARTY

23 North Lime Street
Lancaster, PA 17602
Phone Toll-Free: 1-800-2-VETO-IRS (1-800-
    283-8647)

Phone: 717-390-1993
Fax: 717-390-1996
Website: http://www.constitution-party.net/
Formed in 1992 primarily as a vehicle for Pat
    Buchanan to run for president.

INDEPENDENCE PARTY

P.O. Box 40495
St. Paul, MN 55104
Phone: 651-487-9700
Fax: 651-917-7145
Website: http://www.mnip.org/
Created as a vehicle for Jesse Ventura's
    gubernatorial run.

LABOR PARTY

P.O. Box 53177
Washington, DC 20009
Phone: 202-234-5190
Fax: 202-234-5266
Website:
    http://www.thelaborparty.org/index.html
Started by several major union groups. Leans
    left.

NATURAL LAW PARTY

Website: http://www.natural-law.org/
Gained some ground in 2000 elections.
    Scientific approach to politics. Yoga, TM, etc.

PROHIBITION PARTY

Prohibition National Committee
P.O. Box 2635
Denver, CO 80201
Phone: 303-237-4947
Website: http://www.prohibition.org/

Claims to be oldest third party in America. Ultra conservative.

AMERICAN PATRIOT PARTY

National Headquarters
P.O. Box 0226
Pensacola, FL 32591-0226
Website: http://www.patriotparty.us/
A new party that wants to return power to state governments. Wants to abolish the IRS.

WE THE PEOPLE PARTY

P.O. Box 253
Jackson, NH 03846
Phone: 603-383-4285
Cell: 603-387-6689
Fax: 603-383-6793
Website: http://www.wethepeople-wtp.org/
Centrist and small.

MY POLITICAL IQ

The Free Market Foundation (www.freemarket.org) has published a handy resource guide that puts a citizen's involvement in the political process into perspective. Answer the following questions and calculate your score. There is no "magic" number to hit, but out of 100 possible points, if you find your score is low, you may want to get more involved in your state's politics. You can't impact your leaders if you don't know who they are or what they do.

_____ 1. Registered to vote. (5 points)

_____ 2. Voted in 2004 primary (10 points) and general elections. (6 points)

_____ 3. Attended Democratic or Republican precinct, county/district, or state conventions. (10 points)

_____ 4. Name your elected officials: (2 points for each)

            U.S. Senator: _____

            U.S. Senator: _____

    U.S. Congressman: _____

        State Governor: _____

    State Lt. Governor: _____

         State Senator: _____

  State Representative: _____

_____ 5. Communicated with one of the above during the last two years. (10 points)

_____ 6. Worked as a volunteer or contributed financially to a candidate in the last two years. (15 points)

_____ 7. Wrote letter to editor concerning legislation or election in last two years. (5 points)

_____ 8. Name one organization that provides information on your state's legislative issues: _____ (5 points)

_____ 9. Name one organization that provides information on the voting records of your state legislators: _____ (5 points)

_____ 10. Prayed for your country, state, or elected leaders in the past year. (15 points)

                              _____ Total points scored

21

MADAME MAYOR — YOU WERE SUPPOSED TO LOSE!

Such as we are made of, such we be.

—WILLIAM SHAKESPEARE

FIRST MET LAURA MILLER when she and two other candidates for mayor of Dallas agreed to a debate on my radio show. I was relatively new in town, and neither she nor the other two candidates had a clue as to who I was, but they all agreed to come on after I assured them separately that the others were coming too. As the event got under way, I watched the candidates as they tried to get around some tough questions without really answering them. That is, they didn't want to answer the questions but had to make it appear as if they could. The uncomfortable nonanswers came with the first question, and I was convinced that my first segment would be wasted. But then I noticed an interesting deviation. Something was different about Laura Miller when her time came to speak. She engaged in the debate without notes or handlers, and she was willing to go for the jugular of her adversaries. I remember thinking, *This lady could be an exciting player in the race for mayor.*

I always want my audience to get the facts they need to make a decision and form an opinion, but since there is a fair amount of show biz that goes along with a morning radio show, I knew I needed to add some entertainment into the hour as well. So to avoid the typically boring give-and-take of a political debate, I decided to mix things up midway through the allotted time by giving bicycle horns to the candidates and asking them to answer stupid questions like "What's your favorite song?" "Tell me which candidate said his favorite movie was *The Wizard of Oz*?" and a half-dozen other lame questions. If the candidates were uncomfortable with the tough questions (and they were), they were in full-fidget mode with the easy ones. Nervous laughter and a sense of uneasiness entered the room—except for Laura Miller. She honked the horn for all it was worth and shouted out the answers like she was going for the big money on *Jeopardy*. I liked her. Here was an outsider who could change gears midstream and cause the others to believe that any nervousness was theirs alone.

After the debate was over I remarked to a co-worker that Candidate Miller was going to be the next mayor. I was swiftly rebuffed: "She doesn't have a chance because she doesn't have the big money or support. Besides, she's pissed off more than her share of people around this town."

Laura Miller went on to win the primary and force a runoff election with the big-money candidate. After we concluded a second debate between the two, I was more convinced than ever that Laura Miller was going to be the next mayor. Though I couldn't make such a proclamation, I did go out on a limb to ask her to make weekly appearances on my show if she won. She smiled. I never asked her if it was an "I know I'm going to win too" or a "You flatter me" smile, but the glimmer in her eye suggested the former.

Weeks later she did win—in a pretty major upset—and popped into my studios like a giddy girl who had just been invited to the prom. She clutched the bicycle horn from the first debate in her hand, managing to honk it every now and then to remind people that there was new blood at city hall. As she asked me to autograph the horn, Mayor Miller explained that she would have an open relationship with the media and the citizens. If people wanted answers, all we had to do was ask.

So I decided to take her up on her offer by asking this journalist-turned-politician to fill us in on some of her thoughts and feelings about running for the highest office in the eighth largest city in America:

D.A.: You were an established journalist who dropped it all to run for mayor. Why?

L.M.: I loved being a journalist, especially my last six years at the *Dallas Observer*, which let me write a strange hybrid of weekly opinion columns and long investigative pieces—mainly about city hall. I always thought of myself as the perfect outsider, throwing verbal grenades at a building whose occupants seemed outrageously dysfunctional. It seemed to me that local politicians always ran on a populist theme but inevitably turned conformist and confused once they got into office. The turning point for me came when former mayor Ron Kirk and former city manager John Ware spent a year behind closed doors negotiating with Ross Perot Jr. and Tom Hicks and emerged with a tax-subsidized deal for a new stadium for the hockey and basketball teams (which Perot and Hicks owned).

As an ardent city hall observer and taxpayer, I thought the deal was wildly lopsided in favor of the team owners. The proposal was hurriedly pushed through the city council, and no one tried to put the brakes on. I remember the day the matter came to the council for approval to put the stadium proposal on the ballot, and a long document with all the points was given to them at the start of the meeting. There was no time to absorb it, but the issue was overwhelmingly approved anyway. I remember sitting in the press pit, and for the first time since I'd been a reporter, I wished I was on the other side of the velvet ropes and serving as a council member, because so few of them were aggressive about asking the right questions.

Shortly after the voters narrowly approved what the council had passed, one of the city council members, who represented my part of the city, quit in the middle of his term to run for another office. A light bulb went off in my head, and I decided to run for his seat. My newspaper was almost as shocked as was the city council. My husband despaired. Knowing how passionate and driven I was, he thought he'd never see me again. Plus we already had a politician in the house—him! He is retiring this year from the Texas legislature, where he has served for twenty-four years. In retrospect, the transformation from hard-core, in-your-face journalist to big-city, let's-try-to-be-a-coalition-builder council member was remarkable—almost as remarkable as the transformation from not-so-good-at-being-a-coalition-building council member to successful bridge-building mayor.

D.A.: Describe your process, starting with the first thought of running and going through to your acceptance speech. Since this information is aimed at people thinking about running for office, please share what registration forms, charges, and governmental hoops you had to go through.

L.M.: It is a bit of a bureaucratic nightmare to run for public office, so you have to really want to do it. You have to file a form to appoint a campaign treasurer, file another form to get on the ballot (and in Dallas that has to be accompanied by petition signatures, which must be validated as current and notarized). Then you have to file numerous campaign reports showing how much money you are raising and spending. Everything has to be filed according to a timetable, otherwise the media typically nags you for being irresponsible and unethical. Some of the most frightening moments I've had as a politician were waiting for my petition signatures—some 250 when I ran for mayor—to be validated by the city. If you mess up and are short by even one, you are thrown off the ballot with no second chance to file again.

In Dallas, once you are elected, you must file a financial disclosure form, which lets everyone see what stocks and property you own, who you owe money to, and who you and your spouse get income from. Fundraising is also a difficult business because it's extraordinarily humbling to call on people and ask them for money. It's far worse when they say no, especially if they delight in telling you no and telling you *why* they're saying no. Of course, there is no greater feeling (except the love you get from your spouse/partner and children) of satisfaction than having people tell you they'd be happy to write you a check because they believe in you and admire you and think you are ethical and genuine. That gets you through all the paperwork and petitions and pleading for money.

I believe strongly (I learned this from my husband) that the sure-fire way to win a local election in an area no bigger than one hundred thousand people (roughly the size of a Dallas city council seat) is to campaign door-to-door. Not haphazardly. Not kinda sorta. But methodically and scientifically. You buy computer lists of hard-core (i.e., voting histories) registered voters, glue the info on separate index cards, sort them in file boxes by voting precincts and then streets, and then start walking. I walked to twenty-four hundred houses for my first council election in 1998. I walked weekdays and weekends. For four months. If the voter wasn't home, I left a personal note scribbled on preprinted campaign cards just to have a point of contact. When I got home, I took a different preprinted card (either "Sorry I missed you" or "Glad I met you"), jotted a personal message on it, and sent it in the mail. I won that election with 81 percent of the vote and two (pretty unchallenging) opponents. My husband won his first legislative seat in 1980 against eight formidable opponents (had a runoff, etc.) only because he walked door-to-door . . . twice. A man named Dan Weiser taught us both how to do it. It works.

D.A.: What kind of support system should a person have who is thinking of running for office?

L.M.: I can't imagine running for office without a strong family support system. There are two reasons. The campaign trail is an emotional roller coaster—each day has unexpected crises and pitfalls. Unfounded rumors about you get reported by the media. Money doesn't come in. Mistakes get made by the campaign team. You say dumb and regrettable things and can't take them back. Chaos in general. There are rarely nights that you don't come home either exasperated or sobbing. My husband was my rock. He cheered me, gave me great advice, and put everything into perspective because I knew all day every day that if I lost the election, my life would still be full and happy without the job.

Perspective is important in the shallow world of politics, which is built on the shaky foundations of ego and posturing. Sure you need a campaign manager (for three council elections and two mayoral elections I had my best girlfriend, Robyn, whom I trust implicitly). I only hired professional (and expensive) campaign handlers when I ran for mayor—a wonderful guy named Rob Allyn is honest and ethical and idealistic and became one of my closest friends because I loved talking to him and getting his advice. He cared about me, and I felt it every day. He did my TV ads, brochures, strategizing, press conference organizing, speech writing. Running for office in a city of 1.2 million people is just a whole heck of a lot more complicated than walking to twenty-four hundred homes and writing love notes. I feel extraordinarily lucky to have found Rob and convinced him (I had to beg him to represent me because he disagreed with everything I wrote about as a journalist and thought that helping me would ruin his political consulting career). As for the rest of my support group, I had Rob's staff (they become your buddies, including your bouncers on election night when things get crazy),

Robyn's husband, kids, and friends, who licked envelopes every night until midnight. And dozens of citizens appeared out of nowhere to assemble yard signs and place them (a critical part of the campaign) and gathered petition signatures and showed up at my paltry campaign events where every warm body in the room was grossly appreciated because the reporters are always counting.

D.A.: You were victorious in your run for office, but are there certain things you would have done differently?

L.M.: There are always day-to-day things a candidate would like to have done differently. There are hundreds of times I wish I had been more articulate, more focused, more engaging—less fuzzy, less pointed. The biggest question in any very competitive campaign is how negative and hard-swinging to be. There are no formulas that tell you the best way to do that. Because I often argued with the previous mayor when I was a council member, it was a great leap for some voters to see me as a coalition builder when I decided to run for mayor. It became the theme of my opponent's campaign. That's where having a good consultant comes in. He took my opponent's theme and turned it on its head: "My opponent accuses me of fighting with my predecessor. But he doesn't tell you what I was fighting for. I was fighting for *you*." And then I explained my platform of change. Big regrets? Nope.

D.A.: You were the dark horse who didn't have a chance of winning. How did you pull it off? What kind of personal satisfaction was there in knowing that you had turned the establishment upside down?

L.M.: It's interesting—I ran on a platform of change, and I had a formidable opponent (well-known, unblemished solid reputation, backed by the establishment, he raised more money—$2.2M versus my $1.7M as I recall). Plus he *looked* like a big-city mayor, and I didn't. I won for one reason: people wanted change at city hall. Yet when I got into office, I found that our city charter pretty well had my hands tied when it came to letting me implement change. The city manager ran everything—he'd been there twenty-four years, did everything pretty much the way he had always done it, despite decades of loud grousing about city services from residents. No city council had ever fired a city manager—in fact, I inherited a police chief who had created one scandal after another in the three years he had been chief, and the city manager wouldn't pull the trigger on him, and the city council wasn't doing anything about encouraging that firing either.

I spent my first two years creating task forces (on the Trinity River Project, housing, downtown development, city real-estate transactions, job creation), all in an attempt to turn glaring city problems around by pushing from the outside in (since I had no authority to do it from the inside). It was effective (only because the city manager didn't fight it by drawing a city charter line in the sand, which I appreciated), but it was also frustrating. One, because it all took an enormous amount of time and political capital; the city council ultimately had to embrace each committee's work or it was pointless. And two, if I was elected to change the way business was done at city hall, why not be able to do it? Although we impaneled a charter review commission to look at changing the form of government, the outcome was predictable: since each council member got to pick a member of the commission, and the council opposed a strong-mayor form of government because they believed it diluted their power, the commission opposed it too. Two years into my mayoral duties, the local newspaper hired a nationally recognized consulting firm to compare Dallas to other cities and published a twenty-page special section criticizing city hall and calling for . . . change. (But not for a strong-mayor form of government or a new city manager.)

D.A.: You have been elected and reelected but are known as a shoot-from-the-hip, no-nonsense leader. We know where you stand. What can other leaders/candidates learn from your candor?

L.M.: One of the comments I hear most from citizens is that they like me because I don't sound like a politician. I don't sound gauzy, smoky, two-sides-of-the-mouth, or in careful middle-of-the-road-don't-offend-anybody mode. I think like a journalist. I always hated interviewing an elected official and getting absolutely nothing out of it. Of course, I'm no longer a journalist. To be an effective leader, you have to remember that you're representing an entire city, and people want to be proud to say you are their mayor. You have to have a few rules when it comes to speaking. At least I do. (1) I don't swear publicly. As a journalist, I took pride in using profanity around my peers. (2) I don't criticize individuals, especially not my colleagues on the council. Even the person I'm most frustrated with professionally I don't criticize aggressively or make personal comments about. (3) Although I usually have my speeches written for me, I rarely read from them. I use them for background purposes (reading them on the way to the engagement) but always speak extemporaneously. There is nothing worse than an elected official who's reading from prepared scripts. It's boring. Everyone tunes out. It's cowardly. The best speakers speak from experience, knowledge, and passion. People always like to hear unscripted comments. Always. But I will read a speech occasionally if I'm not totally familiar with the material or it's a terribly formal event like a State of the City where I want to get all my facts in.

D.A.: I haven't asked you the obligatory "You're a woman playing in a man's playground" questions. Is there anything you really want to say on the subject?

L.M.: No. It makes no difference.

D.A.: Are you treated differently by friends and family now that you hold such a high office? If you are, do you notice that you have to create a "distance" with people so that you can adequately do your job? Do friends still feel like they can tell you exactly what they are thinking?

L.M.: My best friend is my husband, Steve. My second best friend is my sister Heather, who lives in Connecticut. My third best friend is my longtime campaign manager and fellow soccer-school-mom Robyn Mirsky. They are the only three people I tell everything to, and that hasn't changed. They are also very pointed about telling me everything they are thinking (including when I do too much "mayor stuff" in relation to family time), just as they always have when I was working as a council member and, before that, as a journalist.

What has changed completely—and this affects the family dynamic—is that I can no longer go anywhere without makeup. I used to go without makeup when I was just running errands around town—that's a thing of the past. I can't go anywhere without people recognizing me (that includes Italy, where my husband and I just took my kids for spring break . . . people from all over the DFW area stopped to talk to me in every city we visited). The downside to that is that my kids practically despaired over it because they feel we never have any quality time together. My eight-year-old will pound me with his fists when I turn to respond to someone in the grocery store or gas station or bookstore.

What my husband has said for all twenty-four years while he was in the Texas legislature rings true to me every day and keeps my work and family priorities balanced: When you leave elected office, you go from being a peacock to a feather duster. Nobody needs you. Nobody calls you. Nobody cares what you think. So you'd better have your family and friends intact and happy, or you're destined for a very lonely life. This is the bottom line. And it's great advice. So many politicians get insanely disproportionate egos when they get elected and mistakenly believe they are somebody. They they throw their families and friends under the bus. It's lonely for them when it's all over. It's so important to remember that, at its base, politics is just the exercise of people wanting to use you to get something for themselves. It's all shallow, orchestrated flattery and fawning. You have to be able to keep it in perspective while you're going through it. If you don't, you become a bad politician and a worse parent and spouse.

D.A.: What is the best way for a citizen to contact you? How can we be assured that you are getting our messages? Are there things a citizen will do to get noticed by you that make you *not* want to respond?

L.M.: There is nothing that I won't respond to—except e-mails or letters containing profanity or racial or sexual orientation slurs. Sometimes I diplomatically rebuff those e-mails (occasionally strenuously rebuff them if they touch a nerve with me), but most of the time I ignore them. All criticisms and complaints are welcome. I read all my e-mail and respond to all of it, and I respond to letters that require or cry for a response. Phone calls are hard to answer in a timely fashion. Sometimes an e-mail or letter causes me to pick up the phone and call the person—that always surprises people. (A lady with a long-leaking and eventually disconnected fire hydrant got a call from me recently. And that hydrant was fixed the next week.) E-mail is the best device to get me. I'm always carrying a folder of e-mail to respond to.

D.A.: What is the one thing you wish you would have known before tossing your hat in the ring?

L.M.: When I ran for city council the first time in 1998 I wish I had known how closed a society city hall really is. I had this vision of collaboration and teamship on every single council issue—that if I had a new perspective on an issue (in part from my ability as an investigative reporter to find and amass new information), my colleagues would greet me warmly and welcome my contributions and energy. Wrong. Of course, it didn't help that I had written unsavory things about half the council. Or that I still carried a reporter notebook around with me wherever I went.

When I did do some issue digging, and stayed up half the night to write it up for my colleagues for a meeting the next day, they recoiled when I handed it out. It taught me (the hard way, because I never succeeded in building coalitions until I became mayor and made it my number-one priority) that the group dynamic is key in politics if you want to accomplish anything. Establishing trust is what gives you successes, not finding the best or most information. My unique, anti-political background in journalism—a world where everything is black or white, right or wrong—gave me a very slow learning curve when it comes to politics. But then I'm still learning. Every day is a new goal and a new strategy on how to get the consensus to get there.

D.A.: Now that you have tasted political victory, do you daydream of shooting for a higher office? Governor? Congress? The White House?

L.M.: The only political race I may do after this is reelection for mayor. I'm so determined to turn Dallas around—and I know I can do it—but it will take longer than just the next three years (the rest of my term) to do it. As a journalist, city politics was always my fascination—never state or local issues that tend to be more policy-driven and less interesting to me. I want the potholes filled, the trash picked up on time, flowers in the medians, no empty buildings, big street carnivals, and safe and pretty neighborhoods. That's what turns me on.

22

. . . .

Q&A WITH POLITICAL PROS

Elected leaders who forget how they got there won't the next time.

—MALCOLM S. FORBES

BEFORE YOU SERIOUSLY TOY with the idea of running for elected office, you need to have a general understanding of the lay of the land. You will find a variety of sources in this section and in the appendixes that are aimed at giving you the needed details, but there is nothing better than to have insiders share candid answers.

I asked two seasoned political pros to share a few of the ins and outs: John Gonzales, a shoot-from-the-hip communicator, and Charles Bauer, best known for his organizational prowess.

Let's go to John Gonzales for the first set of questions. He is the district director for Congressman Michael Burgess and worked as deputy regional director and deputy state director of constituent services for Senator Kay Bailey Hutchison and performed similar duties for Senator Phil Gramm. He has also worked on several campaigns, including Gramm's reelection campaign and the 1992 reelection campaign of George H. W. Bush and Dan Quayle.

D.A.: I want to run for an elected office. What are the typical steps in the process?

J.G.: Tell people. Your family, friends, and neighbors. If you belong to the local Rotary, Chamber of Commerce, or Association, share the news. You have to build a foundation of support and trust. This takes time and volunteer hours.

D.A.: How do I get publicity?

J.G.: You have to create your own publicity. You don't need television, radio, or print publicity in the beginning. Walk the neighborhoods door-to-door, passing out information about your candidacy and who you are. Ask groups if you can attend or speak at one of their meetings.

D.A.: How do I raise funds?

J.G.: Ask. Asking people not only to support you but to give you money is probably one of the most difficult aspects of running for elected office. Money is the mother's milk of politics. It isn't a guarantee for success, but if you don't have money, people will not take you seriously. So if you don't have your own money, marry someone who does. Ask friends to host coffees and/or get-to-know-you events at their homes.

D.A.: How important is it for me to join forces with a particular party?

J.G.: Very important. You have to meet the local party chairman. Yes . . . kiss the ring. The two-party system makes it very, very difficult not to be affiliated with one. The party can make you and/or break you. The local Democrat or Republican Party office controls a wealth of information. They gather names; track events, donors, and volunteers; share information with smaller political groups such as the Pachyderms, Republican Forum clubs, Young Republicans, and area specific groups (i.e., the county chapter of a party organization).

D.A.: How important is it for me to have a background in politics? What if I have never served in office but have a passion to run for a state or national post? Describe the obstacles.

J.G.: It is important to have a background in party politics but not necessarily politics. If you have a passion to run for elected office, then start with number one on this list.

D.A.: Where do I go to find volunteers?

J.G.: The first place to look for volunteers are your family and friends. But the owner of volunteers is the local party. The party has hundreds of names and contacts and can direct all the little old ladies who will do anything to get out of the house, drink some free coffee, and chat with their friends.

D.A.: What is the dumbest thing I could do as I gear up?

J.G.: Forget to tell your spouse. Avoid renting office space and purchasing expensive equipment or printing.

D.A.: What is the smartest thing I could do as I gear up?

J.G.: Tell your spouse. Meet with a political consultant. This will save you time and money.

D.A.: What personal advice would you give me?

J.G.: A very small percentage of voters will determine whether you win or lose. You have to focus on registered voters. You will be wasting your time and money trying to convince people to register to vote for you before you've been elected. Work on that in your second term. Getting your base to the polls on election day will make the difference. The local party activists will make life easier; however, your own foundation of loyal family, friends, and neighbors is the most important base you can have. Your own voting bloc will get people's attention. Passion is great . . . money is great . . . party support is great, but people will vote for someone who has built personal relationships on a foundation of trust and honesty. Likability really helps too. Get your voters out, and other voters will follow. If you build it . . .

ANOTHER PERSPECTIVE

Charles Bauer is the chief of staff for Texas operations in the office of Congressman Pete Sessions, having served the congressman through his loss in 1994 to his win in 1996. Chuck served as Session's deputy chief of staff in Washington, D.C., for two years before moving back to Texas to run things locally. He also served as volunteer advance staff for Speaker of the House Newt Gingrich in 1998.

D.A.: Charles, I don't want to just watch from the sidelines anymore. I want to run for office so I can make a difference. Any thoughts?

C.B.: Running for political office is a life-changing, rewarding, frustrating, exhilarating, and difficult experience. It provides you an opportunity to meet hundreds, if not thousands, of people who you would never have met before. And running for office provides a platform for you to express your views about the direction of your city, state, and/or federal government. Being a candidate will teach you things about your personal resolve, inner strength, and allow you to do things you never thought possible, like public speaking, debating, and interacting with strangers.

D.A.: I don't have a clue what to do first.

C.B.: The easiest thing to do is to get on the ballot. Most elections are partisan contests between the two major parties, Republicans and Democrats. Each party will have a primary. To become a candidate, generally, all you have to do is fill out an application and submit a check made out in the proper amount to the party, and your name is on the ballot. Different offices have different requirements, so some background research may be required to ensure you are qualified to run for that particular position. There are other options, including petitions in lieu of a filing fee, which for Congress requires that you get five hundred signatures from registered voters within the district, and that waives the filing fee.

D.A.: So getting on the ballot puts me in the game? Well, let's go.

C.B.: While filing to be on the ballot seems easy, this is not a decision that comes lightly. The decision to run, if taken seriously, will impact your life for the entire campaign cycle. You become a public figure, people have expectations that you will be at certain events and you will behave in a certain manner. Everything you do will be scrutinized. Plus there is always somewhere to be, and people expect you to be everywhere all the time. There is a breakfast somewhere every morning and a dinner somewhere every evening, six and seven days a week.

D.A.: It seems like people running for office know a lot about everything. What if I am on a mission to change just a few things?

C.B.: Most likely there are one or two specific things that have motivated you to run for office, whether it was something happening in Congress (i.e., tax cuts or tax increases), the state house (school finance), or the city council (increased funding for parks), this is your opportunity to make a difference. It is likely that your passion for this particular issue has been discussed around the breakfast table, among friends, in the halls of your church, and at social gatherings.

D.A.: Money, organization, and contacts—where do I start?

C.B.: My first direction to a potential candidate is to take a weekend and write down on a single sheet of paper the names of every person you know who lives in and around the district and how you know them. Then categorize them (i.e., potential for money, helpful with other people, worker bee, etc.). Prioritize the list and pick the top five to ten people that you are closest to and feel the most comfortable. Ask to visit with them, and pitch them with the idea, asking for their vote and for financial support. If you can't get your closest friends to support you, how are you going to convince people that don't know you that you are the person for the job?

D.A.: Who do I look to for help?

C.B.: If you have a relationship with any elected officials, I would suggest that you find time to sit down with them and ask for their input and advice. Next, I would sit down with the local chairman of the party you align with or the primary you plan to run in. Sell him on your candidacy, ask for his support, and ask for the key people you should meet with to lay the foundation for your campaign. In essence, the embryonic stages of a campaign are giant networking exercises. In fact, most of campaign life is just a giant networking exercise, trying to meet as many people as possible who will vote for you and make a financial contribution to support you.

Getting involved in the retail side of politics—volunteering, contributing, and making relationships with the Democratic or Republican Party—is essential in my mind because it helps you understand who the players are that help make things happen, gives you a recognizable face as someone who has been supporting the party, and gives you credibility within the party. This can be sweat equity, thus not limiting candidates to those who have the big bucks.

D.A.: I have to face it: I'm a novice. Do I really have a chance?

C.B.: Having never run for office does not preclude you from being successful. Obviously, starting out by running for Congress requires that you have been active in either charitable or civic organizations or have been deeply involved in the party, because these campaigns are highly competitive races in which many high-profile people want to run and current elected officials try to step up. So the stakes are high. But that's not to say it can't be done.

D.A.: If I run, I want to win.

C.B.: The three keys to a successful campaign are money, message, and media, in that order. Without money, you can't get your message out and don't have money for media. Money must first come from the list of people you compiled. If you've been involved in politics or a party, you will know or recognize the top twenty-five to fifty money names you need to call in town to solicit support for your campaign. The key is to collect the names of people who will support you and then put together a coffee. If you get a big name behind you, like an elected representative, ask him to be the special guest at a reception. Ask everyone you meet at these functions to support your campaign. Twenty-five-dollar checks add up if you collect enough of them. Most important, learn the rules surrounding finances, so you don't make any mistakes and you know exactly how much people can donate.

D.A.: Great, that's money. What was the other one?

C.B.: Message—as I suggested earlier, there are probably one or two events that pushed you to run for office. That means you are very passionate and can articulate your beliefs on that issue well. Study up on all the issues in the race so you can speak to them, but find three issues that you want to drill home, know them inside and out, and learn how to speak about those three issues in every conversation you have. Test the three issues on your closest friends to make sure you know you are hitting three hot-button issues for the race, not just your three hot-button issues. For example, manned exploration to Mars may be critical to you, but where is it on anyone else's radar?

D.A.: And media?

C.B.: To get publicity. Once you put together a solid team, hold a kickoff press conference. Send press kits about you to all of the media outlets. Determine what shows and reporters cover politics. Try to set up time to visit with them over the phone or make appointments for personal visits to get them interested in your candidacy and to see if they will cover your race and campaign events.

THE EVEN DOZEN RULES TO VICTORY ACCORDING TO CHARLES BAUER

1. Anyone can run. Make sure your head and heart are in the right place. If you aren't committed, it will be hard to get people passionate about your candidacy.
2. Make sure you vote in every election.
3. Learn the campaign rules surrounding your race.
4. Determine what party you want to belong to and get active.
5. Make sure you are also active in charitable and civic organizations.
6. List out your closest friends and sign them up first.
7. Ask everyone you meet for their vote and for a contribution. You can't afford to be shy about asking for money.
8. Ask everyone you meet for five people they know who you should call.
9. Network, network, network.

10. Determine what you believe in, stick to your message, and hammer it home.

11. Figure out your plan toward victory, and don't let anyone or anything sway you off course.

12. Keep detailed notes and create a database of all the people you meet (a simple spreadsheet will work).

IT'S YOUR GOVERNMENT

I don't make jokes. I just watch the government and
report the facts.—WILL ROGERS

This limited list of websites will get you started when you decide that it is time to contact your local, state, or federal government about an issue. Treat these links and addresses as nothing more than a "get to know you" session for your government because there are more than a thousand federal agencies and tens of thousands more at the state and local levels. Do not give up hope about finding what you want or the department you need. One good thing about the government: since it breeds so many bureaucracies, you should be able to track down whatever you need to even the most obscure agency.

GETTING STARTED

These first four sites may be the only ones you ever need because of their exhaustive coverage of departments, links, addresses, and search details. As a talk-show host, I couldn't get by without these quick and friendly sites when I'm researching some hot topic.

www.firstgov.gov: This is a first-stop website that has contact information for almost every aspect of American government.

http://thomas.loc.gov/: One of the best government-maintained search engines for all things governmental, including all bills, activity in the House and Senate, law changes, the Congressional Record, and much more.

http://clerk.house.gov/: The Office of the Clerk online information center. You can obtain copies of House documents, including public disclosure forms, made available by the clerk as part of his official duties. You can also find quick links to:

House floor proceedings	roll call votes
bill summary and status	conference committee reports
congressional biographical directory	Congressional Record
Federal Register	House calendar
how our laws are made	lobbying registration information
member office mailing labels	

http://www.statelocalgov.net/: A privately maintained website with links to state and local government agencies nationwide. One of the most comprehensive government websites available.

CONTACTING SPECIFIC GOVERNMENT OFFICES

The White House

http://www.whitehouse.gov/
The White House website includes up-to-the-minute information about current issues, news events, appointments and nominations, offices, and major speeches. This is the first place to look for the latest information on the executive branch.

The White House
1600 Pennsylvania Avenue, NW
Washington, DC 20500
Comments: 202-456-1111
Switchboard: 202-456-1414
Fax: 202-456-2461
E-mail: president@whitehouse.gov

Legislative Branch

http://thomas.loc.gov/home/legbranch/legbranch.html
Contains information on the organization, history, and structure of the legislative branch. Also provides a list of legislative agencies and commissions and a congressional directory an links to Senate and senators' websites.

http://www.senate.gov/
The official site of the U.S. Senate with members, biographies, contact information, and a rudimentary tracking tool.

http://www.house.gov/
The official site of the U.S. House of Representatives.

Judicial Branch

http://www.uscourts.gov/
From the website: "This page is maintained by the Administrative Office of the U.S. Courts on behalf of the U.S. Courts. The purpose of this site is to function as a clearinghouse for information from and about the Judicial Branch of the U.S. Government." You may contact various offices of the judicial branch via this website or by phone. To reach the Administrative Office of the U.S. Courts, Office of Public Affairs, call 202-502-2600. Or write to Office of Public Affairs, Administrative Office of the U.S. Courts, Washington, DC 20544.

Department of Defense

http://www.defenselink.mil/
The site provides the latest information from the Department of Defense, including press releases, website links, and updated information on the War on Terror. You may e-mail directly from the website or send regular mail to:

Honorable Donald H. Rumsfeld
Secretary of Defense
1000 Defense Pentagon
Washington, DC 20301

Directorate for Public Inquiry and Analysis
Office of the Secretary of Defense (Public Affairs)
Room 3A750—The Pentagon
1400 Defense Pentagon
Washington, DC 20301-1400

Federal Bureau of Investigation

http://www.fbi.gov/
The FBI is the investigative arm of the Department of Justice. This website includes information about how to apply for a job, submit a tip, and information about the various programs and history of the FBI. You may also find contact information for local field offices. You may contact the FBI via this website or through regular mail:

Federal Bureau of Investigation
J. Edgar Hoover Building
935 Pennsylvania Avenue, NW
Washington, DC 20535-0001
Phone: 202-324-3000

Homeland Security Department

http://www.dhs.gov/dhspublic/
From the website: "We will lead the unified national effort to secure America. We will prevent and deter terrorist attacks and protect against and respond to threats and hazards to the nation. We will ensure safe and secure borders, welcome lawful immigrants and visitors, and promote the free-flow of commerce." You may contact the Department of Homeland Security via this website or by mail:

U.S. Department of Homeland Security
Washington, DC 20528

Central Intelligence Agency

http://www.cia.gov/
From the website: "We support the President, the National Security Council, and all who make and execute US national security policy by providing accurate, evidence-based, comprehensive, and timely foreign intelligence related to national security; and conducting counterintelligence activities, special activities, and other functions related to foreign intelligence and national security as directed by the President."

Central Intelligence Agency
Office of Public Affairs
Washington, DC 20505
Phone: 703-482-0623
Hours: 7:00 a.m. to 5:00 p.m., U.S. Eastern time
Fax: 703-482-1739
Hours: 7:00 a.m. to 5:00 p.m., U.S. Eastern time
(Please include a phone number for callback.)

Alcohol, Tobacco, Firearms and Explosives

http://www.atf.gov/
The Department of Alcohol, Tobacco, Firearms and Explosives is a branch of the Department of Justice. You may contact certain departments via this website. From the website: "The Bureau of Alcohol, Tobacco, Firearms and Explosives cannot respond to e-mail inquiries relating to technical, policy and/or legal questions. Inquiries of this nature can only be addressed through a letter outlining your questions to the following address":

Bureau of Alcohol, Tobacco, Firearms and Explosives
Office of Public and Governmental Affairs
650 Massachusetts Avenue, NW
Room 8290
Washington, DC 20226

Social Security Administration

http://www.ssa.gov/
This official website includes current information, news releases, and publications. From the website: "The Social Security Administration is the Nation's primary income security agency. It administers the Federal retirement, survivors and disability insurance programs, as well as the program of supplemen-

tal security income (SSI) for the aged, blind and disabled, and performs certain functions with respect to the black lung benefits program. SSA also directs the aid to the aged, blind and disabled in Guam, Puerto Rico and the Virgin Islands." Jo Anne B. Barnhart serves as the commissioner. You may contact the Social Security Administration via this website or by mail or phone (from a touchtone phone 7:00 a.m. to 7:00 p.m. EST: 1-800-772-1213).

Social Security Administration
Office of Public Inquiries
Windsor Park Building
6401 Security Boulevard
Baltimore, MD 21235

Internal Revenue Service

http://www.irs.gov/
Contains current information about the IRS, its scope, and its organization. You may also access forms and publications from this site. The site suggests you contact your local office with questions. You may most efficiently access the IRS through the website's "contact us" link.

Department of Education

http://www.ed.gov/index.jhtml
The stated purpose of the Department of Education is "Promoting excellence in education for all Americans." This website contains information about current laws and information about financial aid and grants, etc.
E-mail: customerservice@inet.ed.gov
Phone: 1-800-USA-LEARN (1-800-872-5327)
TTY: 1-800-437-0833
Fax: 202-401-0689

U.S. Department of Education
400 Maryland Avenue, SW
Washington, DC 20202

No Child Left Behind
E-mail: NoChildLeftBehind@edu.gov
Phone: 1-888-814-NCLB (1-888-814-6252)
TTY: 1-800-437-0833
Fax: 202-401-0689

Centers for Disease Control and Prevention

http://www.cdc.gov/
From the website: "The Centers for Disease Control and Prevention (CDC) is recognized as the lead federal agency for protecting the health and safety of people—at home and abroad, providing credible information to enhance health decisions, and promoting health through strong partnerships. CDC serves as the national focus for developing and applying disease prevention and control, environmental health, and health promotion and education activities designed to improve the health of the people of the United States." Contact via this website or by phone:

Hotlines:
National AIDS Hotline: 1-800-342-2437
National HIV/AIDS Hotline (Spanish): 1-800-344-7432
National Immunization Hotline (English): 1-800-232-2522
National Immunization Hotline (Spanish): 1-800-232-0233
National STD Hotline: 1-800-227-8922
Traveler's Health: 1-877-394-8747

Office of Management and Budget

http://www.whitehouse.gov/omb/
Contains updated information on the president's budget, management agenda, agency audits, and various departments supporting the president's budget policy.

The Office of Management and Budget
725 17th Street, NW
Washington, DC 20503
Fax: 202-395-3888
Information: 202-395-3080
Jobs website: http://www.usajobs.opm.gov/

General Accounting Office

http://www.gao.gov/
The official site for the General Accounting Office with access to key information about the U.S. budget, political spending habits, and a link to report fraud and abuse by your elected officials.

23

• •

PEOPLE CAN MAKE
A DIFFERENCE,
EVEN IN AMERICA

Write injuries in dust, benefits in marble.
—BENJAMIN FRANKLIN

IN ISRAEL THERE IS a body of water known as the Dead Sea. So concentrated is its salt and mineral content (no other body of water in the world has more) that a person cannot sink underwater. With this one-of-a-kind phenomenon comes another: nothing can live in it. It is dead. When asked why, scientists explain that the Dead Sea is carved out in such a way that water flows freely into it but it has no outlet. It loses the value of the fresh water and becomes a stagnant pool of rich resources with no life.

In a way, America is like that sea. We have the greatest resources, wealth, opportunities, and freedoms on the planet, yet many of us bathe in our splendor and share nothing with others. Things flow to us. We horde them.

One of the greatest things about reclaiming the spirit that is America is that we still have the ability to look back and recall how things used to be. Cooperation, volunteerism, and neighbor-helping-neighbor concepts were keys to our success. We have to find a way to reinvent ourselves, using those character traits both for the good of our nation and the perspectives that others have about us.

"People can make a difference, even in America." That was the headline blaring from the British newspaper I was reading, and I could feel the blood drain from my head. *What undeniable trash talk*, I thought. How dare they suggest that somehow, in spite of ourselves, we were still a benevolent nation? Later, after thinking about it awhile, the headline made sense—at least from a non-U.S. perspective.

Many parts of the world see America as greedy, lust-driven, and lawless. They don't have images of George W. Bush as a sheriff in a make-believe cowboy town for nothing. So, of course, when they see good things coming from our nation, they are able to take their focus off our government and put it back on our people—which is where it rightly belongs anyway. That British headline caused me to realize that *we* are the ones who have always made the difference, not our bureaucratic programs. We have to get back into the game.

This section is all about reclaiming that which rightfully belongs to us via the vote, civic involvement, and volunteerism. Every one of us has a unique gift or talent that we can share with others for a few hours a week and enrich our own lives as well as change them.

Read how just a few of our country's charities and movements got their start. They are in no particular order, but there is a noticeable thread running through each. See if you can catch what it is, and I'll have the answer at the end of this section.

MAKE-A-WISH FOUNDATION

MOST OF us have heard of the Make-A-Wish Foundation, a program that has served up more than 110,000 wishes for terminally ill children. Most probably believe it started as some corporation's "feel good" mission. Not true. U.S. Customs officer Tommy Austin became friends with Linda Greicius and her very ill seven-year-old son, Chris. From the time he saw Tommy, Chris loved everything there was about police work, yelling, "Freeze, I'm a cop!" at their first meeting. Tommy had promised Chris a ride in a police helicopter, and in the spring of 1980—when Chris's physical condition worsened—Tommy contacted the Arizona Department of Public Safety (DPS) about making Chris's wish come true. DPS arranged for a helicopter to pick up Chris and escort him around the city of Phoenix, landing at the DPS. Chris was even sworn in as the first ever and only honorary state trooper in Arizona history.

On May 2, 1980, Chris was back in the hospital. He was so proud and happy about being a patrolman, he asked that a uniform the officers had made for him be hung in the window of his room and his motorcycle helmet and "Smokey the Bear" hat be placed on his dresser so he could see them. The following day Chris Greicius died, but not before having realized his greatest dream. When DPS officer Scott Stahl and officer Frank Shankwitz were returning from Chris's funeral, they began reflecting on Chris's magical experience. They saw how happy Chris was that his wish had come true, and that the wish seemed to take some of Chris's and Linda's pain away—replacing the anguish with smiles and laughter. They thought that if one boy's wish could be granted, maybe the same could be done for other children. At that moment the idea of the Make-A-Wish Foundation was born.

THE SUSAN G. KOMEN BREAST CANCER FOUNDATION

BEST KNOWN for the Susan G. Komen Race for the Cure, this charity program was born out of a promise to a dying woman. In 1980 Susan Goodman Komen fell victim to breast cancer at the age of thirty-six, and besides leaving a grieving husband and two children behind, her sister, Nancy Goodman Brinker, was devastated. Young women just were not supposed to die from breast cancer, and so Nancy made a promise to Susan to dedicate the rest of her life to breast cancer research, education, and treatment. Two years later Nancy established the Komen Foundation, which has become an international organization with a network of volunteers working through local chapters in 111 cities across the United States. Thanks to its volunteers and supporters, the Komen Foundation has raised more than $600 million to become the largest private funding charity of research dedicated solely to breast cancer in the United States.

RONALD McDONALD HOUSE

IN 1974 Philadelphia Eagles tight end Fred Hill's three-year-old daughter was diagnosed with leukemia. After spending countless sleepless nights in hospitals, along with many other parents, he and his wife worked to find a better solution. When he heard that Dr. Audrey Evans, head of the pediatric oncology unit at Children's Hospital of Philadelphia, had been dreaming of a house that could serve as a temporary residence for families whose children were being treated at the hospital, Hill rallied his teammates to raise funds to help families like his. The Ronald McDonald House was born.

Now, thirty years later, there are 211 houses in 19 countries with more than three million families helped. Ronald McDonald House Charities, a nonprofit 501(c)3, creates, finds, and supports programs that directly improve the health and well-being of children through its network of 173 local charities currently serving 44 countries. To date the charity has awarded more than $300 million to children's programs. All because one man could feel the pain that other families felt.

911 COMMISSION

THOUGH MUCH of it turned into a partisan slugfest, the congressional commission that was set up in early 2004 to look into the horrific terrorist attacks on September 11, 2001, would never have happened had it not been for a few family members of victims who refused to back down. The families were told there would be no commission hearings and no top officials testifying. Someone apparently forgot to ask the family members if this was okay with them, because they immediately took their stories to radio, television, and newspapers.

"There's no question that the momentum for the creation of the commission came from the family groups," said commission spokesman Al Felzenberg. "That's beyond dispute." Stephen Push, whose wife, Lisa Raines, was on the plane that hit the Pentagon, says family members spent more than a year "slogging through Congress" and demanding an independent hearing. "We were told we were dead in the water, and that we should forget about it. They were opposed to any investigation whatsoever." After the Senate voted 90-8 in favor of the commission, the family members saw the kind of response they were looking for. These were just average citizens who were impacted by an extraordinary life-changing event, and they used their newfound prowess on government to get what they wanted.

MOTHERS AGAINST DRUNK DRIVING (MADD)

MADD WAS founded in 1980 by two small groups of women on opposite coasts of the United States. Enraged after her five-and-a-half-month-old daughter became one of the world's youngest quadriplegics when a repeat drunk-driving offender traveling at more than 120 mph slammed into her vehicle, Cindi Lamb and her friends waged a war against drunk driving in their home state of Maryland. Less than a year later thirteen-year-old California resident Cari Lightner was killed at the hands of a drunk driver. Just two days prior the offender had been released on bail for a hit-and-run drunk-driving crash. He already had two drunk-driving convictions with a third plea-bargained to reckless accident. At the time of Cari's death, the drunk-driving offender was carrying a valid California driver's license.

In Sacramento, Cari's mother, Candace Lightner, gathered friends to discuss forming a citizen's group to fight drunk driving. Thus MADD was born with a name that would sweep the nation. Today it is the largest crime victims' assistance organization in the world with more than three million members and supporters. According to the group, alcohol-related traffic fatalities have declined by 43 percent.

BIG BROTHERS BIG SISTERS

IT WAS the turn of the century and Ernest Coulter, a clerk of the juvenile court in New York City, had had enough. Every day he went to work he saw more and more young people going the route of crime and jail because they didn't have positive influences in their lives. Coulter told friends that his heart broke daily. He asked a group of civic leaders and businessmen to join him at a hastily called meeting where Coulter hoped to garner some support for an idea. At that December 4, 1904, meeting, Coulter appealed to those present to take on the role of a Big Brother. He wanted each man to agree to befriend one boy who had been in trouble. All forty men present stepped forward, creating the movement that is now Big Brothers Big Sisters of America. Today the program, which matches caring adults with children ages five to eighteen years old in one-to-one relationships, has five hundred agencies in more than five thousand communities across America.

HABITAT FOR HUMANITY INTERNATIONAL

IN 1965 Millard and Linda Fuller visited Koinonia, a small farm outside Americus, Georgia. What they saw there became a life-changing experience for them and the Christian farm's director, Clarence Jordan. Fuller and Jordan collaborated on an idea they called "partnership housing"—where those in need of adequate shelter would work side by side with volunteers to build simple, decent houses. In 1968 Koinonia laid out forty-two half-acre house sites, with four acres reserved as a community park and recreational area. Capital was donated from around the country to start the work. Homes were built and sold to needy families at no profit and no interest. The basic model of Habitat for Humanity was begun. In September 1976 the Fullers called together a group of supporters to discuss the future of their dream. Habitat for Humanity International (HFHI) as an organization was born at this meeting.

Their program gained nationwide interest when, in 1984, former U.S. President Jimmy Carter and his wife, Rosalynn, took their first Habitat work trip. Since its founding in 1976, Habitat for Humanity International has built and rehabilitated more than 125,000 houses sheltering more than 625,000 people in some 3,000 communities worldwide.

PRISON FELLOWSHIP INTERNATIONAL

PRISON FELLOWSHIP International was founded in 1976 as a way of reaching out to the country's prison population. Its founder, Chuck Colson, knew the need firsthand because he had just been released from prison after serving time for a Watergate-related conviction. By 1980 representatives from Prison Fellowship groups could be found in Australia, Canada, England, New Zealand, and the Bahamas. And since that time PFI has seen organizations develop in more than 105 countries around the world. It is the world's largest Christian ministry working in the criminal justice field. Colson could have come out of prison with a chip on his shoulder as one of a few to face the fallout of Richard Nixon's Watergate. Instead, he knew what the "power of one" would do for the world.

OPERATION IRAQI CHILDREN

ACTOR GARY SINISE (*Forrest Gump, Apollo 13*) toured Iraq after Operation Iraqi Freedom and was surprised to see how dilapidated the schools were in the land of Saddam Hussein. When he returned home, he contacted his daughter's school with the hope that it would help collect some supplies to send to Iraq. The school came through with twenty boxes, and the Sinise family was elated. He then teamed with friend and author Laura Hillenbrand (*Seabiscuit: An American Legend*) to create Operation Iraqi Children, a program that enables Americans to send school supplies and Arabic translations of *Seabiscuit* to Iraqi children.

"Imagine sending your child to a school in which there are virtually no books, no pencils, no paper, no blackboards," says Hillenbrand. "This is the reality for Iraqi children. The future of the Iraqi nation is being squandered for lack of basic school supplies." The American soldiers will bring these gifts to them and will win the Iraqi people's goodwill, admiration, and trust. Over and over again, they will hear the words like those that one Iraqi parent spoke to a soldier as his child opened a box of supplies from America: "We will never forget this day."

FARM AID

IN 1985 America's farms were in crisis as properties were failing in record numbers. A group of musicians like Willie Nelson and Neil Young decided to do something about it and created a concert experience that could be used to raise funds to help the nation's farmers. Since the first concert in September 1985, Farm Aid has been committed to providing real help to rural America and family farmers through direct aid, credit and financial counseling, and supporting efforts to strengthen family farm agriculture. Farm Aid has raised more than $24 million to support its mission in the midst of a massive farm crisis through a group of dedicated artists bound together to support the rural communities that raised them.

SO WHAT about that thread I mentioned earlier? Figured it out? The simple answer: the American spirit still lives! You have just read about men and women from a hundred years ago and from today, rich and poor, in jail and out, educated and not so educated, happy and sad. All of them took what they knew and turned it into a way to help others. Tens of millions of people have been positively affected by the few short stories in this section, but the stories center on less than a dozen dreamers.

Start a project or find a group to join and do it. Before we can reclaim America, we must first decide that it's salvageable and that we can be part of the solution.

THE STARTING POINT FOR VOLUNTEERISM

The world is a dangerous place to live; not because of
the people who are evil, but because of the people
who don't do anything about it.
—ALBERT EINSTEIN

This is a short listing of charities, agencies, and service organizations where anyone who is willing to get involved can go to start the process. What you will find is that your gifts and abilities will manifest soon after you have plugged into a program. As you get an idea about the things you like and don't like, you will find new and exciting opportunities that never would have materialized if you had not made the effort to volunteer. It really doesn't matter where your strengths lie, there is a place for you. Community service, tax-cutting initiatives, feeding the poor, national service programs, and women's issues are five out of thousands of projects available, but you won't find one if you don't look for it.

The first section, One-Stop Volunteer Resources, is a great place to start your quest for service opportunities across America.

ONE-STOP VOLUNTEER RESOURCES

POINTS OF LIGHT FOUNDATION AND VOLUNTEER CENTER NATIONAL NETWORK

Website: http://www.pointsoflight.org/
An excellent resource for volunteer prospects of every kind.

50+ VOLUNTEERING

For information about 50+ volunteer initiatives utilizing the skills and abilities of older Americans, contact chjohnson@pointsoflight.org or call 202-729-3215.

Phone: 1-800-Volunteer.org
Website: http://www.1-800-volunteer.org/
Provides volunteers with a direct connection to local volunteer opportunities that match interests, skills, and the common desire to make a difference.

VOLUNTEER MATCH

Website: www.volunteermatch.org
A web-based service designed to help corporations better serve their communities. It is an easy way for employees to get involved in their communities and for corporations to manage and track results.

IDEALIST.ORG

Website: http://www.idealist.org/career.html
A one-stop volunteer and work preparation website.

FIRST GOV NONPROFIT

Website: http://www.firstgov.gov/Business/Nonprofit.shtml
An excellent resource to learn more about volunteering, nonprofits, and especially grant-writing techniques.

NPGUIDES

Website: http://www.npguides.org/guide/links.htm
A very good resource on raising funds for service and volunteer organizations.

THE VIRTUAL VOLUNTEERING PROJECT

Website: http://www.serviceleader.org/old/vv/
"To encourage and assist in the development and success of volunteer activities that can be completed, in whole or in part, via the Internet."

From the Virtual Volunteering website: "The Virtual Volunteering Project is the only organization of its kind: it encourages and assists in the development and success of volunteer activities that can be completed via the Internet, and help volunteer managers use cyberspace to work with ALL volunteers. The Project is not a matching service; instead, it builds the capacity of both agencies and volunteers, to make online service possible."

OUTDOOR SERVICE OPPORTUNITIES

U.S. ARMY CORP OF ENGINEERS VOLUNTEER CLEARINGHOUSE

Website: http://www.orn.usace.army.mil/volunteer/
From the webpage: "The U.S. Army Corps of Engineers Volunteer Clearinghouse is a nationwide, toll free hotline number for individuals who are interested in volunteering their time with the Corps. By calling the hotline a potential volunteer can express interest in any Corps project nationwide. The Clearinghouse in turn, gives the individual a point of contact for the area they have requested, as well as written information about volunteer opportunities there."

Opportunities include everything from campground host, trail construction and maintenance, docent, visitor center staff, to tour guides.

VOLUNTEER CLEARINGHOUSE, CELRN-OP-R

P.O. Box 1070
Nashville, TN 37202
Phone: 1-800-865-8337
Fax: 615-736-7643

VOLUNTEERS IN PARKS (NATIONAL PARK SERVICE)

Website: http://www.nps.gov/volunteer/index.htm
From the webpage: "The National Park Service Volunteers-In-Parks Program (VIP) was authorized by Public Law 91-357 enacted 1970. The primary purpose of the VIP program is to provide a vehicle through which the National Park Service can accept and utilize voluntary help and services from the public. The major objective of the program is to utilize this voluntary help in such a way that is mutually beneficial to the National Park Service and the volunteer."

VOLUNTEER FIRE (USDA FOREST SERVICE)

Assistance Program
Website: http://www.fs.fed.us/fire/partners/vfa/help/guide.htm
From the webpage: "The purpose of the Volunteer Fire Assistance (VFA) Program, formerly known as the Rural Community Fire Protection (RCFP) Program, is to provide Federal financial, technical, and other assistance to State Foresters and other appropriate officials to organize, train and equip fire departments in rural areas and rural communities to prevent and suppress fires. A rural community is defined as having 10,000 or less population. This 10,000 population limit for participation in the VFA Program facilitates distribution of available VFA funding to the most needy fire departments."

USDA FOREST SERVICE

Fire and Aviation Management
P.O. Box 96090
Washington, DC 20090-6090
Phone: 202-205-1503

ANIMAL RESCUE

AMERICAN SOCIETY FOR THE PREVENTION OF CRUELTY TO ANIMALS (ASPCA)

Website: http://www.aspca.org
"Our mission is to provide effective means for the prevention of cruelty to animals throughout the United States. We offer national programs in humane education, public awareness, government ad-

vocacy, shelter support, and animal medical services and placement. Our New York City headquarters houses a full-service animal hospital, behavior center, adoption facility, and Humane Law Enforcement Department. We are a privately funded 501(c)(3) not-for-profit corporation."

AMERICAN SOCIETY FOR THE PREVENTION OF CRUELTY TO ANIMALS (ASPCA)

424 E. 92nd Street
New York, NY 10128-6804

NATIONAL AND COMMUNITY SERVICE

Website: http://www.cns.gov/
The corporation's mission is to provide opportunities for Americans of all ages and backgrounds to engage in service.

OTHER OUTDOOR DISASTER PREPAREDNESS, VOLUNTEERING, AND VOLUNTEER MANAGEMENT OPPORTUNITIES

NATIONAL EMERGENCY MANAGEMENT ASSOCIATION

Website: http://www.nemaweb.org

NVOAD—NATIONAL VOLUNTARY ORGANIZATIONS ACTIVE IN DISASTER

Website: http://www.nvoad.org/aboutnv.htm

AMERICAN RED CROSS

Website: http://www.redcross.org/services/disaster/

ASSOCIATION FOR VOLUNTEER ADMINISTRATION

Website: http://www.avaintl.org/education/edopps.html

CITIZEN CORPS

Website: http://www.citizencorps.gov

CITYCARES OF AMERICA

Website: http://citycares.org/national/network.asp

CORPORATION FOR NATIONAL AND COMMUNITY SERVICE

Website: http://www.nationalservice.org/news/homeland.html

INTERNATIONAL ASSOCIATION OF EMERGENCY MANAGERS

Website: http://www.iaem.com

INTERNATIONAL ASSOCIATION OF FIRE CHIEFS

Website: http://www.iafc.org/downloads/index.shtml

NATIONAL ASSOCIATION OF PLANNING COUNCILS

Website: http://www.communityplanning.org/meetour.htm

USA FREEDOM CORPS

Website: http://www.usafreedomcorps.gov

SOCIAL OUTREACH

HABITAT FOR HUMANITY INTERNATIONAL

Website: http://www.habitat.org/
Habitat for Humanity brings families and communities in need together with volunteers and resources to build quality affordable housing. Habitat homes are built with no profit made. Homeowners contribute "sweat equity" and housing payments are recycled into other homes.
121 Habitat Street
Americus, GA 31709-3498
Phone: 229-924-6935

AMERICORPS

Website: http://www.americorps.org/
From the website: "The Corporation for National and Community Service provides opportunities for Americans of all ages and backgrounds to serve their communities and country through three programs: Senior Corps, AmeriCorps, and Learn and Serve America. Members and volunteers serve with national and community nonprofit organizations, faith-based groups, schools, and local agencies to help meet community needs in education, the environment, public safety, homeland security, and other critical areas. The Corporation is part of USA Freedom Corps, a White House initiative to foster a culture of citizenship, service, and responsibility, and help all Americans answer the President's Call to Service."

NATIONAL AND COMMUNITY SERVICE HEADQUARTERS

Website: www.nationalservice.org
A national agency that promotes strong communities through volunteerism.

AMERICAN RED CROSS

Website: http://www.redcross.org/

From the website: "The Red Cross depends on volunteers, who constitute 97 percent of the total work force, to carry on their humanitarian work: 175,000 volunteers worked to prevent, prepare for and respond to nearly 64,000 disaster incidents last year."

Over 15 million Americans turn to the Red Cross to learn first aid, CPR, swimming, and other health and safety skills. Last year more than 230,000 people volunteered to teach those courses.

Half the nation's blood supply—six million pints annually—is collected by more than 190,000 Red Cross volunteers.

Among the emergency services for the men and women of the armed forces is the delivery of urgent family messages—one every 22 seconds.

More than 24,000 volunteers serve as chairs, members of boards of directors, or on advisory boards for local Red Cross units—chapters, blood services regions, and military stations.

As part of the International Red Cross Movement, the organization works to ease human suffering on a global scale.

American Red Cross National Headquarters
2025 E Street, NW
Washington, DC 20006
Phone: (202) 303-4498

MEALS ON WHEELS

Website: http://www.mowaa.org/index.shtml

"The Meals On Wheels Association of America represents those who provide congregate and home-delivered meal services to people in need. Our mission is to provide visionary leadership and professional training, and to develop partnerships that will ensure the provision of quality nutrition services."

1414 Prince Street
Suite 302
Alexandria, VA 22314
Phone: 703-548-5558

MEDISEND INTERNATIONAL

Website: www.medisend.org

MediSend recycles medical surplus to developing countries. "Each year in the United States alone, more than $6 billion worth of medical surplus is generated. Normally, this surplus would be discarded, costing our health care system more than $700 million in disposal charges. For environmentally responsible humanitarians, MediSend is the organization that makes a direct, high-value impact to both its donors and recipients."

MediSend International
9244 Markville
Dallas, TX 75243
Phone: 214-575-5006

UNITED WAY

Website: http://national.unitedway.org/

From the website: "United Way of America is the national organization dedicated to leading the United Way movement in making a measurable impact in every community in America. The United Way movement includes approximately 1,400 community-based United Way organizations. Each is independent, separately incorporated and governed by local volunteers."

701 North Fairfax St.
Alexandria, VA 22314
Phone: 703-836-7112

EXTRA MILE

Website: http://www.extramile.us/

A tribute in honor of our country's greatest volunteers—those who have changed the world by going the extra mile for others.

FAMILY CARES

Website: www.familycares.org

Provides resources for parents, teachers, and community leaders who want to engage families in volunteer activities.

JOIN HANDS DAY—YOUTH AND ADULTS VOLUNTEERING TOGETHER

Website: http://www.joinhandsday.org/

A day of service that builds relationships between youth and adults while they work together to plan, organize, and implement volunteering activities in their communities.

THE RONALD McDONALD HOUSE CHARITIES

Website: http://www.rmhc.com/

Has awarded more than $400 million in grants worldwide to make an immediate and positive impact on as many children as possible.

AMERICA THE BEAUTIFUL

Website: http://www.america-the-beautiful.org/
A program dedicated to beautifying America.

ASSOCIATION OF JUNIOR LEAGUES, INTERNATIONAL (AJLI)

Website: http://www.ajli.org/
An organization of women committed to promoting volunteerism, developing the potential of women, and improving communities through the effective action of trained volunteers.

CITYCARES

Website: http://www.citycares.org/
An innovative alliance of volunteer organizations with 3,600 nonprofit organizations and schools across the country.

MISSIONFISH

Website: http://www.missionfish.org/
Helps nonprofits raise money on eBay. Through an exclusive relationship with eBay, the website makes it possible for sellers to donate some of their proceeds to nonprofits.

THE SALVATION ARMY

Website: http://www.salvationarmyusa.org/
An evangelical wing of the Universal Christian Church, its mission is to preach the gospel of Jesus Christ and meet personal needs without discrimination. Some of the services provided are housing for homeless people, vocational guidance, welfare-to-work programs, after-school programs, and character-building programs (boys and girls clubs-scouts).

VOLUNTEERING WITH YOUTH

BOYS AND GIRLS CLUBS OF AMERICA

Website: http://www.bgca.org/
To inspire and enable all young people, especially those from disadvantaged circumstances, to realize their full potential as productive, responsible, and caring citizens.

NATIONAL AND LOCAL MENTORING INITIATIVES

Website: http://www.mentoring.org/
A national program to promote mentoring with today's youth.

JUNIOR ACHIEVEMENT

Website: www.ja.org

"Junior Achievement uses hands-on experiences to help young people understand the economics of life. In partnership with business and educators, Junior Achievement brings the real world to students, opening their minds to their potential. After all, kids are our future."

Junior Achievement, Inc.
One Education Way
Colorado Springs, CO 80906
Phone: 719-540-8000
Fax: 719-540-6299
E-mail: newmedia@ja.org

BIG BROTHERS BIG SISTERS

Website: www.bbbsa.org

"Founded in 1904, Big Brothers Big Sisters is the oldest and largest youth mentoring organization in the United States." The long-term mission of Big Brothers Big Sisters is to help one million children by the year 2010. Today Big Brothers Big Sisters serves more than two hundred thousand children, ages six through eighteen, in five thousand communities across all fifty states.

Big Brothers Big Sisters National Office
230 North 13th Street
Philadelphia, PA 19107

KIDS CARE CLUBS

Website: http://www.kidscare.org/

Designed to develop compassion and the spirit of service and philanthropy in elementary- and middle-school-aged youth.

PRUDENTIAL YOUTH LEADERSHIP INSTITUTE

Website: http://www.pyli.org/

Provides youth with the encouragement, networks, and skills to make meaningful contributions to their communities and to learn how to become strong leaders.

CITIZENS' SCHOLARSHIP FOUNDATION

Website: http://www.csfa.org/

To support students.

AMERICA'S PROMISE

Website: http://www.americaspromise.org/
Mobilizing people to build the character and competence of the nation's youth.

YOUTH SERVICE AMERICA (YSA)

Website: http://www.ysa.org/
A resource center of more than three hundred organizations committed to increasing the quantity and quality of opportunities for young Americans to serve locally, nationally, or globally.

COMMUNITIES IN SCHOOLS

Website: http://www.cisnet.org/
Connects community resources with schools to help young people successfully learn, stay in school, and prepare for life.

MILITARY SUPPORT

USO

Website: www.uso.org
From the website: "The USO mission is to provide morale, welfare, and recreation-type services to uniformed military personnel. The original intent of Congress—and enduring style of USO delivery—is to represent the American people by extending a touch of home to the military. Thus, although some USO programs/services are similar to those provided by other agencies, the hallmark of the USO has been and will continue to be HOW—as much as WHAT—services are provided. Key focus/atmosphere/purpose differences are: nonprofit oriented v. profit-oriented; charitable v. business; volunteer v. employee emphasis."
Phone: 202-610-5700
For donations, contact 1-800-876-7469

OPERATION MILITARY PRIDE

Website: www.operationmilitarypride.org
A service organization dedicated to boosting the morale of deployed military personnel in a variety of ways including letters and care packages. Motto: "If it wears a uniform—We support it." The website also includes many links regarding the military.

THE DEPARTMENT OF VETERANS AFFAIRS

Website: http://www1.va.gov/volunteer/
A program that opens up volunteer opportunities for people wanting to help our nation's veterans.

VETERANS OF FOREIGN WARS OF THE UNITED STATES (VFW)

Website: http://www.vfw.org/

Provides support for programs that increase awareness of the sacrifices of veterans.

Don't forget to check out MarineMoms.org, NavyMoms.org, ProudArmyMoms.org, and Air-ForceMoms.org to see many other opportunities to serve our Americans in uniform.

24

. . . .

CAN I GET
A VOLUNTEER?

To keep a lamp burning we have to keep putting oil in it.
—MOTHER TERESA

VOLUNTEER AGENCIES AND SOCIAL organizations have their own way of finding, growing, and training volunteers, though almost all require that interested participants complete an application or questionnaire. Instead of trying to create an exhaustive commentary on the process, I spoke with a couple of people to get two perspectives on the mindsets of the leadership of these groups.

Celeste H. Faro is the executive director of the North Collin County Habitat for Humanity (www.ncc-habitat.com). Habitat for Humanity is a grass-roots organization managed by a local board of directors, volunteers, and an executive director. They sell homes at no profit to partner families with 0 percent interest mortgages for a fixed period of time. Currently a Habitat home in Faro's area costs an average of $60,000. Habitat relies on volunteer labor, donated materials, sponsor partners, and tax-deductible donations.

D.A.: Will the educational or work-related background of a volunteer dictate where he or she serves?

C.F.: Yes, we like to place volunteers according to their experience so that they will be satisfied and we will benefit from their expertise.

D.A.: What is the procedure for an individual volunteer to work with your organization?

C.F.: We have an application and a one-hour orientation, which includes a video about Habitat and a safety video for working on the building site. Volunteers also receive information about our local affiliate and where our volunteer needs are.

D.A.: What types of questions should a citizen ask before volunteering?

C.F.: Do I have time to dedicate to the organization? Is this a one-time volunteer opportunity or is this an ongoing program? What can I give to the organization? What do I hope to get out of volunteering?

D.A.: What percentage of volunteers go on to work for wages with your group?

C.F.: Since we only have one paid staff and are a 100 percent volunteer organization, less than 1 percent work for wages. In the future all positions created will come from current volunteers.

D.A.: When you get feedback, what are the two most fulfilling things people say they get from volunteering?

C.F.: Personal satisfaction, the chance to meet the families the home is being built for, and knowing that they are really making a difference on a very personal and local level.

D.A.: When you get feedback, what are the top two negatives they say about volunteer work?

C.F.: Not having enough opportunities to volunteer and lack of adequate training (mainly on building sites), since we have so many differently skilled volunteers.

D.A.: In your opinion, where are the top five areas where a person can volunteer and make a difference?

C.F.: In our organization: building, family support, family selection, fundraising, and the carpenter's club.

D.A.: If you receive funds from the state or federal government, how difficult is it to meet all of the bureaucratic demands?

C.F.: Just a lot of reporting requirements and huge amounts of paperwork to actually get the funds. It's worth it, though.

D.A.: Did you start in your position or work your way through the system?

C.F.: I started in my position but had worked for twelve years previously with other organizations.

D.A.: If you could get people to understand only one thing about volunteering, what would that one thing be?

C.F.: How personally rewarding it is.

D.A.: If you could change anything about volunteer-oriented programs, what would it be?

C.F.: More recognition for volunteers.

D.A.: What is the best way for you to get publicity?

C.F.: Have great relations with the media and constantly keep them informed of what we are doing. Come up with something different and unique.

Kelly J. Shackelford is president of the Free Market Foundation (www.freemarket.org) and chief counsel of its legal division. Free Market serves as the statewide public policy council associated with James Dobson's Focus on the Family.

Before joining the organization in 1997, Shackelford was the regional coordinator for the southwest and mid-America regions of the Rutherford Institute and the director of Texas Rutherford. He has argued before the U.S. Supreme Court and has testified before the U.S. Congress and the Texas legislature. Shackelford is routinely sought out by media outlets because of his expertise, including *Ankarlo Mornings*, NBC's *Today Show*, CNN, the National Associated Press, the *New York Times*, the *Washington Times*, the *Washington Post*, and the *L.A. Times*, among many others.

D.A.: Let's look at a citizen's involvement from a different perspective. I have three questions. What should I do first if I want to make a difference in the future of America?

K.S.: I would start by getting registered. Also get a voter's guide to help you vote. Almost every state has a good conservative guide—Focus on the Family has a list of their state-approved groups who have them. Get on an update list (like ours) to see what is actually going on. They need to find a good state group. Heritage.org is a good national site.

D.A.: Why are people reluctant to volunteer time or get directly involved in a way to create change?

K.S.: People are busy and intimidated because they feel they don't know much. The reality is that 98 percent of politics is just showing up. My answer to the first question above will start the process of changing this, especially the update list (like our weekly e-mail alert).

D.A.: The Free Market Foundation has been filling the gap for a long time. If my readers could take one thing away from a lesson you learned, what would it be?

K.S.: About ten years ago students at Southlake Carroll were given the freedom to do their own pep rallies. Attendance was not required, and it was run by students. During their time of speech, they decided to spend the last minute to pray for the safety of the players and families coming to and from the game.

The ACLU drafted a student to file a suit to stop this (so much for the ACLU believing in free speech). The case ended up in the court of a judge who was a former ACLU attorney. We met with and signed up as clients more than three hundred parents and kids in a meeting there. They were incensed. This was attacking the very reason many of them had moved to this conservative community.

We could not figure it out. How did an ACLU judge get elected in such a conservative area? The county Republican chair answered our question. Every Republican who had run for office in this conservative area was successful. When it came to the position of judge, the chair begged for someone to just put their name on the ballot. No one would.

The community got exactly what they deserved. Anyone just willing to put their name on the ballot would have had this prayer suit land on their desk instead of the ACLU.

That last answer demonstrates exactly how far we have drifted, by default, from our nation's heritage. Two hundred, one hundred, even fifty years ago, we would have seen willing participants line up to take the post if it meant saving a basic American freedom. Today we are lackadaisical, afraid, or too busy to see how we are slowly slipping into the abyss.

It doesn't matter where you get plugged in—just as long as you find someplace to serve.

You are the answer to our nation's needs.

25

· ·

A SOCCER DAD
COMES THROUGH

No winter lasts forever;
no spring skips its turn.

—HAL BORLAND

MﾠATTHEW SCHONHOFF HAD IT all—three great kids, a beautiful wife, his own business. He was his kid's soccer coach and lived in a great house, but something was missing. As a private investigator, he knew about life's ups and downs and possessed a driving will to make an impact. It kept pulling him in the direction of young people.

One day at church an idea kept pounding his brain. It was a concept he had only recently heard about, but he knew this was exactly what he was meant to do. The best part about it was how he could harness the power of volunteerism by linking it directly to local churches and families in need.

The ministry he eventually spearheaded is called Clothe A Child, and in a few short years it has already impacted thousands with a simple concept of caring. This is the spirit that built America—see a need and figure out a way to address it while allowing recipients to maintain their dignity.

D.A.: Matt, you are the executive director of Clothe A Child. Describe the program.

M.S.: Clothe A Child is a church-based community involvement program designed to meet the back-to-school clothing needs of underprivileged children in the community. Children are recommended for service in the program by their schools. Working closely with area churches and businesses, Clothe A Child raises donations and recruits volunteers for a one-day annual event. The children and their families come to a department store early one Saturday morning a few weeks after school starts and are matched with a volunteer who assists them in their shopping. It is a wonderful time of fellowship as each child enjoys the excitement of choosing new school clothes.

D.A.: What was going on in your life that caused you to get involved?

M.S.: My wife and I had just moved to the area and joined a church. I tried to get involved in several ministries, but they never seemed to fit my talents or desires. This was the first time I had ever been involved in any church activities other than attending. I had an overwhelming desire to lead and to start something new that would fit my passion: helping children. God brought this ministry to mind as a way to benefit local children. I contacted the church about duplicating their program locally, and they were more than willing to help. I received guidance and direction that first year. After the first year, much of what we did was directed by the ideas and talents of a small group of people who became involved at a much deeper level. This enabled us to tweak this program to serve many more children.

D.A.: Did you go into this thinking, *I'll help this year and move on*, or *This is a dream come true*? Why?

M.S.: When I approached a friend with the idea, he said, "Great! Go do it." In the beginning I had such a burning desire to make this work. It did not get off the ground in 1999, but we kept at it and God blessed our efforts in 2000. I took this very personally and poured everything I had into the program to make sure it was successful at helping the children. I have always had the attitude, right or wrong, that adults can do whatever they want. They can mess up and hurt themselves, but they just can't hurt the kids. My thought process was never that this is a dream come true; I was just consumed with making this program work. Each year I stood back to evaluate and saw that many more children applied than could be served. This was my motivation to continue pursuing every avenue possible to grow this ministry to make a larger impact each year.

D.A.: How did you get the news about your program to the masses?

M.S.: The first year we prayed. Truthfully. We went from twelve volunteers two days before the event to seventy-two volunteers at the event. In the years following we gave talks, put together fliers, and talked to anyone who would listen. Word of mouth and spheres of influence were huge. That is how we ended up at one of the discount department stores to start. That is how we got hooked up with a coffee shop and a doughnut chain to provide refreshments. Each year we approach new churches about partnering with us in our efforts.

D.A.: How do you get volunteers?

M.S.: Most come from area churches. CAC is promoted heavily during the summer months in the community churches. Volunteers from these churches help out on the morning of the event. We also have many volunteers who come through the school district. Many are teachers, counselors, principals, and students. Last year 435 volunteers helped at our local event. Of those, nearly 40 were high-school Spanish students. They were given the opportunity by their teacher to earn credit for their class by assisting Spanish-speaking families at the event. Many were so moved by the tangible experience of love that they volunteered to help at another event the next week.

D.A.: Did stores rush to work with you or brush you aside? How did you finally succeed?

M.S.: Stores did not rush to work with us. Initially, one of the department stories would not even talk to us since we weren't incorporated. Another was only interested in guarantees and what we could provide for them. We ended up at where we did that first year through my mentor. In a chance phone call she told me that one of the people who had helped to launch CAC in 1989 was now a store manager who would most certainly work with us. When that store eventually closed locally, God made it apparent which store we should call next. Interestingly, now that we are incorporated and have had so much success in our community, many stores want to work with us, including some very large department stores and retail chains.

D.A.: What is the role of the area churches in your efforts?

M.S.: They are absolutely vital. Nearly all our funds are raised in the area churches. Most of our volunteers come from the same churches. This program is the epitome of a church-based community ministry. Without church involvement, CAC could not have the impact it does today. It is my belief that CAC will always remain a church-based effort, because this is the only place I know of where the desire to help others permeates the entire congregation. Where else can you find more than four hundred volunteers eager to love others for four hours at 5:30 a.m. on a Saturday morning?

D.A.: How are you involved with the growth of the program elsewhere? Is it true this is spreading across America?

M.S.: CAC birthed its first expansion in 2003 to a neighboring city. That event clothed 208 children and involved more than 125 volunteers and 6 area churches. There are plans for further expansion to at least two more communities next year. We have had inquiries about CAC from churches as far away as Connecticut and Utah and are packing CAC as a ministry in a box that any church can pick up and utilize in their community. That should be ready by 2005. We are willing to assist any church that desires to bless their community through the framework of this ministry.

D.A.: What kind of reaction have you had from families who have been touched by Clothe A Child?

M.S.: My favorite question. The response has been overwhelmingly "Thank you. You will never know how much this means to us." CAC allows the families to maintain their dignity. There are no hand-me-downs. No worn clothes. No scuffed shoes. The families are provided with a voucher and a volunteer to help tabulate their totals. From there the families are free to address any and all of their clothing needs.

As a community-based program, many relationships have grown to the point that the volunteer and family keep in touch, allowing a personal and comfortable setting in which the family can continue to be helped. Many of our volunteers cry when they finish shopping with their families as they are so moved by the experience. Their love for serving others is reflected in their volunteering again each year. I hear feedback from our volunteers that they feel they have been blessed far more than the families they served.

Here are some of the letters we received from school administrators regarding the children served by CAC:

> You all really made a difference in one of my second graders. She was so excited to have something that was not a hand-me-down that she modeled her new clothes every day that she wore them. Her teacher thanked me for that because her self-esteem has just skyrocketed.

> I can't tell you how much I appreciate what you all have done for our kids. The week after everyone went shopping there was a sense of pride and excitement in these children. They held their heads a little higher and seemed happier. It always makes me proud as a Christian to see other Christians put feet to their faith. Thank you so much for your sacrifices.

> I wanted to say thank you for your Clothe a Child Program. I teach in McKinney, Texas. I had a little child who was wearing pants that were six inches too big on each side. We tried to pin them on, but they were still falling off even with a belt, which was wrapped around him two times. His parents' house had recently burned, and he moved to our community. He had no clothes or shoes. . . . He was so proud of the new things he received through your program. . . . Thanks!

D.A.: What advice do you have for other people who are civic-minded and want to start some type of program in their community?

M.S.: No impact is too small. CAC met with many obstacles in the beginning, but our attitude was that if we help even one child, it was worth all our efforts. Surround yourself with people who have a passion and commitment for serving others. Give yourselves at least two years of working, praying, and evaluating to get your program established.

Never forget that the love and compassion you show someone today could impact thousands for generations to come.

D.A.: Anything else?

M.S.: I have been blessed beyond belief in the results of CAC. I can't describe what it feels like to see and hear all the smiling faces and joyous laughter of the children. Many come having never experienced the opportunity to pick their own new clothes. I thank God for giving me this opportunity to serve him in a manner that creates such joy in the children. In four years this ministry has grown from 72 volunteers and clothing 100 kids to having over 550 volunteers and clothing 758 children. To God be the glory.

THE HEART of volunteering is finding a need and then making the decision to do something to fill it.

26

• •

TEXAS UNITED!

When you row another person across the river, you get there yourself.

—CHINESE PROVERB

THERE ARE countless ways to make an impact on society through political involvement and volunteerism, but sometimes events demand that you jump into a firestorm like I did in Springfield, Missouri, and Nashville, Tennessee. Sometimes you need to lead the charge for positive protest.

Saddam Hussein had thumbed his nose at the United States and the United Nations for the seventeenth time, and although countries like France, Germany, Russia, and China wanted to extend him more time, almost everyone around the globe knew what was about to happen.

In the winter of 2003 mass demonstrations against a war with Iraq had become international events with hundreds of thousands marching in Europe and nearly as many in America. Many protesters chanted anti-USA slogans and carried banners depicting George W. Bush as a mad-man along the lines of Joseph Stalin, Benito Mussolini, and Adolf Hitler. In fact, one poster that seemed to turn up at each event included a picture of the president with a Hitler mustache at a swastika-laden podium declaring war on the helpless. Coffins were used as common props.

In New York City several protests were staged by communist groups and left-leaning organizations that enjoyed every moment of ridicule they could bring to the White House and the greatest nation on the planet. They clashed with police, got into fistfights with onlookers, and chained themselves together in the middle of major intersections so they could stop traffic and commerce altogether. I found it quite odd that these people who were so deliberate in their stance against war were more than willing to show their violent side with only the slightest provocation. It just seemed hypocritical to me.

For the record, I was in favor of the effort to stop our country's arch nemesis for the final time. With most pests and vermin, if you take out the nest, the rest scurry away in fear. I was hoping the same thing would happen with Hussein and Al-Qaeda.

Two very important matters were culminating at the time America was posturing for war: Hollywood celebrities were coming out against any conflict, and my second son, Adam, was about to drop a bombshell of his own. He would be joining the fight.

It was early February 2003, and most Americans were mystified by the number of Hollywood elitists becoming so vocal against war with Iraq. It wasn't a shock that the stars from the land of make-believe were against the war, but to see them on every talk show, in every newscast, and on the cover of most newspapers was disconcerting.

I was watching a CBS news program while I prepared to do my morning radio show when an ad came on the television. It was a little before 3:00 a.m., and everything I had been doing seemed unimportant, at least for the moment. Then Susan Sarandon offered an Oscar-caliber performance to make me and the rest of America feel ashamed because the country was bracing for war. She looked in the camera and asked, "What have the Iraqi people ever done to us?"

Typically, I move through the house quietly at that time of the morning, but I couldn't control myself. I half shouted at the TV. I grabbed my TiVo remote to be certain that I had indeed heard what I thought I had heard. As the unit replayed the video, I fetched my mini-disc recorder. Within seconds I was pulling the audio for playback later in my show.

On my way to the studio my foot floored the gas more out of indignation and anger than a need to make up for lost time. We have men and women who are marching to war, and some will die, but a major movie star is already launching a program of disinformation, trying to undermine this effort to control one of the greatest threats to world peace since the end of the cold war. *How dare she!* I thought.

During my show I referenced the story a few times and played the audio. Calls poured in to the switchboard. I played it again. My on-air lines jammed. I played it a third time. I was so angry my voice was shaking. My comments and the audience's responsed were all spontaneous, all impromptu. Needless to say, my listeners soon asked what I intended to do in response. I wasn't prepared to answer that, but I knew something had to be done. During a commercial break, a plan began to take shape.

When my program resumed, I played the audio once more and laid out my idea. We would hold our state's first pro-America rally, an event that was destined to be the first major rally of its kind anywhere in the country. I was fed up with the wall-to-wall coverage of the America haters; I wanted some of us to represent the other side.

"In the next few days, you will know exactly when and where the event will be held, so get ready," I announced at the ending the show. I was feeling supercharged. Those elitist snobs on the other side were going to get a dose of grass-roots patriotism.

As I walked out of the studio I expected to see equally exuberant faces. Instead, abject horror greeted me in expression and demeanor. No one said I was crazy, but they were certainly thinking it.

I went to see Jeff Hillery, my program director. He has always been a great sounding board for my ideas. So I propped myself up against his wall. "Well, if we're going to embrace this, Darrell, it needs a name," he said, letting me know he thought the idea had potential. As we tossed slogans and titles in the air, each fell flatter than the one before it.

Then we began to examine our expectations. The more we talked, the clearer the picture became. Just then, Jeff got an "I have the answer" look. "What do you think of Texas United?" he asked. *Texas United.* I repeated the name a few times and was sold. I headed home to make a list of the items we needed and e-mailed it to the KLIF promotions teams.

Next we went on a mission to find a place for our rally. What a wake-up call that was. One would think most businesses would jump at the chance to host a patriotic rally. Just imagine the goodwill that would come their way. But that wasn't the case. Every business and community leader we contacted said that they loved the idea but were not about to host the event. I was dumbfounded. This was a no-brainer.

I went on the air the next day and explained the situation. I was seething, but not as much as I had been the previous day. A listener suggested we look at Bedford, a small sleepy town between Dallas and Fort Worth. We called the mayor and he was all for it. He even had the perfect venue: a huge park setting and parking lot where the city held a blues fest every year. After calling insurance companies, city leaders, and security experts, we agreed this was the ideal location. Within a week Texas United would start a trend that would be picked up as a nationwide event.

Meanwhile, my son, Adam, slipped into my home office clutching a PR kit. I was on the phone but could see he was anxious to speak with me but waved for him to come back later. He didn't move. When I began to motion again, he gave me a soul-searing look and placed the kit on my desk. My stomach caught in my throat, and for a moment I couldn't say anything. Adam was planning to join the marines. I placed a hand over the receiver and told Adam to leave the packet and come back later, mainly because I had no idea how to respond. He came by twice more before the end of the day, but I still wasn't prepared to talk. Here I was, Mr. Patriot, and I wasn't sure how I felt about my son and the upcoming war.

The next day Adam stepped back into my office. Once again I told him I wasn't prepared to discuss it. Besides my uncertain feelings, I sincerely wanted to know how serious he was. I waved him off a few more times that day, but I could see that he was getting frustrated. Finally, the next afternoon, he walked back into my office and leaned over my desk to stare down at me, arms spread wide in a braced position.

"Dad," he said. "I'm twenty-one, and I don't need your permission to join. I would like your blessing, but I don't need it."

I smiled and invited him to sit. "I really needed to see that you were serious, son," I said as I looked into his idealistic eyes. "Why do you want to join and why now? We're on the verge of war, Adam." I elected a stern but compassionate father role for the conversation. What he said next put everything into perspective—for both of us.

"If a person isn't willing to join the military during wartime," Adam replied, "then why join in the first place?!" What a lesson in sacrifice.

The next day we met with the sergeant in charge of recruiting. He had already met with Adam several times and was prepared to answer the typical five to ten minutes' worth of questions most parents ask. Most parents aren't talk-show hosts, and most parents don't have the four great kids that I do. If you're going to include one of my kids in your plans, then I want details—all the details. For more than two hours I grilled the recruiter on every thing I could think of. I'm convinced he curled up in a fetal position after we left his office.

To my son, I said, "You have my blessing," choking back the emotion as we drove home. I was both very proud and very scared.

February 13, the selected date for Texas United, arrived. It was a miserable day. Windy, rainy, and cold. The weather tied up traffic throughout North Texas. As I inched toward Bedford, I was charged with
nervous energy. People told me that no one in their right mind would
venture out in these conditions just to stand in a parking lot for an hour,
not unless we were offering big prizes. Patriotism certainly wouldn't be
enough to generate a strong turnout. Boy, were they wrong.

I pulled into the parking lot around 6:00 p.m. and saw about 150 people standing in the rain, which was enough for me to declare the gathering a partial success. After all, we had the elements to blame. For the next
hour, trucks and cars streamed in from every direction, and the crowd increased. As I walked through the throng, people handed me small flags
and gave me a few attaboy pats on the back. It soon hit me: there was an
intense desire to show support for America and our troops, and I was
their conduit. I've only felt that sense of pride a few times in my life.

I remember my wife, Laurie, coming back from a flag-buying trip as
excited as a child at Disneyland. She and my two younger kids held piles
of small U.S. flags. "I went to the register to pay for a few of these, and
the cashier looked at me and said she knew who I was and that her store
wanted to 'help the cause,' so she sold me a few and gave the rest so the
crowd could wave them." Everyone wanted to play a part.

By 7:00 p.m. folks were already singing patriotic songs and creating
spontaneous cheers that echoed from one end of the gathering to the
next. All events will have problems; Texas United had some that seemed
insurmountable. The audio feeds back to the radio station were problematic because the crew wasn't fully prepared. The speaker system was inadequate and covered in plastic throughout the entire event. And no one
followed up for staging. Thank God for a gentleman who brought a full-
size Liberty Bell replica; his flatbed trailer became the platform, and a
bullhorn we found in another truck became our loudspeaker system.

Some events take on a life of their own; even major problems will
have a difficult time sidelining them. This was one of those nights. It is
also important that I stress the absolute need for lists, plans, and systems,
and for a leader to make sure they are carried out. This was an idea born
in my mind and spirit, but I had handed the execution to people with the
time and expertise to facilitate the many needs that would arise. Because
the people entrusted with the system needs did not dream big enough, we
almost had a catastrophe. I'll give you a few tips on that in a moment.

As the evening progressed, I was joined onstage by a former member of the Metropolitan Opera who volunteered to sing. A local band showed up with little notice and led the audience in a few patriotic choruses. A child singing sensation sang the National Anthem. And I floated on and off the stage as the crowd chanted, clapped, and honored America. The energy from the night was contagious.

Toward the end, I invited Adam to the stage. Most knew of his military decision because I had shared the story earlier in the week during my broadcast. As I honored him as a surrogate for all branches of the military, the muscles in my neck tightened, almost to the point of cutting off my air. The gravity of his decision kicked in. I told the audience, "Our men and women in the military are making major sacrifices and some will make the ultimate kind—returning in a body bag." I choked up. Soon it could be my son paying that price. I was honored to have that moment of reflection as he stood by my side.

I stayed well past the end of the program because so many people wanted to stop and talk. They gave me pictures, flags, and keepsakes. For all of us, this time together was almost a religious experience.

Nationally syndicated talk guru Glenn Beck is a friend of mine, and he called to ask for a recap of the effort. When I called him from my car afterward, I told him of the unbelievable success, that more than thirty-five hundred people had turned a cold, wet winter night into one of the greatest events ever. He kept repeating, "You had thirty-five hundred people standing in the rain?! Tell me you're not making this up—thirty-five hundred people!" He was staggered because he knew everything was put together in just six days. "Darrell, I plan to host some of these. Are you cool with that?" he asked. I assured him that this was all about letting people express themselves; it was greater than any one person.

The next day I talked with Beck and some people who work with his show so they would have an idea of what I believed had worked for me and what hadn't. With that, Texas United left a rural field and headed for the national spotlight. Beck's Rally for America kicked into high gear a couple weeks later, and when his many stops were complete, hundreds of thousands of Americans had joined in the effort.

But just as soon as Glenn's rallies began, both he and the company that syndicates his show, Clear Channel, came under tremendous fire from the liberal press, the *New York Times* and other newspapers and mainstream media, because they were convinced the Rallies for America were controlled by the Bush administration and manipulated by the Republican National Committee. (Did I say LIBERAL media? Forgive me. As they continue to tell us, no such thing exists.)

Two people know for sure how everything started: Glenn Beck and me. We were the ones on cell phones shortly after the Texas United rally. I suppose if the *New York Times* really wanted to check the facts they could call my wife and two teenage children, because they were in the car with me while Glenn and I spoke.

Texas United began as a heartfelt expression of support for America, and so did the Rallies for America. There were no "suits" or corporate players pulling the strings. And no matter how hard the liberal machine wants to sell such lies, Karl Rove, George W. Bush, and Ed Gillespie were not sending in the plays from the sidelines. It was something that two talk-show hosts decided to do with and for the people of this great country because citizens were feeling their patriotism and pride but couldn't find an outlet. It was pure. It was honest. It was all American. I hate it when the press distorts something and then prostitutes it to sell more papers and fill airtime.

Several weeks later our radio station was contacted by the Dallas Cowboys, which also owned the AFL Desperados, an indoor football team. They had followed our success in February and asked us to put together Texas United II. The Cowboys franchise is one of the best in the world, and to remain that way, they control every aspect of a deal. When we first met with them, I felt they were willing to give enough leeway to satisfy their needs and ours. The last thing I wanted was to become a sellout to corporate America. Everyone agreed to terms, but as time drew closer, I had the sinking feeling that we had sold out.

When I looked at the planned program, almost every move and word was sponsored. I tried to rationalize my uneasiness, but it persisted. Texas United was too pure, it was too right. After several negotiations we finally agreed to open the game, provide running commentary from the audience, and lead in halftime festivities. We couldn't duplicate the raw emotions of the night in Bedford, but as the seventeen thousand people we put in the stands cheered and waved their banners, I knew Texas United II would also be a success in its own way.

Dare to let the dream develop in your heart, but don't sit back thinking it is a terrible idea or one that others will fulfill. If it's in your head and heart—it's in there for a reason. Become a conduit for great change.

In the following chapter, I interview one of the country's best promoters, but here are a few lessons or tips I would pass along from events
I have created and promoted:

1. Always have a plan and work it to the very end. Try to have a fail-safe
   in place. If the ball is dropped, how do you get things moving again?
2. Be sure the person you entrust with leadership responsibilities shares
   your vision. Can he get the job done? Does he dream big? Can he
   lead the charge but also accept direction and feedback? You must be
   willing to keep an active eye on the process because people will remember you—not your support team—in times of success and failure.
3. If you are inviting people to gather for an event, never leave the object of attention on the ground or at the same level as those in attendance unless you have no other options. In my case, I demanded a
   stage and was assured that one would be provided. In fact, no one really followed up on the need. Imagine how difficult it would have
   been to be seen and heard by thirty-five hundred people if I had remained at street level and encircled by them.
4. Plan for more than you believe will actually show up. In our case, I
   asked for a sound system that would cover an area with the potential
   for thousands. The sound system that was provided could handle
   hundreds, and the engineers left plastic covers on the speakers because of the rain. Spend the extra money to do it right.
5. Lead. Don't just put your event together and hope that the magic
   will arrive. More often than not, magic misses the plane. Who is
   going to sing? speak? perform? How long does each segment last?
   Will you include the crowd? Choreograph each stage in your mind.
   Contemplate what your reaction should be in the face of disaster.
6. Security in today's world is mandatory. Because this was a pro-America rally in the shadow of a war on terror and post-9/11, I had police,
   undercover officers, FBI, and Homeland Security personnel on
   alert. They were in the crowd that night. Know your situation inti-
   mately in order to properly plan.
7. Secure your area. As I was heading to the platform, I was encircled
   by people and could barely move. I had to direct people to shift from
   one area to another to ensure safety.
8. Enjoy the moment. As soon as it arrives—it is gone.

27

●●●

WINNING EVENT
STRATEGIES FROM
A PREMIER PROMOTER

*Never underestimate the apathy of people, nor their capacity
to complain.*

—CHAZ CORZINE

IF YOU are feeling an inner nudge that says you're the person who has to
lead the next charge, then be advised that putting an event together takes
a lot of work, multiple strategies, and a little know-how. Thus far you've
read about what I've done (or should have done) to make an event succeed. But there are some powerful things to learn about how to stage
something that will make a difference in your community, your city,
your county, your state, your country.

Chaz Corzine is a partner with Blanton Harrell Cooke & Corzine.
He is considered one of the foremost experts in promotion and entertainment management, and he has served as personal manager to stars
like Amy Grant and Michael W. Smith. I sat down with Chaz to get a
better idea how to properly stage an event to get the results we want.

After Texas United, I knew the concept was powerful, but in several
ways I believe it succeeded in spite of us all. I hate that feeling. I made
meticulous notes and to-do lists for the people around me since I had
hosted similar events in the past. It didn't matter. With one or two people in the wrong place, everything nearly fell apart.

D.A.: Let's look at a few concepts that you use to create a winning program. Start at the beginning. I have a grass-roots event and would like others to know about it. How do I promote it with little or no money?

C.C.: We look for people we call "gatekeepers." These are men and women who have a great amount of influence and can help get the word out to the masses in short order. Radio and television personalities would be an example of gatekeepers. I can try to tell six thousand people about my event, or I can find five or six gatekeepers to do that for me.

D.A.: Do you have a method for involving groups and teams to spread the word?

C.C.: Know who your audience is and know where they congregate so you can easily target them. I promote a lot in the Christian marketplace. At least once a week I know exactly where they are going to be. A cause is neither sacred nor secular; instead, it is "why you do what you do." I have a plaque in my office that reminds me of this concept every day. It's from A. W. Tozer: "It is not WHAT a man does that determines whether his work is sacred or secular, it is WHY he does it." Man, that's powerful stuff. If you have a strong event or cause, there is no reason why you shouldn't go after religious people because that's a sure direction to take. You can branch off from there.

D.A.: What if I know my event needs a performer, but they are too costly? How can I negotiate so I don't go broke and the talent is financially satisfied?

C.C.: Find a talent who identifies with your cause and has a passion for it. It's a huge challenge because there are a billion and one great causes. This will be one of your biggest challenges. If you can't find a star who will come in and join your effort because they believe as you do, you can still negotiate their fees. Remember, everything in show biz is negotiable. For instance, maybe the artist gets ten thousand dollars for a Friday night date, but you know he will be near your area on Thursday. You may want to consider changing your date to Thursday because you can probably get him to come for less than half his normal price. If you can remain flexible, you will win in the end.

D.A.: What if I don't know how to negotiate these kinds of deals?

C.C.: Most cities have four or five very strong promoters, so if you're not great in this area, I would recommend finding one of them or someone else you may know to take this task. The easiest way to find good promoters is to call a couple of local venues and find out who they work with. Once they give you a few names, call and explain what you want to accomplish. If a promoter can catch your vision, you will have one of the best resources ready to guide you through the project. If you have never booked an artist, you probably won't even get a call back from an artist or their management.

D.A.: If there is no way I can get the artist I want, do you have any suggestion how I would find another who may be traveling through my area or is in between concert dates?

C.C.: This is where a local promoter will help immensely. I would encourage people putting on an event to not be afraid to spend money to ensure the quality of an event. For example, if you use a local promoter to help secure your talent, you may want to consider hiring that promoter to produce the event too. That is *not* giving up control. You retain control, but you are using the promoter's experienced people to make sure the event goes off without a hitch (from a technical standpoint).

D.A.: Are there any sure-fire methods for recruiting volunteers? Is there a specific way I should approach candidates?

C.C.: I don't think you can motivate volunteers without a good cause, and this may be your litmus test. If people aren't getting excited about your event and volunteers are hard to come by, it may mean you don't have a strong cause. It may mean you have something that is important to you but not to a lot of other people.

D.A.: If the event grows to a level where I can't do it alone, what are the first areas of responsibility you would fill (security, traffic, etc.)?

C.C.: Insurance. Always make sure you have a ton of insurance because the guy who stubs his toe is coming after one guy—you. If you are holding your event in a community center or public building, they should have this covered for you or at least provide the information you need. Speaking of the building, this is another area that is very negotiable. Be prepared to whittle the price down and always be sure to read this contract very carefully. Building owners have a lot of extraneous details you should be aware of. Next comes advertising and marketing. This will take the bulk of your time, so be sure to budget your time wisely here.

D.A.: What is the biggest mistake a small-time or volunteer promoter makes when trying to stage an event?

C.C.: Don't just assume people are going to show up. Never make such assumptions, because as soon as you do, you're going to lose your shirt. If I bring Michael W. Smith to town and ten thousand people show up, I always work from the belief that no one will show up when I bring him back to town the next time. Never take this for granted. Promote, promote, and promote again.

D.A.: You have put together major concerts. What aspect of producing and promoting gives you the most jitters?

C.C.: Early on, I always had butterflies, mainly because I didn't know what I was doing. If I thought I had made a mistake and was promoting an event based on my heart and not my head, then I would have a lot of butterflies. Here's an example: if you have a fundraiser planned and your heart says to book Willie Nelson, but your head says he isn't in the demographics of your core supporters, then listen to your head. You will thank me for this advice.

D.A.: What part provides the greatest satisfaction?

C.C.: I believe that people's lives are touched by what we do. I am not a great orator or public kind of person, but I am very strong behind the scenes. I know I can handle everything for Amy Grant or Michael W. Smith, and they will be able to hit the stage and make a valuable contribution. On a bigger scale, I think entertainment is a huge gift to others; it transports us to a different place. In fact, a great entertainment package, coupled with a strong cause, can deliver some of the best results a promoter will ever see.

D.A.: Has one of your events ever bombed? How did you handle it and what did you learn?

C.C.: Fresh out of college I promoted some concerts for the late Ray Charles. It seemed like a no-brainer. Ray Charles at the Fox Theatre in Atlanta. How could a guy go wrong? I lost a lot of money on that deal. For years I carried one of those ticket stubs in my wallet as a reminder to never get into something I don't know. I was a young white kid trying to promote a black superstar. I didn't know the first thing about how to reach African Americans. I still have that stub in my office at home. That was an expensive lesson.

D.A.: Anything else you wish event promoters/organizers would know before they jump into the thick of things?

C.C.: (1) If you don't know how to promote, then have people around you who do. (2) Know your audience—who you're trying to reach *and* how to reach them. (3) Do it right or don't do it. I went to a fundraiser recently, a sit-down dinner kind of deal, and the group ran out of food. They ran out of food! I didn't sit there thinking, *Well, this is a pretty frugal bunch. I think I want to support them financially.* I walked away extremely angry. If they aren't smart enough to budget for a fundraiser dinner, then how many other areas will they fail in? (4) Be smart. Think things through. Don't pinch a penny and lose a dollar. (5) Promote. Promote. Promote.

28

●●●

OPERATION
ENDURING SUPPORT

He stands erect by bending over the fallen.
He rises by lifting others.

—ROBERT GREEN INGERSOLL

BY MAY 2004 A discernible rift was becoming more evident with each passing headline and news story. Americans were becoming more concerned about the war in Iraq, and the media were exploiting every nuance of it. President Bush's job approval numbers were in trouble, and questions about the treatment of prisoners by U.S. soldiers dominated water-cooler conversations nationwide. In my radio program, all I had to do was mention the situation and the phones would ring off the hook. It was time to hear from We The People yet again.

After thinking about some of the lessons from the systems failures we encountered with Texas United, I decided to take another shot at honoring our troops and our country. It was time someone stepped up to the task.

I was brainstorming with my producer, AnnMarie Petitto, about new ways to show our support since we had already covered the meat-and-potatoes elements like guest speakers, singers, and patriotic images. We both knew we needed that special touch. It was then that the highly creative master of morning drive radio shot me her famous look; it's the one that says, "Watch out! this is gonna be good!" Her idea wasn't just good, it was outstanding. Then she said, "Let's make a sea of flags as a genuine show of support." I knew we were on to something. Within weeks I took our afternoon host, Greg Knapp, out to lunch to invite him to join our efforts so we could really create a memorable afternoon.

Several weeks later, on Armed Forces Day, Operation Enduring Support became a reality. This time we called very few people for help. Congressmen called us. Bands called us. Television crews called us. Volunteers called us. Even the name of the event and the logo we used came from volunteers. There is nothing better than to watch a massive grass-roots campaign take shape. With less than three weeks to put everything together, I knew we had little room for error, so I made a checklist of what we needed and handed it off to the promotions people. But this time I checked with them daily, sometimes several times a day, to make sure everything was falling into place. In the end, with approximately five thousand people congregating in a local park, our show of support couldn't have come together better. When people believe in something and work together toward the goal of making it happen, success usually follows.

During Operation Enduring Support, we moved forward with the AnnMarie's idea of a sea of flags. The concept reminded me of Arlington National Cemetery, so that's how I explained it to my audience. The goal was to make people feel the impact of war through the images we were creating. We asked everyone to bring a flag for a "flag planting ceremony." Before they pushed their small wooden flag staffs in the ground, I had each person write on it the name of someone they knew in the military. If they didn't have a name, they were instructed to inscribe the staff with "Unknown military person." After the attendees spread out across the vast acreage, every man, woman, boy, and girl quietly, somberly, took a moment to imagine the face of our nation's bravest and then plant their flag. After a twenty-one-gun salute and "Taps," I asked the audience to find someone else's flag and pull it up. "Put this small flag somewhere that you will see it daily, and then pray for this country and the person represented on the staff." It was a moving moment for all of us.

Later, as people headed home, several veterans openly wept in the midst of some of the Stars and Stripes we had planted earlier. The power of support is life-changing.

29

•••••••••••••••••••••••••••••••••••••••

GOOD PR IS
NOT MAGIC!

MOST PEOPLE BELIEVE THAT public relations work requires some sort of supernatural or magical powers when all it really takes is careful attention to detail and a little bit of common sense. Good PR is essential if your organization hopes to get the word out about your event through non-news channels, and it is usually the single most important facet that is responsible for the image you are trying to project. A person who has strong PR skills will be able to look at your strengths and weaknesses and devise a plan that will put those strengths front and center, hopefully taking attention off the negatives. No matter where you choose to operate within the battle to save America, you will need to know the essentials of getting other people to catch your vision.

Jayne Cravens runs a virtual volunteering website and since 2001 has been the online volunteering specialist at United Nations Volunteer Programme in Bonn, Germany. She was named one of the Top 25 Women of the Web in 2001. Kelly Taft is president of the Phoenix chapter of the Public Relations Society of America and one of the most highly respected leaders in the public relations field. I asked each one of these talented professionals for some perspectives on how to go about creating an event.

D.A.: Assume I have a nonprofit or civic-oriented group and I want to stage an event or spread the word about my organization. How do I create a buzz with limited dollars?

K.T.: Knowing your audience is crucial. Where do they get their information? To whom do they listen most? Where do they hang out? What's hot among this demographic? Knowing this information can give you tremendous insight into what type of event will work best. Never underestimate word of mouth or the power of e-mail. If you can reach a few key messengers among this group who are willing to spread the word, you can create the buzz you're looking for without investing a lot of advertising dollars.

J.C.: Publicity isn't just a function, it's a way of thinking. It's a commitment. Everyone at an organization has to see themselves as promoters of the organization. Can all paid staff and volunteers recite a ten- to twenty-second easy-to-understand description of your organization? Are they enthusiastic about providing this description to others? As far as no-cost publicity: speaking at civic groups, e-mailing press releases to local papers and media outlets, and calling reporters to pitch stories have no financial costs to undertake. What all these tasks *do* require is commitment.

D.A.: Will I need tens of thousands of dollars to get the word out about my event?

K.T.: Following the advice above, you could do it for much less than that.

J.C.: I could do it with no money. What is needed is human resources, commitment, and *time*.

D.A.: What is the biggest mistake my group could make when trying to get publicity?

K.T.: Not understanding the audience and using the wrong message for that audience.

J.C.: Not identifying what exactly they want someone to do as a result of hearing the organization's message and not tailoring all activities to that goal. Of course one of the biggest mistakes would be throwing money around before you really know what to spend it on.

D.A.: Are there ways you would suggest to manipulate the media or market in a positive way to provide coverage for an event?

K.T.: First, you shouldn't be thinking in terms of manipulation. You should believe in your product or message and tell your story with honesty and passion. If you have a message worth telling or a product worth promoting that provides important value to your community, you don't have to manipulate the media; they will be eager to spread the word. Find a message worth telling and make the event worth covering. Use lots of visuals and try to understand what parts of the media you want to attract. Know what they like to cover and who they are trying to reach. Seek outlets that have the same audience you want to reach.

J.C.: Invite people from the media to the event, not just to cover it, but to participate in it. If there is going to be something particularly visual in the preparations, fax the TV stations on the day of the event and let them know what would be the best times to send a camera out.

D.A.: Are there a few key ingredients a group can use to create a theme and message that will hit their target with information?

K.T.: If you believe in your product, company, or mission, you will have a far better understanding of what you want your message to be. What is it that your organization does that no one else does better? Why is what you are promoting valuable to me? How will my life be better if I behave the way you want? Try this tactic: Come up with one-word descriptors of what you are trying to promote. Put one word on each page. Then, as quickly as possible, underneath that word write anything that comes to mind that the word emotes. Then take those words and do the same thing. You may end up with some interesting descriptors you hadn't thought of before. Test various one-liners on different focus groups and see if the descriptors evoke the same ideas and thoughts that you want to get across.

J.C.: Publicity is not a mathematical equation. It's not a soup to prepare. It's more of an ongoing garden that changes with the seasons. Different activities for different seasons.

D.A.: Any special advice to groups or persons trying to get publicity?

K.T.: Be honest with both customers and the media. Don't overpromise. Don't entice journalists to an event that falls short of expectations. Don't waste their time with non-events or they will stop trusting you. Seek publicity when you have a legitimate message to tell or a truly newsworthy event to attend. Understand what it is you want out of the publicity. If what you really want is for people to donate to your organization, make it clear that is your intent, first explaining the great benefits to them personally if they donate (peace of mind, warm glow for knowing they helped a child, making the world a better place, whatever that benefit is). Don't try to prevaricate or bait and switch, making the event seem like something other than a fundraising event if fundraising is the intent, etc.

D.A.: Assuming a civic, community, or nonprofit group needs publicity but has no money to spend, what ways would you suggest for them to get the word out?

K.T.: As described above, if you have a story to tell, you don't need money to get the word out. Key is knowing who wants to hear it and how they want to hear it. There are lots of community sections in many daily newspapers. Consider starting there. Or start with a city-run cable station that does public affairs programming. Become an expert in your area. And when national news is topical to your agency's services, call up and offer the local angle.

Once you start tasting success, use it to gain even more publicity. A big part of a strong PR campaign is to create momentum. Sometimes that Big Mo happens naturally just because of the way things play out, but more often than not it is prestructured and controlled. Remember, media outlets never want to feel like they have missed out on a big event or story, so use this to your advantage.

Let's assume you have an event that must have sold-out numbers and let's also assume that you have done your homework to make sure you have the right performer or attraction, location, and plans for exposure. If May 1 is your target date, then prepare to start the initial PR wave a few months earlier, unless it is a huge event—then you may want to shoot for several months' advance notice.

Ask yourself what the main draws are for the event and then look at all the angles to get the word out via a PR campaign—which can be done in several ways:

1. Advertising. Unless you are highly skilled in the purchasing of advertising, *do not* attempt to do it alone—unless you have unlimited capital to spend. Instead, get to know a successful sales representative from the market who may share your dream or civic-mindedness. In this case, he may help you for little or no fees. Otherwise, in a strictly freelance manner, offer to help this person with a little side cash in exchange for information on high and low advertising rates, which media outlets are in a position to offer price discounts, value-added opportunities, and other specials. I have seen radio and television stations make advertising available at 50 percent to 70 percent reductions based on the campaign schedule and options on the table.

If you cannot find a local rep then you may want to consider using an ad agency or PR firm—though both can be costly. Don't believe it if the sales representative for a media firm says they are just here to help you. They exist to get your money. If they see you as a one-hit wonder with one event, then you are just there to help them meet their monthly revenue goal. But if they see you as a person who will be in the market with a variety of advertising needs in the weeks, months, and years to come, they will be more inclined to work to make the ads stretch further than your budget. Again, it is very difficult to get an advertising representative to catch your vision on the first phase of advertising.

2. If at all possible, look for a popular local singer or band that has an established following. Their audience will come for them but stay for you.

3. In putting the buzz into the media, consider all the positive and negative aspects that surround your event and be prepared to capitalize on them. For instance, if your group is planning a big fight on income taxes, and you plan to dump a ton of tea in a local river to stage a revolt, then get the message into the media. If the story is big and controversial, news organizations rush to it. If you believe it can turn into a powerful event, but none of the media outlets will work with you, one strategy

that has been effective is to plant a story. But be warned: media outlets and reporters *hate* being manipulated in this way, though sometimes it is the only way to gain interest. Just be advised if the organization finds out in advance of your event that you have planted the story—they will probably drop you cold. This is purely a judgment call. Come up with all the possible hooks and see how you can push one or two forward. Obviously, if your event is a very positive, civic-minded kind, then try to accentuate the positives to get the interest you want. If you alienate your core audience, then you have killed your chances for success.

4. Create the buzz within your population. This is not easy to do, but it can be very effective. Get the people in the community who share your vision to help spread the news. You must work hard to make sure these volunteers work within your timetable and do not disappear after a few hours' work. There is nothing worse than to make plans around the distribution of fifteen thousand fliers only to find out that less than five hundred were distributed. It's almost worse than starting over.

Besides fliers and other person-to-person handouts, you may want to consider what items and performers at your event may be of keen interest locally. If you have a strong pop singer or television personality, have your volunteers share that information via word of mouth and handout campaigns. "Hey did you hear that Brad Pitt was going to be at that event Saturday night?" Don't lie. Don't spread rumors. But if a powerful personality will be in attendance or onstage, use this information to create the buzz. (It's usually a smart idea to be sure the high-profile person doesn't mind the momentary exploitation, because he can change his mind at the last minute, leaving you hanging.)

If you are able to get media exposure, use it to keep your momentum rolling. Sometimes you will have to pay a TV or radio station to make copies, but the expense is worth it. Newspapers and magazines can put printed materials in your hands in little time. Tip: If you are buying ads or plan to, go through your sales representative to secure a copy of a news article or story that has appeared on their station or in their publication. Sales representatives are good for this. They are also great for getting complimentary passes to a wide variety of events locally. Use those to your advantage. Perhaps the sales representative offers you two tickets to a big playoff game. You may want to consider giving the tickets to a contributor or supporter, or at least invite the person to join you for a night of relaxation. They will remember you later.

HOW TO GET NEWS COVERAGE

YOU ARE ready to impact your community with an important event, campaign, or blow-the-lid-off-corruption story, but if your local, state, or national news doesn't pick up on it, you will be stuck light-years away from accomplishing your goals. Knowing how to get to a news reporter is the important first step, but knowing what to do after you have his attention is make or break time.

Imagine you are on the other side of that call, letter, or e-mail. If you are a broadcast journalist, you are not working on a single deadline but one of many. You may have to gather information for the four, five, six, and ten o'clock newscasts. On top of the deadlines and reports, you are also fielding calls aimed directly at you as well as general calls that somehow get routed to your extension. On top of that, you are researching stories, doing follow-up, and checking e-mail. That's when you're in the newsroom. If you have been sent to cover a story, you are continuing to handle all of those tasks and adding travel, traffic, interaction, and more. Now ask yourself, "How would I want to be contacted by a stranger with a story to tell?"

TIPS ON SENDING PRESS RELEASES TO NEWSPAPERS[1]

LET'S HEAR it for the *Los Angeles Times* and the *Oregonian*. Those are the only two major national dailies (with circulations over three hundred thousand) whose websites offer guidelines for submitting press releases to their staffs. Their guidelines are combined, organized, and summarized below. The source of each is also noted (LA or OR).

WHAT IS A PRESS RELEASE?

IN GENERAL, a good press release is a concise, complete description of an upcoming news event, a timely report of an event that has just occurred, notification of important personnel or procedural changes in an organization, or other news or feature tips. (LA)

The press release is the tool most often used to share information with newspapers when the story is not breaking news. The press release is a concise, informative, and straightforward piece of writing that describes what you want the public to know. It also can convey ideas of potential stories to editors and remind them of upcoming events. (OR)

NEWSWORTHINESS

To BE newsworthy, your information or story should meet one or more of the following criteria (OR):

TIMELINESS: information that is currently relevant or has some immediate impact on readers.

NOVELTY: a story that is unusual or unique. You know the adage: When a dog bites a man, it's not news; when a man bites a dog, it is. The first, the best, the worst, the tallest, the shortest. If something stands out from everything else, it may be newsworthy.

CONSEQUENCE: information about a development that will have a significant impact on some or all of the paper's readers.

HUMAN INTEREST: a story that reveals something quirky, colorful, or otherwise dramatic about the human condition or character.

PROMINENCE: information or news about a public figure, organization, or recognizable person.

PROXIMITY: information or news that has an effect on people living in the area.

WRITING THE RELEASE

A WELL-PRESENTED press release, typewritten or printed clearly, observes the following guidelines (LA, OR):

INVERTED PYRAMID: The structure of the press release puts the most important and indispensable information at the beginning of the story, the most expendable at the end. Address the who, what, where, why, and when in the first two paragraphs.

PAPER: Use white, inexpensive 8½" x 11".

LENGTH: Just the facts please. Make every word, sentence, and paragraph count. Keep it tight—no longer than two double-spaced pages.

CONTACT: Identify the organization or individual sending the release and include the name and daytime and evening phone number (with area code) and e-mail address of someone a reporter can contact with questions. If possible, give a website address where further information is available.

DATE: Date the release and include whether the material is for immediate use or for release at a later date.

SIMULTANEOUS SUBMISSION: If you send materials to more than one of the newspaper's sections simultaneously, attach a note indicating this. It will assist the editors in avoiding duplication.

PROTOCOL: If the release is longer than one page, add "more" at the bottom of the first page and identify following pages with either the subject of the release or the name of your organization. Type "end" or "30" or "###" at the bottom of the last page.

COMMON MISTAKES

HERE ARE the most common mistakes people make that hurt their chances of getting any coverage (LA):

1. Providing insufficient, incomplete, inaccurate, or vague information
2. Omitting the name and phone number of someone the editors can contact with questions
3. Writing releases that are too long
4. Submitting a release too late for a particular deadline
5. Most newsrooms are organized by sections of the newspaper or by general subject areas. If you don't know which individual reporter or editor to send a release to, address it to the appropriate news desk (e.g., business desk, city desk, national news desk, sports desk, etc.).

If possible, send your release to the appropriate editor or reporter, the one whose beat includes the subject of your release. Many newspapers provide a directory of editors and reporters at their websites. You can also call the newsroom or managing editor to find out to whom you should send your press release.

WHAT JOURNALISTS WISH YOU KNEW

I ASKED five journalists from across the country to offer some insight into how best to use them to get a story out. They were very candid. Maria Arita is an anchor/reporter with CBS 11 News in Dallas/Fort Worth; Andy Ludlum is news director at KFWB in Los Angeles; Angela Anderson is news director at KXNT in Las Vegas; Terese Arena is news director at KLIF in Dallas/Fort Worth; and Sara Dorsey is a reporter with WOI-TV in Des Moines, Iowa. They have more than a hundred years of journalistic experience between them, and their backgrounds include editing, beat reporting, anchoring, investigative reporting, and writing. Their answers should help you in your quest to get your story, campaign, or organization into the news.

What is the best way for a person to get a story idea to you?

A.L.: E-mail.

M.A.: In order of the most effective to the least: e-mail, phone call, letter. A conversation would follow if my curiosity is piqued.

T.A.: The best way to contact the media is by e-mail, fax, or letter. Phone calls rarely work because we're often too busy to return the calls, if they even get to us. Personal conversations are good because you can get the chance to explain your story. But don't seek out specific media members. Chances are you'll never get to talk to them. Personal conversations are better in a casual or networking setting.

S.D.: The best way to get in touch with busy journalists on strict deadlines is via e-mail. I have time to read the idea, digest it, hand it off if it doesn't apply to me, or call back when I have time.

What is the worst way and what are the common mistakes individuals or groups make when trying to involve a news department?

A.L.: Blind contacts with no awareness of the station's needs/format or proper method of contact.

M.A.: Worst way to get to a news department: Do *not* send gifts. I'm far less likely to consider a story this way for ethical reasons. Even if I did decide to do it, I'd have to send the gift back. Common mistakes: (a) Never try to pitch something for personal gratification or self-promotion. If it's not newsworthy, it won't be done. (b) Not a good idea to try to leverage us by mentioning the competition. (c) Many try to get coverage without having even the basic facts. They should do their homework first. Requests to the media do best when the meat and potatoes are close to the surface with the details as an attachment. (d) News organizations true to their integrity are not interested in titillating viewers at the expense of their credibility. Don't exaggerate or embellish. We usually see through that stuff pretty quickly, and once you lose our trust it's hard to get it back.

T.A.: The worst mistake a person or group can make is to disguise a non-story as a real story. Be up front and tell us exactly what you're doing and why it benefits the community. We'll make the decision. The other big mistake is to send reams of paper with your information. We rarely have time to wade through it, and most likely all you're doing is killing trees. The KISS (keep it simple, son) principle should always be used.

A.A.: Not being flexible. Newsrooms are getting smaller, and sometimes there aren't enough reporters to cover each story. Especially in radio. Sometimes just making the person available for a phone interview can make all the difference.

S.D.: Don't call too many times. Just because you don't get an immediate call back doesn't mean yours is a lost cause. Calling too much, though, could seal your fate. A journalist on deadline hates to have five voice mails from the same person.

Do you mind if the same person sends duplicate information to other reporters who work with you?

A.L.: This can be a problem at times, though some of my reporters specialize in certain areas and I certainly don't need to micromanage every story idea.

M.A.: Not usually. We understand that sometimes people aren't sure who the best person might be for a story. Reporters suggest stories that come their way to their peers all the time, especially if they believe someone else might be better equipped. It's all in a good day's work.

T.A.: We don't mind if you're sending your information about a news event to the other media outlets. It will improve your chances of getting coverage. But if you have a big, juicy story (the kind that might blow the lid off some scandal or a trial, for example), you should carefully choose the reporter you give it to. If he turns you down, try the next name on your list. A good reporter will recognize the importance of the story and will appreciate it that you gave that story exclusively to him.

S.D.: In my newsroom we work as a team. Often we don't share the same days off, so if the event is urgent, it's probably best to send it to more than one reporter so you can be sure someone sees it in time. A good, well-run newsroom will quickly work out the kinks of two reporters with one story idea. If you have a specific reporter you've worked with before, mention that to the other reporters you send the information to.

What goes through your mind if a person says, "I was going to take my story to your competition but wanted to give you first crack at it"?

A.L.: It almost always means the story is so lame that neither of us would really want it.

M.A.: Well, I'd get crackin' if I were you. (I'd smell a big one.)

T.A.: Reporters want exclusive stories and appreciate it when someone thinks enough of their work to give it exclusively to them. But use that tactic wisely and judiciously. Burn a reporter on a nonstory and you could lose that contact forever.

A.A.: If a person says he is going to give the story to you first, I always ask why. Is it because you have a relationship with this person and have covered similar stories in the past? Is it because it may not be the type of story your competitor will cover? Or is he lying to you to try and make the story seem more important than it really is?

S.D.: That comment usually makes me laugh because it sounds like he is doing me a favor, when in fact he's the one who wants the information out. But if someone says that to me, I will still take the story and just make him agree to not call the competition.

How do you handle it if a person tries to control you in the background, investigation, and creation of a story?

A.L.: It probably wouldn't be that easy for someone to get into a controlling position on a story. But if he became increasingly persistent, we'd probably break contact and go at the story from another direction.

M.A.: It depends on who it is. Reporters often collaborate with each other. It's all about teamwork. The investigational aspects may require various members of the news team to work together. But once I've got my facts and resources, I need to have free rein and creative control.

T.A.: I will usually back away from a person who tries to control a story. It appears to me he has an agenda he's trying to promote. But sometimes you have to play by the contact's rules. For example, I received an anonymous call once about a prominent member of a Dallas sports team who had been booked into the county jail. That's about all the caller could tell me. Using other sources, we were able to confirm and break the story. As a result of that call, that person gave me other tips about good stories inside the jail, but I had to take them on his terms and on his time because of fears he would be discovered and lose his job. He never steered me wrong.

A.A.: If someone tries to control me in the background and investigation of a story, I listen to what he has to say and then move on. I then ask why he is trying to control information. I believe in using at least three sources for every story and always go for the opposite angle. The person who is trying to control the investigation often has something he does not want you to find out. I try to find that out.

S.D.: I let people believe they have input, but ultimately I have the final say. I like to listen because that person may have more information than I do or have a different perspective that might help me out. But as a journalist, I decide what the true story is, not one person's version or side that he wants told.

Are there a certain number of times a person should call or write to find out if you are progressing with a story?

A.L.: Never! At least on a routine basis. Such contact would most likely be seen as pressure or an intrusion rather than any meaningful help in completing the story.

M.A.: If you're speaking of the subject of a story, it's very appropriate for them to call and check in a couple of times, especially if a time frame has been discussed. Unfortunately, the nature of the news is that anything can be bumped for priorities: breaking news, local news, weather.

A.A.: Checking in once a week is usually okay with me, unless there is a prior relationship. People sometimes need to understand a story may get pushed aside for a few days because of a larger story.

S.D.: I would say checking in once is not bad. After that I tell sources I'll let them know if I need anything. I usually like to let them know when the story will air if they have something invested in it.

In a couple of sentences, what do you wish John Q. Public knew about reporting a story?

A.L.: Our job isn't to make you happy or necessarily tell you about something you agree with—that's talk radio. Unlike some talk radio, we are interested in all sides of a controversy.

M.A.: Stories for television broadcasts must have some visual value, and their content must reflect the needs of the community without compromising the integrity of our news department.

T.A.: I want John Q. Public to know that the majority of reporters are fair and balanced individuals who do not have an agenda when reporting a story. That does not mean they're not affected by a story, but they try to keep their opinions to themselves.

A.A.: I wish the general public would understand that reporters are people. We are compassionate people who really do not like asking the fire victim how does it feel to lose everything. We do get satisfaction from getting the story first and right. Reporters are biased, but hopefully not in their reporting. We do have opinions but work very hard to keep them out of the story, which is why I talk with so many different people before doing a story. Also, people need to understand reporters often do not choose what story gets covered; they are assigned.

S.D.: I wish everyone knew that most reporters are not out to make people look bad. They are trying to uncover the truth in an issue, but doing that is not always foolproof. Journalists make mistakes especially in breaking news situations. . . . When things are fly by the seat of your pants, even the cops get things wrong. So if the information we get is wrong, sometimes the information the public gets will have to be changed as more information becomes available.

What are press credentials used for? What have you used them for? Are there other types of credentials for the average American?

A.L.: Press credentials are not as cool as folks may think. They're not free movie passes, and they don't get you out of speeding tickets. We don't even have to use them that often. The ones that are of any value are issued after a background check by a respected agency such as the LAPD. Most common uses: getting in to see high-ranking folks who have some sort of protection or security—or perhaps gaining less restricted access to certain disaster scenes. I would not encourage average folks to try to obtain press credentials; you'd just get in the way or get hurt. And I don't try to hang around your job, do I?

T.A.: Press credentials are issued by several agencies: the county sheriff, the local police department, or the department of public safety. Reporters use them to identify themselves and gain access to a breaking story that would be off-limits to the general public. Some reporters have been known to use them to gain free access to sporting events and things like that. Because you must be able to prove that you work for the media outlet you represent, I know of no credentials that would be available to the average person.

HOW TO LEVERAGE YOUR MEDIA EXPOSURE*

You worked hard to get media coverage. You sent out press releases, made follow-up calls, answered tough questions, and used some persuasion to get the media to appreciate your point of view. Then you got some hits—your name and your message are out there in print, on the air, and in cyber-space. But your job is not finished.

Maximum Exposure

How many clients and prospective clients actually read, viewed, or heard that message? How many were tuned to that station at the right time or read that particular issue of the publication that features your company? Probably not many. That's why you need to take one more step to fully ex-ploit the media coverage you earned: distribute those media appearances directly to individuals in your market.

In Print

It's easy to distribute copies of a printed article with your byline or one that quotes you as an expert. You can make photocopies and mail them to your list of clients and prospects, or specific segments thereof. It's sometimes smart to also include on your distribution list associates, influential colleagues, directors, and officers of professional and trade associations, regulatory agencies that affect your clients' interests, and—if the article is in a national publication—local reporters and columnists.

But don't simply put the photocopied piece in an envelope and mail it. Enclose a carefully worded cover letter, one that imparts a personalized message, draws attention to the article, puts it into context, and summarizes it for those who don't have either the time or inclination to read the whole piece.

On the Radio

There are two ways to leverage a radio show that features an interview with you or that mentions your company favorably. First, if it's truly interesting, entertaining, or instructive, you can tape the show, make duplicate copies of the audiotape, and distribute the dupes to your list. (Most radio stations will provide a high-quality recording of the show if you request that they do so in advance.) Be sure to label the cassette with your company's name and address; the name of the program and radio station, includ-ing its call letters and frequency; and the date of the show.

---

*David Freedman, "The Afterglow: How to Leverage Your Media Exposure: Distribute Photocopies, Transcripts, Tapes, and/or Photos of Your Media Appearances." Used by permission of Eminent Publishing Company, Highland Park, Illinois 60035, www.empub.com.

Duplicating and distributing cassette tapes is expensive. Moreover, if it's boring, not many listeners are going to slog through the entire tape. A more economical alternative, and in many cases a more effective one, is to transcribe the interview and distribute photocopies of the transcript. You can edit the transcript to remove extraneous material and digest it to the most essential information. You can add minor clarifications or make minor corrections without substantially changing the substance of the program.

Whether you distribute an audiotape or a transcript, you should mail it with an introductory cover letter.

As Seen on TV

Distributing a videotaped interview of yourself, or a videotaped show that features your company, can sometimes be the most effective tool of all—not only because people tend to be quite impressed (often unduly) with anything that appears on the flickering screen, but also because your message will be seen as well as heard. Many studies have shown that people remember information longer and more accurately when they experience it both aurally and visually as opposed to one or the other. (Television studios are usually willing to provide a high-quality video recording of the show if you provide the videotape.)

But videos are more expensive to dupe and mail. Again, you can save money by transcribing all or part of the show and simply distributing the transcript. Be sure to edit the text, because the printed words don't always make as much sense as when they're spoken.

Here's another way, sort of a hybrid solution, to make use of a TV program. Take your videotape to a video production studio and have a technician make a few freeze-frame photos from the tape. A good production facility can take you through the videotape frame by frame and let you pick the shots that portray you at your best. The technician can capture these stills on a computer floppy disk or CD-ROM. Take the disk to a printer (or a good photocopy shop) and ask a designer to create a cover page for your transcript with a title, brief explanatory text, and your best photo with a caption under it. Print the cover page in color if you can afford it, because it'll attract more attention than black and white.

Another alternative is to simply create a flier, without a transcript, to include in your media kit.

e-Publicity

The best way to herald an Internet appearance—either an online newsletter or an e-zine—is to send e-mail messages to as many people on your list as possible, giving them a hypertext link to the webpage on which you make your appearance. Then your correspondents can simply click on the link and travel to that page. If it's hard news, appearing on a site that's updated daily, be sure you download the page or print out a copy of the piece immediately, because it may not last more than a day.

You'll no doubt have many people on your list whose e-mail addresses you don't know. In those cases, you'll have to mail them the URL, send them a printout of the webpage, or both—with a cover letter.

Permission to Reproduce

In general you should ask the publisher or broadcast station for permission to reproduce the piece that you intend to distribute. As long as you're not selling the copies or using them to promote a product that competes with the original owner of the copyright, you should have no trouble getting permission. As a courtesy, even if it's not required, you can note on the reproduction itself, or in your cover letter, that the piece "originally appeared in the January 1999 issue of *Good Business* magazine and has been reproduced with permission of the publisher" or a similar credit for a broadcast station.

The Cover Letter

Any mailing will be more effective with a semipersonalized cover letter, addressed to "friends" or using some appropriate salutation. In the letter introduce the enclosed reproduction and let readers know that it addresses a subject relevant to their business or personal finances. Provide a brief summary of the piece. Here's your chance also to append additional comments, clarifications, corrections, or elaboration that you didn't have a chance to include in the original piece.

If the piece is truly valuable and instructive to your correspondents, it's most effective to send it (and the cover letter) without any other correspondence or materials. If you're using the piece simply as a flier that says, "Look, I'm in the media!" and it's not particularly instructive on its own, it may be better to enclose the piece along with other routine correspondence.

Once it's out the door, and you've exploited your media appearance in a dignified way, your job is done, except for one little thing: remember to save a copy of each mailing for your media kit. Once you collect several pieces in your media kit, you can use it to earn yourself more and bigger media appearances.

30

· ·

THE RAINBOW THAT
IS AMERICA

Dream lofty dreams, and as you dream, so shall you become.
Your vision is the promise of what you shall one day be; your
ideal is the prophecy of what you shall at last unveil.
—JAMES ALLEN

ABUNCH OF PAGES ago I started this work with a chapter entitled "The Brewing Storm," so I feel it is only appropriate to end with something a little less ominous. For such a young nation, we have endured our share of triumphs and defeats, but other countries around the globe are still extraordinarily jealous of our grand experiment and how well it is working. When our forefathers put together the pieces of this representative democracy, our republic, they went to great pains to see as far into the future as they could to head off or diminish the problems we might face. As an old farmer friend of mine would say, "They done good."

Yes, they done good, but with anything that is living and growing, if we don't provide the proper care, we risk losing everything. As was demonstrated in the opening chapters, America doesn't know how to do things halfway, which means when we veer off course, we give that our all too. We have a lot of ground to make up if this country is going to represent the ideals, morals, and values that it once treasured. And restoration will take time, energy, and commitment, but it is doable. We have to get our hearts right again and begin exercising that small but strong muscle called resolve. Resolve right now to find an area to apply your gifts and then do it. Give it your all, and watch what happens.

I use an analogy from my days as a cassette music fan to describe the condition of this country. If I go out and buy a cassette of the Beatles' *Let It Be*, I have an original. If my brother copies that recording onto another cassette—aside from violating the copyright—he has a second-generation tape that's not quite as good as the original. If someone else copies his copy of the tape, they wind up with a third-generation recording that has a lot of distorted highs and muffled lows. If the duplication process continues in this manner, eventually the last copy of a copy will bear little similarity to the original. The end result is so degraded that the words and tunes will hardly be distinguishable.

America has fallen into that trap. We started with a good thing. A very good thing. But over the years we settled for anything but the original. Our faith has withered, our trust is rusty, our political leaders are suspect, our tax dollars seem stolen, and outside agendas dictate policies. With each new issue where we settle for something less than best and where we continue to allow attacks on the vision our founders had for this promised land, we move another generation away from the American Dream. Eventually, we can't discern if our slumber-filled thoughts are pleasant hopes or demented nightmares. That's what happens when we lose sight of the source.

In just a few months, from late 2003 to early 2004, the forces for change and division were highly visible. A ban on partial-birth abortion, which tries to stop the most gruesome of deaths, was overturned by a federal judge, though President Bush vows to fight on.

In an effort to win approval in the Latino community, the president floated a trial balloon aimed at aiding illegal aliens. It was dressed up as a wonderful way to help several million lawbreakers (as many as eighteen million from Mexico alone) find forgiveness and waiting arms. When word spread, the majority of Americans were outraged, and the idea was soon shifted to a back burner. Our illegal immigrant situation is very complex, but the answer should not be one of forgive and forget, unless we want to treat all lawbreakers in a similar fashion.

Pharmaceutical drug prices have soared to such heights that our elderly are forced to choose between trying to feel better and having food on the table. Just as more and more people started buying their medicines from Europe, Mexico, and Canada, the big drug companies, one of the great lobbying powers in America, applied pressure to stop the practice. Since many of our government leaders receive a fair share of campaign contributions from the legal pushers, the poor and aged didn't stand a chance. The FDA started cracking down on the practice of heading north and south for cheaper drugs, while the pharmaceutical industry threatened to withhold drugs from drugstores selling to Americans.

Saddam Hussein was captured in December 2003 while he hid like a rat in a little hole in the ground. He threatened to take his own life, though in the end he didn't have the guts to pull the trigger—even though he had no problems doing so with tens of thousands of others. America thought this would usher in change for the better in war-torn Iraq. Instead, more U.S. military personnel were killed and injured in the days that followed Hussein's arrest than during the combat involved in ending his reign of terror. U.S. Marines were held at bay in a medium-sized city called Fallujah because the demands to "do little harm" to the enemy handcuffed their efforts. A nation without a resolve to win will most certainly lose.

Just when we thought it couldn't get any worse, word started circulating that some of our soldiers had gone to extreme lengths to interrogate Iraqi prisoners. They stripped them, made them pile into pyramids of human flesh, and forced them to masturbate while photographs were made. Some were beaten, others psychologically manipulated, and humiliation was a daily occurrence. Each of those few soldiers said they were just doing their jobs when asked about the abuse. Were they going to great lengths to get information about terrorism? Or has a society that no longer embraces values, morals, and ethics begun to see its underside exposed to the world?

Shortly after the pictures of abused prisoners began to make the rounds in Congress, the media, and on talk shows, five terrorists beheaded a young American civilian whom they had kidnapped in Iraq. They proclaimed his execution was in retaliation for the mistreatment of the Iraqi prisoners. Though America was outraged by the event, our evening news still gave approximately twelve to fifteen times more coverage to naked prisoners than they did to the murder of an innocent man who was in the wrong place at the wrong time.

The pressures are still on the American Dream to survive—more involved and convoluted than ever before, but our fighting spirit has to wage on. And we can do it one issue at a time.

What went wrong with America? We watered down the message, altered our beliefs, and inevitably gave up.

How do we fix it? Look in the mirror, stand on a subway platform during rush hour, visit a government meeting, hold a dying child in your arms, or watch a veteran hobble down the sidewalk because his country forgot that sacrifice and dignity are brothers, not strangers. Then struggle. Struggle with the absolute knowledge that the only person who has any chance of affecting any kind of change in the future of America is you.

Sure, there is a brewing storm, but unless it flattens you and steals your vision (which it can only do with your permission), you will live to be better for it. You will learn to take nothing for granted, to fight leaner, and to refuse to stop short of the goal.

Reclaim the power that is yours. A hefty price was paid for it. Rivers of blood spilled over their banks and tears flooded the countryside to give you the chance to carry on the legacy that is America. Get involved. Stand as our founders stood. Stop at nothing.

What went wrong with America? Plenty. What is right about America? The spirit that sets us apart from all other nations in history is still very much alive. It is the spirit of the original American Dream, and it resides in you.

CONCLUSION

AN OPEN LETTER TO MY READERS
(AND RADIO AUDIENCE)

AMERICA IS THE GREATEST nation on the planet; even its detractors know this. Our citizens have invested lives, blood, and destinies to give us something most of the world longs for—freedom.

It is human nature to take something for granted, no matter how precious. And by doing so, we have a tendency to neglect or exploit it. My wife is one of my greatest treasures because she is such a beautiful human being. She has been the perfect partner, mother, and friend, but there are still times when I forget how lost I would be without her. I have to create opportunities to hug or kiss or tell her how much I love her.

As Americans, We The People must create the same kinds of opportunities to remind ourselves of the value of this country. We can vote, drive through states unfettered, protest decisions of our elected officials, and worship freely, along with tens of thousands of other blessings.

We are a very fortunate people. We are the envy of millions.

Meanwhile, forces gather to destroy and rule us. Look at Al-Qaeda and radical Islamic extremists as an example. Their blueprint is to destroy America and advance the cause of Islam. For decades these and other radicals have been preparing for the day they will dance on our bones. They represent just one faction that wishes to see our way of life demolished.

Choose to fight for this country. In small ways and big ways we must all choose to get involved, to make a difference. My hope is that I have given you at least a starting place for your efforts.

May God continue to bless America.

NOTES

Chapter 2: They Lied to Us

1. Boston College Libaries, Ogilvie, John, ca. 1580–1615, http://infoeagle.bc.edu /cgi-bin/search.cgi?LIFE&index_0=SUBJECT/STRUCTURE:PHRASE&term _0=Ogilvie%20John%20ca.%201580-1615; Library of Congress, http://lcweb .loc.gov/exhibits/religion/rel01.html.
2. Biography of martyr John Rogers, http://home.att.net/~bryantrogers/Martyr .htm; Library of Congress, http://lcweb.loc.gov/exhibits/religion/rel01.html.
3. Mayflower Compact 1620. Agreement Between the Settlers at New Plymouth. The Federal and State Constitutions Colonial Charters, and Other Organic Laws of the States, Territories, and Colonies Now or Heretofore Forming the United States of America Compiled and Edited Under the Act of Congress of June 30, 1906 by Francis Newton Thorpe (Washington, DC: Government Printing Office, 1909).
4. Library of Congress, http://memory.loc.gov/ammem/today/jul20.html.
5. Library of Congress, http://lcweb.loc.gov/exhibits/religion/rel01.html.
6. State Library of Massachusetts, http://www.state.ma.us/lib/legishistory/liberties .htm.
7. The Laws and Liberties of Massachusetts: reprinted from the copy of the 1648 edition in the Henry E. Huntington Library (Cambridge: Harvard University Press, 1929); Library of Congress, The General Laws and Liberties of the Massachusetts Colony: Revised and Reprinted (Cambridge: Samuel Green, 1672), http://memory.loc.gov/ammem/today/jul20.html.
8. Christopher Columbus to the King and Queen of Spain, 1494, http://odur .let.rug.nl/~usa/D/1400-1500/columbus/extract.htm.
9. Christopher Columbus, *Personal Narrative of the First Voyage of Columbus to America: From a Manuscript Recently Discovered in Spain* (Boston: T. B. Wait and Son, 1827); "America a Christian Nation?" http://www.moralconcerns.org/past/Amer1492 .htm.

10. John Jay, *The Correspondence and Public Papers of John Jay*, ed. Henry P. Johnston (New York: Putnam, 1890), 4:365.

11. Patrick Henry quotations, http://www.usiap.org/Legacy/Quotes/PatrickHenry .html.

12. http://www.buchanan.org/pray-quotes.html.

13. Congressional Thanksgiving Day Proclamation, November 1, 1777, Rare Book and Special Collections Division, Library of Congress, http://lcweb.loc.gov /exhibits/religion/rel04.html.

14. Proposed Seal for the United States, Manuscript Division, Library of Congress; http://lcweb.loc.gov/exhibits/religion/rel04.html.

15. Lewis Henry Boutell, *The Life of Roger Sherman* (Chicago: McClurg, 1896), 272–73; David Barton, *Original Intent* (Aledo, TX: Wallbuilders, 2000), 138.

16. National Archives. Declaration of Independence, http://www.archives.gov/ national_archives_experience/declaration.html#more.

17. The National Archives, Virginia Declaration of Rights, June 1776, http://www .archives.gov/national_archives_experience/virginia_declaration_of_rights.html.

18. Aitken Bible, January 12, 1781, http://www.wallbuilders.com/resources/search /detail.php?ResourceID=79.

19. Religion and the Congress of the Confederation, Library of Congress, 1774–89, http://lcweb.loc.gov/exhibits/religion/rel04.html.

20. Mode of Disposing of Lands in the Eastern Territory, 1785, Rare Book and Special Collections Division, Library of Congress.

21. An Ordinance for the Government of the Territory of the United States, North-West of the River Ohio, 1787, Broadside, Continental Congress, 1787, Rare Book and Special Collections Division, Library of Congress.

22. *Runkel v. Winemiller*, 4 Harris and McHenry 276, 288 (Sup. Ct. Md. 1799).

23. *Church of the Holy Trinity v. U.S.*, 143 U.S. 457 (1892), 12 S.Ct. 511, 36 L.Ed. 226.

24. *United States v. Macintosh*, 283 U.S. 605 (1931).

25. *Zorach v. Clauson*, 343 U.S. 306, 307, 313 (1952).

26. *School District of Abington Township v Schempp*, 374 U.S. 203, 212, 225, 21, 71 (1963).

Chapter 3: A Clear and Present Danger

1. W. Cleon Skousen, *The Naked Communist* (Salt Lake City: Ensign, 1958).

2. U.S. Congress, *Congressional Record*, 88th Congress, 1st sess., 1963. Vol. 109, appendix pages A1-A2842.

3. Pacific Justice Institute, February 2003, www.pacificjustice.org.

4. Senate Committee on Foreign Relations, *A Decade of American Foreign Policy: Basic Documents, 1941-49* (Washington, DC: Government Printing Office, 1950).

5. http://www.newsobserver.com/24hour/nation/story/1129047p-7857651c.html.

6. Copyright © 2004 AP Online, Matt Gouras, January 2004.

7. http://www.nytimes.com/2004/02/04/national/04CND-MASS.html?hp.

8. John MacArthur, "The Seeker-Sensitive Movement."

9. *Santa Fe Independent School District v. Doe et al.*, 530 U.S. 290 (2000).

10. Douglas Kennedy, "Texas History Gets New Mexican Twist," May 30, 2002.

11. Vicente Fox on Fox News Sunday, January 12, 2004, http://www.foxnews.com/story/0,2933,108050,00.html.

12. All Change in Mexico, BBC, September 30, 2000, http://news.bbc.co.uk/1/hi/programmes/from_our_own_correspondent/945199.stm.

13. D. J. Kirby, "Sex Education in the Schools," in *Sexuality and American Social Policy*, ed. J. A. Garrison, M. D. Smith, D. J. Besharov (Menlo Park, CA: Kaiser, 1994).

14. Centers for Disease Control and Prevention, "Youth Risk Behavior Surveillance—United States, 1993"; *Morbidity and Mortality Weekly Report*, 1995; 44:1–56.

15. Department of Health and Human Services, *Healthy People 200: National Health Promotion and Disease Prevention Objectives*, DHHS Publication No. 91-50212 (Washington, DC: U.S. Government Printing Office, 1990).

16. P. S. Rosenberg, R. J. Biggar, and J. J. Goedert, "Declining Age at HIV Infection in the United States" (letter), *New England Journal of Medicine* 330 (1994): 789–90.

17. HIV/AIDS Surveillance Report: U.S. HIV and AIDS Cases Reported Through December 2002, vol. 14.

18. Adams Media Research, Forrester Research, Veronis Suhler Communications Industry Report, IVD.

19. Ann Burgess, noted clinical researcher and author, testimony to the U.S. Attorney General's Commission of Pornography, 1985.

20. http://www.winwithoutwarus.org/.

21. *New York Times*, March 4, 2003.

22. "Aziz: We Will Fight to the Last Bullet," *Pravda*, March 11, 2003.

23. "Oscar-winning Actress Susan Sarandon Has Accused Organizers of the Academy Awards of Being Obsessed with Control," BBC News, May 27, 2003.

Chapter 4: The Separation of Church and State Myth

1. Annals of Congress, August 15, 1789, 729-31.

2. Senate Journal, September 9, 1789, 2 B.

3. Robert S. Alley, "Public Education and the Public Good," *William & Mary Bill of Rights Journal* 4, no. 1 (Summer 1995).
4. Albert Lipscomb, ed., *The Writings of Thomas Jefferson*, 20 vols. (Washington, DC: Thomas Jefferson Memorial Association, 1904–5), 16:281–82.

Chapter 5: No More Springfields!

1. Luther Campbell, et al., "Me So Horny," Two Pepper Music.
2. Luther Campbell, "Face Down. Ass Up," Lil Joe Wein Music, Inc.

Chapter 6: The Absurdity of It All

1. *Seattle Times*, March 4, 2004, http://seattletimes.nwsource.com/html/localnews/2001870852_littleleague04e.html.

Chapter 8: The Slope to Destruction

1. Consumers Against Supermarket Privacy Invasion and Numbering (CASPIAN), http://www.nocards.org.
2. U.S. Bureau of the Census, Population Profile of the United States, 1997, http://www.census.gov/prod/3/98pubs/p23-194.pdf.
3. *Lawrence v. Texas* (02-102), 41 S.W. 3d 349 (2003).
4. Consumers Against Supermarket Privacy Invasion and Numbering (CASPIAN), http://www.nocards.org; Greg Jacobson, "Technology Revolution Underway," *Chain Drug Review*, October 22, 2001, http://www.chaindrugreview.com/articles/tech_revolution.html.
5. "Auto Center Joins UK Group," *MIT Tech Talk*, January 24, 2001, http://web.mit.edu/newsoffice/tt/2001/jan24/auto.html.
6. Introduction to Auto-ID, http://www.autoidcenter.org/technology.asp.
7. Electronic Product Code (EPC), http://www.eretailnews.com/Features/0105epc1.htm.
8. Charles W. Schmidt, "The Networked Physical World," http://www.rand.org/scitech/stpi/ourfuture/Internet/sec4_networked.html.
9. Cheryl Rosen and Mathew G. Nelson, "The Fast Track: Radio-frequency Devices Promise to Make It Easier to Monitor the Flow of Inventory Across the Supply Chain," *InformationWeek*, June 18, 2001, http://www.informationweek.com/shared/printableArticle?doc_id=IWK20010618S0001; Indrani Rajkhowa, "Shop-

ping Gets Smarter," *Computers Today*, June 16–30, 2001, http://www.india-today
.com/ctoday/20010616/marvels.html.

10. U.S. House of Representatives, Subcommittee on Domestic and International
Monetary Policy, Committee on Banking and Financial Services, September 19,
2000, Washington, DC, http://commdocs.house.gov/committees/bank/hba66988
.000/hba66988_0.HTM#68.

Chapter 9: All Fed Up: Red States–Blue States

1. The Canadian Society of Muslims, P.O. Box 143, Station P, Toronto, ON Canada
M5S 2S7, http://muslim-canada.org/muslimstats.html.
2. Based on data collected from *The Economist*, January 20, 2001.
3. Ibid.
4. Based on a map that appeared in *USA Today*, November 20, 2000.
5. Based on data collected from ibid.

Chapter 11: Oh, the Hypocrisy!

1. U.S. Department of State, Treaty on the Non-Proliferation of Nuclear Weapons
(1968). Entered into force March 5, 1970.

Chapter 12: Does "The Star-Spangled Banner" Still Make You Cry?

1. *West Virginia State Board of Education v. Barnette*, 319 U.S. 624 (1943).

Chapter 16: Talk Radio Saved Democracy—Sort Of

1. James Bowman, National Review Online, August 2003, http://www.nationalre-
view.com/flashback/flashback-bowman080103.asp.

Chapter 17: The Governor's Gone Mad!

1. Patrick Poole, "Tennesseans Stage Tax Revolt! Massive Revolt at State Capitol
Stops New Income-tax Plan," July 13, 2001, http://www.worldnetdaily.com/news
/article.asp?ARTICLE_ID=20024.
2. "Protesters Storm Tennessee Capitol Over Income Tax Plan," July 13, 2001,
http://www.foxnews.com/story/0,2933,29445,00.html.

Chapter 19: The Politics of It All

1. Federal Election Commission, see http://www.fec.gov/pages/faqs.htm.
2. Disclaimer per https://electionimpact.votenet.com/dnc/?CFID=33364&CFTO-KEN=28115774.
3. Federal Election Commission, http://www.fec.gov/pages/faqs.htm.